MIND
A Comprehensive Study on Mind and Its Dynamics

MIND

A Comprehensive Study on Mind and Its Dynamics

by

Dr. Krishanu Das
B.Sc. (Hons.), M.B.B.S.

Please send any comment regarding this book to
e-mail : dr.krisdas@yandex.com

First Edition : February 2016

Graphics Design :
FORTUNE GRAPHICS

INTRODUCTION

I am not a psychologist, I am a general physician.

But being in medical service over more than ten years, I have come through the contacts of a sea of people.

This always has stirred my mind to probe into and understand the basic structure and nature of our human mind.

The patients, who were suffering from physical illnesses, were often found to be associated with various psychological illnesses. Precisely, in treating a patient, whatever he might suffer from, his psychological back ground had always been taken into consideration.

All these observations, along with my years-long experience, developed in my mind an understanding of the real framework and functioning of our human psyche. Though, this did not always go with the conventional teaching, yet my own mind never could throw it off.

In this book, I have tried to explain and portray a detailed description of structure and functioning of our human psyche. The reader can go through a beautiful journey while reading this book as well as unbolt all the secret doors in core of his own inside.

The book has two parts. The part I has some original ideas of my own. And the part II is based mostly on established booked knowledge.

I would be glad to receive any constructive criticism that will sharpen my knowledge.

Another point is, I have written this book not only for academics in the related field, but for the individuals in any other discipline also.

So the text has been written with lucid terms and in easy understanding manner, as far as possible.

01.01.2016   - Dr. K. Das

"If you can't explain it simply, you don't understand it well enough."

— Albert Einstein.

Dedicated to
The Creativity of Human Mind

CONTENTS

MIND - PART - I
(Dynamics of Mind)

CHAPTER I

FOUR HOUSES
OF MIND

Man's desire to know his own 'mind', or his inside 'self' has been bred through a long time. From prehistoric time, our querying mind has not only tried to understand the mystiques of the nature and the universe, but also strained to explore the mysterious depth of his own enigmatic self. ' Who am I ?', and 'what's happening within my mind ?' - unfathomed mystery surrounding these questions has intrigued our mind to think and probe forever. Concurrently, our mind has also aspired to comprehend the meaning of the life and uncover the causes of morbid mental sufferings.

This quest or pursuit of knowledge, on one side, has led into man's philosophical and scientific works; and on the other, this endeavor has been conceptualized within his faith, beliefs, and religion.

Ancient Egyptians believed that human soul was made up of five parts. These are the Ren (name), the Ba (personality), the Ka (vital spark), the Sheut (shadow), and the Ib (heart).

According to their notion, the Ib or heart is the seat of emotion, thought, and motivation or will power.

Ancient Egyptian physicians had some understanding of brain and its functions, but they largely neglected the study of it unlike other organs. The famous Edwin Smith papyrus first described the anatomy of human brain, yet the author did not take the leap to describe it as the center of thought, emotions, and voluntary physical activities.

Ancient Greek philosophers conceptualized 'soul' or 'psyche' with breath or 'Pneuma'. They used the term 'Nous' to describe the mind or awareness. Sometimes the term was also used to mean reasoning or understanding.

Plato (428-348 B.C.E) postulated that, the soul is immortal, and the body is mortal. When death occurs, the mortal body of a person dies. And the soul escapes from the body, unharmed and indestructible, to merge with the universal soul.

This merger is accomplished by the power of 'the cause', which is one of the four elements. Other three elements are 'the Finite', 'the Infinite', and 'the Combination'.

Plato also identified three distinct parts of the soul. These are 'Reason' (Nous), 'Passion' (Thumos), and 'Appetite' (Epithumia).

Aristotle (384-322 B.C.E), his disciple, divided the soul into three parts : Nutritive Power - concerned with nutrition and growth, which belongs to both plants and all animals; Sensory Power - a faculty and activity of sense organs, that is vision, hearing, taste, smell, touch, as well as internal senses of imagination and memory; and Intellectual Power - concerned with understanding, reasoning, and discursive thinking.

Animals have the nutritive and sensory powers, but they lack the intellectual power.

According to 'Samkhya', the oldest school of Indian philosophy or Hinduism, which originated in the 1st millennium B.C.E, the universe is divided into two realities. These are 'Purusha' (consciousness) and 'Prakriti' (nature). 'Jiva' (a living organism) is a state where these two realities merge together into a form. And from this fusion emerges out intellect and self-consciousness (I-feeling).

Significant efforts on understanding of mind also came from the medieval Muslim and Jewish philosophers, like Al Farabi, Avicenna, Averroes.

Medieval Muslim physician Ahmed Ibn Sah al-Balkhi (850-934) related diseases to both the body and mind. According to him both can be balanced or unbalanced. Imbalance of the body can result in fever, headache, and other physical illness, and imbalance of the mind can result in anger, anxiety, or other psychological symptoms.

The relationship between 'mind and mental processes' and 'body and its activities' was the main area of work engaging a series of philosophers pioneered by Rene Descartes (1560-1650).

This relationship was also known as Mind-Body problem or Mind-Body dualism.

Descartes posited the idea that pineal gland in our brain is the seat of our soul, and mind (or soul) interacts with the body at the pineal gland.

Philosophers in western Europe in early modern period of 17th and 18th centuries, like Bacon, Hobbes, Lock, and Hume, established the idea of 'Empiricism' - the theory that all of our knowledge are based on experiences derived from the senses.

According to them, intellect is something that develops from the experience of the sensations, being interpreted by the brain in a physical way, and nothing else.

In the middle of the 19th century, a series of neuro-physiologists made significant discoveries in areas of the functions and mechanisms of the brain and nervous system. These discoveries very decisively established the foundation of current knowledge and modern concept of brain and its dynamic functions.

Charles Bell (1774-1843) and Francois Magendie (1783-1855) discovered the difference between sensory and motor nerves independently.

Emil-Du-Bois Reymond (1818-1896) founded modern electro-physiology, through his researches on electrical activities in nerve and muscle fibers.

Pierre Paul Broca (1824-1880) and Carl Wernicke (1848-1905) identified areas of the brain responsible for language and speech.

Gustav Fritsch (1837-1927), Edward Hitzig (1839-1907), and David Ferrier (1843-1924) detected the locations of sensory and motor areas of the brain.

All these discoveries had immensely contributed to our understanding of the brain and nervous system, and their mechanisms of activities.

By the turn of the 20th century, Sigmund Freud (1856-1939) from Vienna, through a series of works, developed a completely independent approach to explain and analyse the structure and functions of the mind. And he employed his theories in his therapy for the patients.

The principal theme of his therapy was 'interpretation' of mental sufferings, based on his theories; so that the patients can get their own insights into their pestering psyches and apply efforts to correct them on their own. He coined the term 'Psychoanalysis', to entitle this.

In 20th century, rapid development of science in the fields of Molecular Neurobiology, Neurophysiology, Psychopharmacology; and the advent of modern investigating techniques like CT, MRI, PET scanning enriched us with further knowledge to know and interpret the mechanisms of brain's functions and related mental processes.

In this book, in the following pages, there is an overall approach for the understanding of the basic infrastructure and functions of our mind and its dynamic processes. All these are not only based on current scientific knowledge, but also on my years-long experiences, observations, and interpretations. I must ask the reader to read carefully and to read every line as I have tried to give a clear description of the whole functioning of our mind. If there is something that is to be discussed, the reader can communicate with me through mail.

So let us start.

Four Houses of Mind

All of ours brain's activities can be divided into three regions; these are 'Conscious', 'Subconscious', and 'Unconscious'.

First we will come to Mind's conscious activities. Mind's conscious activities are those which occur in the awaken state of the organism along with the awareness of it. In normal sense, what we feel to be our 'mind', comes under this domain. Our thinking, emotional affections, volitional activities are all part of our conscious mind. All these conscious activities of ours are centered within the four major houses in our brain. Though, all of these houses are assigned to perform in their respective areas of work, but they are interconnected with each other through a number of joining corridors or neural pathways, that means each of the houses has influence on others, and actions of them are inter-related.

Not only that, though the activities of them are located predominantly in our conscious realm of the mind, all four houses have a major subconscious and an unconscious component. They may influence all the unconscious activities of the brain also.

These four houses are :
(1) House of Memory, (2) House of Intelligence, (3) House of Emotions, and
(4) House of Physical Activities.
Each of these houses has again been sub-partitioned into three faculties :
(1) Reflexive Faculty, (2) Short-term Faculty, and (3) Long-term Faculty.

Controlling cabins of all of these houses are situated in different areas of the brain (Fig.1). The house of intelligence is controlled by the frontal area of the cerebral cortex of our brain. The house of physical activity is controlled by the motor and premotor cortex of our brain. The house of emotion is maintained by the limbic system of the brain, which is composed of limbic cortex, a rim of cortical tissue around the hilus of the adjoining cerebral hemispheres, and a number of associated deep structures – the hypothalamus, the amygdala, the anterior nuclei of thalamus, the paraolfactory area, the fornix, the hippocampus, the nucleus accumbens, the cingulate gyrus, the mammillary bodies, the orbitofrontal cortex, and the septal nuclei (Fig. 29). And the house of memory is run by different association areas in different parts of the brain. Sensory memories are stored in the respective sensory association areas for the senses. Like, visual memories are stored in visual association area adjacent to primary visual cortex in the cerebrum. Auditory memories are stored in auditory association area of the cerebral cortex, and so others. Besides sensory or perceptional information, memories of intellectual processes that we've already undergone and memories of past emotional experiences are also stocked in frontal association area and association area in limbic cortex respectively (Fig. 15)

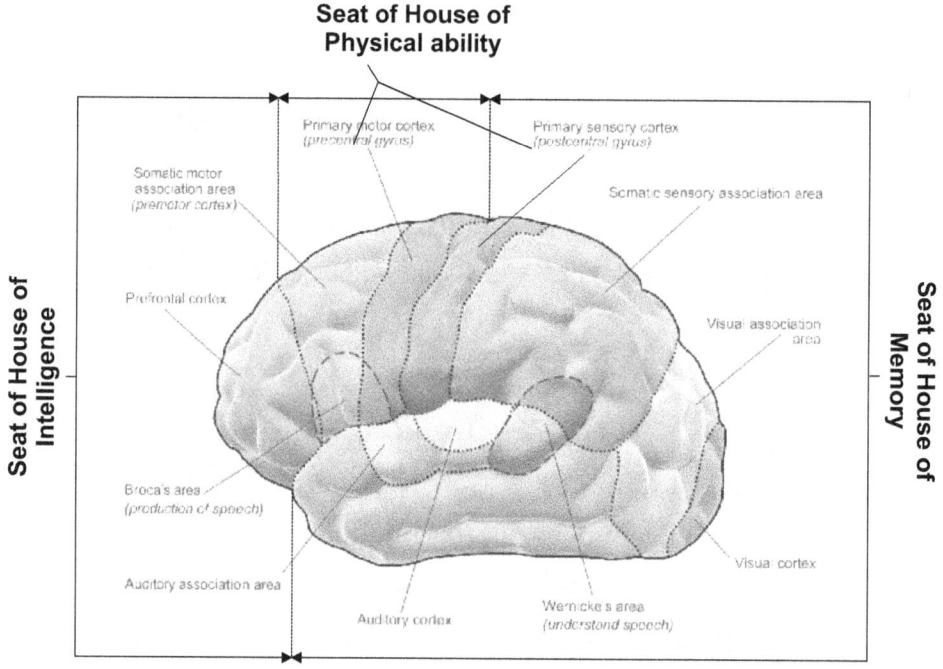

Fig. 1 : Location of Four Major Houses
(Image adapted from Blausen medical gallery)

There are also some other centers in our brain save these four houses, like the area controlling sleep and wakefulness, or the area controlling mood; which have to be regarded as the accessory or regulating parts of our conscious mind. They have been described in chapter IV of this book.

Now, what is our subconscious? Our subconscious though remains predominantly beyond the reach of our conscious mind, many of our conscious activities are processed in subconscious. And we, sometimes, get projection of it through intuition or sudden retrieval of a memory; or through dreams into our consciousness. We become tired to solve some problem, suddenly solution comes to our mind in some relaxed moment or when away from thinking about it. It means that subconscious was working on it all the time. So it functions as a backstage to our conscious mind where many of our conscious activities are processed, rehearsed, evaluated and finalized for actions like – storage in long-term memory, or projection into our consciousness through different ways. So we may call it subconscious mind.

Our conscious activities of the mind, as already described, are conducted by the different parts of our brain. So one may wonder – 'Where then resides our subconscious?'. To make it easier, it has to be said that we can think on one subject at a particular time. Even if mind thinks on different subjects, mind does it in quick succession, switching from one to another. But that does not mean that other centers of conscious activities of our brain are shut off at that particular moment. They all work, but are not focused at the same time into our consciousness. So when one enjoying some movie, may be his house of intelligence is working on some of his worries that he had experienced earlier. After the work-up is complete, the resolution suddenly came up in his mind along with the way to resolution. He got surprised as he was not attentively thinking on that problem with conscious effort.

So, our subconscious is nothing but the latent activities of all four houses of the brain, which go on in the back stage behind our conscious mind. The functions of it continue even during sleep and sometimes they are projected into our consciousness through dreams in sleep.

Interpretation of a dream is difficult, as the dreams are not like something that subconscious sends in our conscious awareness in an organized way, as in intuition (a sudden, quick subconscious activities of our house of intelligence), or sudden retrieval of a memory (a subconscious retrieval action of the house of memory). But whatever we see in our dreams, we must know, they are the product of our subconscious' activities, that means the subconscious was working on them. But the projection of the product fails to represent it in an organised manner, for that, the dreams may not follow any logical form or proper time sequence - like surrealistic paintings.

We do not know what is the exact neuronal, molecular and cellular mechanism by which the activity of a particular part of our brain comes into our consciousness, while the activities of the rest remain covered under veil in subconscious mind. There is possibility of existence of some common area or areas in the brain through which a certain activity of any of these four houses comes into our conscious self, leaving all other activities of the houses behind to form our subconscious self.

This common area could be thalamus, or any of the structures of the limbic system, because damage in the limbic system interferes with the declarative memory, that means the person fails to recall memory consciously in coherent form.

Compared to our conscious activities of the mind, our subconscious can be much quicker and faster, as our subconscious' activities do not have the need to serially inform our aware self. For that reason, we sometimes designate the term 'the sixth sense of us', informally for our subconscious, particularly in cases where we receive its alarming projection into aware self, through its rapid undercurrent activities.

Our subconscious' activities are run on their own, not having the necessity of volitional command or whip of our conscious mind. But sometimes, their activities can be initiated by our conscious demand, as in the case of procedural memory, which has been described later in this chapter.

That is the reason, why we remember many insignificant facts that we do not want to; or we recall repeatedly many unpleasant emotional experiences against our will despite our strong resistance; or sometimes we do not feel to like some person or some place though we cannot explain why. But, of course, we cannot say, if the insignificant facts are really insignificant, or emotional experiences are not those which have not to be urgently neutralised, or there is no logic behind our not liking something. As in many a cases, subconscious eventually comes to have proved itself to be utter true. But yes, logic is of course there, as the processes of subconscious follow the same mechanisms as those of the conscious mind; but they could be more quicker and finer, and possibly more intricate than that our conscious mind can follow through its acquired knowledge.

More often than less, our subconscious finally concludes itself to be more reliable than our conscious mind. For that, we very often may be believed that 'our subconscious is wiser than our conscious mind'. In a considerable number of cases probably the answer is 'yes'. But yet, this is not always altogether true. A properly knowledgeable mind can explain subconscious' activities also. And there are scores when our subconscious may be falsified and mislead. For that, here is this book, to get to know all the different quarters of our mysterious mind and the true views within the insides of them. Knowledge makes us wiser, that is necessary for the most intelligent person also.

Activities of the subconscious mind has been described, not under any common heading but in different chapters where it has been related.

Brain's unconscious activities are those which are not regulated by our conscious and subconscious drive – like regulation of the heart beats, regulation of the visceral functions, body temperature regulation, and so others. In majority, these are mediated through the autonomic nervous system, the higher center of which is located in hypothalamus of the brain. But any activity of any of the houses, either conscious or subconscious, may have influence on that part of the brain; like emotion 'fear' produces dilatation of pupil and increased sweating, rigorous muscular activities increase heart rate and respiratory rate, and so many.

So, though by general notion, the 'mind' refers to the activities of our conscious mind; in actual sense, the 'mind' has extensions in all of these three demesnes, that is conscious, subconscious and unconscious.

HOUSE OF MEMORY

House of memory has three major functions - Collect new information; Store them in the respective storage spaces; and Retrieve them when necessary.

Depending on the process of memorization, potentiation and retrieval, the house of memory can be partitioned into three faculties.

(1) Reflexive Memory (2) Short-term Memory and (3) Long-term Memory.

There is no demarcating line between short-term memory and long-term memory; long-term potentiation of short-term memories saves the memories as long-term memories.

But the purpose and way of activities of these three faculties are different.

REFLEXIVE MEMORY

Reflexive memories, as obvious, are those stored information, whose retrieval occurs in unconscious way, within a very short period of time or reflexively. Their retrieval do not involve volitional effort of our conscious mind to retrieve them. For example, we startle to watch something which has association with some fearful knowledge or past significant experience, and take action without much awareness or instructions of our conscious logical thought. Suppose one entered into his room and suddenly watched a large poisonous snake, lying just beyond the doorstep. He would jump back in reverse reflexly. Here he did not think too much, or tried to retrieve any memory. But through his knowledge and experiences, he has learned that it is a dangerous threat to his survival and can cause immediate death.

So the information has been saved as a reflexive memory.

There are so many examples of reflexive memories that we all experience in our practical life. Feeling hungry seeing a delicious food, feeling disgust watching a ghastly scene, grasping romantic sensation seeing someone beloved - all are examples of reflexive memories.

Reflexive memory helps us to take actions in both positive and negative ways. In the first example (snake and fear), it induced the subject to take action in negative way, whereas feeling hungry watching a desired food and taking action is an example of positive phenomenon.

Reflexive memory is helpful in many ways for our survival. Without it we would have been succumbed to many accidents and harmful injuries, even to death.

Reflexive memory may work independently, or its action could be interspersed with reflexive actions of other houses. In the first example, it is not working singularly. As the person sees the snake at very in front of him, also a sudden gust of fear comes into his mind, which in turn triggers the house of intelligence to decide reflexively what to do and by the order of which, desired muscular activities take place. So here all the reflexive part of the houses are acting together in a series to produce a harmonious expression of a conditioned phenomenon.

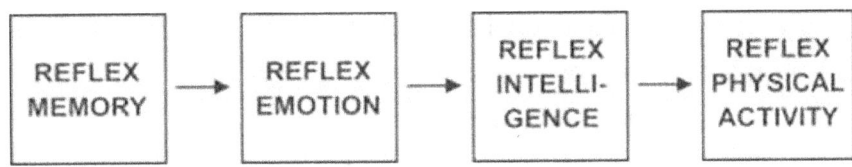

Fig. 2 : Sequential Actions of The Houses

In Pavlov's experiment with dog, the dog was conditioned with the sound of bell and subsequent food. So the dog salivated at the sound of bell, even in the absence of food. Here reflex memory and reflex emotion (hunger) acted serially, but the end expression was secretion of the salivary gland (component of reflex intelligence and reflex muscular activities was also there). It is because the reflex emotion not only triggers the house of intelligence or physical activity, but also triggers the autonomic nervous system; such as reflex fear produces dilatation of pupil, reflex hunger produces secretion of salivary glands, etc. As I have already said, all of the houses have influences on our unconscious brain activities also.

Reflex memory once formed, may remain for varying time or even life-long, depending upon the nature of the stimuli and degree of their potentiation. But reverse experiences and deconditioning processes can change or neutralise reflexive memories.

For example, in Pavlov's experiment the bell was rung as the food was produced before the dog. After repeated occurrence of this incidence, the bell was rung only without presentation of food, but yet the dog felt hungry at the sound of the bell and his salivary secretion increased. This is a conditioned learning. But after several times of incidence when the bell was rung only without production of food, the dog gradually ceased to feel hungry and his salivary secretion stopped at the sound of the bell. This is known as deconditioning (or extinction) of the conditioned learning.

There are two types of learning that can be achieved through conditioning processes : Classical conditioning, and Operant conditioning. Though they follow the same route of processing, they differ in nature.

Classical conditioning is so named, because this is based on the 'classical' experiments of Russian physiologist Ivan Petrovich Pavlov (1849-1936), as the 'dog, food and bell' experiment stated above. Generally, classical conditioning involves with all the reflexive faculties of the houses as well as unconscious activities of the brain. They produce responses reflexively, having been consolidated on the conditioning processes. In the above mentioned experiment of Pavlov, the sound of the bell is a neutral stimulus, as it itself does not evoke any specific response. The presentation of food is an unconditioned stimulus (US) as it is followed by an unconditioned response (UR) - that is 'increased salivary secretion'. When the conditioning process is completed with the increased salivary secretion at the sound of the bell, 'the sound of the bell' is termed as the 'conditioned stimulus (CS)' and the resulting response is termed as 'conditioned response (CR)'.

In case of operant conditioning, the term coined by B. F. Skinner (1904-1990), learning involves all the faculties of the houses rather than reflexive faculties, and the conditioned response emerges out in an elaborated way rather than reflexive actions.

Operant conditioning can be voluntarily set to increase or decrease a specific behaviour. In operant conditioning there are two modalities to increase a behaviour – (1) Positive reinforcement, and (2) Negative reinforcement.

The father gives a chocolate when the child draws a picture. If this reward increases the frequency, duration or magnitude (i.e. the child tries to draw a better picture) of that behaviour of the child, that would be known as positive reinforcement. But the father slaps the child if the child does not draw a picture, if this pain or stimulus increases the frequency, duration or magnitude of that behaviour of the child to avoid that pain or unpleasant stimulus, that would be known as negative reinforcement.

Again the father slaps the child whenever the child spits, and if this decreases the frequency, duration or magnitude of that behaviour of the child, that would be known as punishment. Punishment is a modality to decrease an unwanted behaviour.

In operant conditioning, besides punishment there are also other two modalities to decrease an unwanted behaviour; One is 'Time-out'; – where the reinforcement is withdrawn for some time, contingent upon the unwanted behaviour. Another is 'Satiation' – where the unwanted behaviour is positively reinforced, so that tiring occurs.

'Modelling' is another operant conditioning where the child or a person is exposed to a 'model' behaviour and is induced to copy that. This is applied to both increase and decrease some specific behaviours.

Though generally these processes are applied for behaviour therapy, but these processes can also be made operated in formation or potentiation of memory, like in preparing study materials by the children.

In desensitization process, the physician by repeated exposure to the phobic object without any harm, actually deconditions the subject's phobic memories to that object, which had been conditioned in earlier life with some associated unfavourable experiences.

SHORT-TERM MEMORY

Short-term memories are needed in our day-to-day normal activities.

Suppose one remembers, he has an engagement at 5-30 in the evening. He remembers it as long as the demand of the situation is there to keep it to be remembered. As soon as the engagement is over, there is no demand to remember that particular time and he gradually forgets it, if it is not transferred in long-term memory.

Purpose of the short-term memories is to maintain regular normal activities.

It can also be referred as working memory, as Baddeley and Hitch proposed in their 'working memory' model.

LONG-TERM MEMORY

Long-term memory composes our experience and knowledge for our future action.

Which memory will be taken into long-term memory?

It depends on two factors.

If the short-term information is repeatedly used over a time. For example, some one goes out in the morning to his job and for that he catches 08-30 train in the morning.

Now every working day in the morning, he remembers the same information. Regular repetitive retrieval of the memory over a long period of time, can push his short-term memory to be recorded as a long-term memory.

Even long after he retired from his job, he can remember, I used to catch 08-30 train in the morning to go to work.

Another factor on which long-term memory depends for its formation, is some event that significantly modifies one's life. Any incidence or information that has a major impact on our life and experiences, and that could be valuable for the prospect of our future actions, is stored as long-term memory, even instantly.

One can remember the date of his marriage, the date of his father's death for long time, even for life time because these events significantly modify one's life. Again, in case of some traumatic accidents, like being endangered by fire, injuries, or other harm, the incidents are stored as long-term memories, because these create our knowledge and experience, which protect us in future in similar situation and make our chance of survival better. Usually this type of memories involves emotional charges.

But the processing of memories for storing as long-term memories occurs mainly in our subconscious mind. Subconscious mind chooses which memory has to be preserved as long- term memory.

It is very mystique nature of our subconscious that it may not present any definite logic to our conscious mind for this selection of memories.

Sometimes we remember many trifle facts or incidents for a long time, without understanding why we have remembered them. Maybe, there are some reasons to remember them or they can modify our future life, which seem to be inapparent to our conscious mind. In other words, as I have already said, our subconscious may sometimes be wiser than our conscious mind. Difference between our conscious and subconscious thinking is, our subconscious acts on involving wide area basing on permutations and combinations of bits of knowledge that we gathered already, in a more complex and integrated way, the way which our conscious mind sometimes finds hard to follow, though logical co-relation is there also and mechanisms of actions are the same. On the contrary, our conscious thinking involves more emotions to procreate creative and innovative thoughts.

The students when prepare their studies, they take either of two principles of memorization. That is they repeat the memorization process and retrieve the learned materials from memory regularly over a period of time or throughout the course, so that the repetitive processes of retrieval can store the memories as long-term memories.

Otherwise, they have to have a strong motivation. If he passes the exam., it will give him the opportunity to have a very good job or bring him a higher social status - these future prospects also help his subconscious to store learned study materials easily. Needless to say emotional charges are involved with it.

All of our studies are not examinations oriented all the time. Our inquisitive nature in mind to know the unknown, and to know something which bears direct influence or is related with our real life, definitely help to remember the facts easily. But in all these cases emotional charges act as drives. Our subconscious' discretion also supports them to be memorized for long.

Long-term memory is not fixed in its contents. With the course of time, it changes in its contents. Some are deleted, some new memories are added. Once the poem, one could remember always very clearly in his school days, even recited it in various occasions, in future life, suddenly one day he discovered that he had forgotten that his favorite poem.

Our subconscious is always doing these things in backstage. The items of information which seem to it less important now, are being deleted and newer information which, to it, has more significance, is being added.

Along with our perceptional memories (memories - data of which are received through our sense organs), our emotional experiences, intellectual processes, and motor skills are also stored in our memory as memorigraphic data. The emotions we are feeling in our everyday life, intellectual or logical processes that we are conducting in our house of intelligence, and the motor skills - all are being stored in the respective areas of the brain. When we walk, drive or do cycling, we don't have to consciously remember how to walk, to drive or do cycling, as the motor activities for those actions have been stored in our memory as memorigraphic data. When we do mathematics, the process by which we are solving the problem through the house of intelligence is stored in frontal association area (described later) as memorigraphic data. Same way our emotional experiences that we are encountering in our everyday life are being stored in limbic association area as memorigraphic data. Though emotions help in the hippocampus mediated embedding of all types of memories (that has been described in mechanisms of memory) but they are themselves are stored as emotional data. So activities of all the houses can be stored as short or long term memories in the respective areas of the brain after being converted into memorigraphic data.

But here I will discuss about emotional memories a bit elaborately, because there is significant difference between these type of memories and all other types of memories.

Emotional memories are those memories which record our emotional responses. Suppose one got horrified watching a deadly scene. Here the visual image through the sense organ of vision, i.e. eye, will be stored in secondary visual cortex – and it is a perceptional memory. But the emotion 'fear' attached with it will be stored separately as memory in limbic cortex – and it is an emotional memory.

Both these memories will be associated in large parieto-occipito-temporal association area. So when one will recall the event later imaginatively both the memories will occur to him. One will give him the perception of vision of that incident and another will evoke the emotion 'fear' within him. So at the same time, along with the imagining the incidence, the subject will shudder in 'fear'.

Now what's the difference between theses two types of memories?

On repeated recollections of the memory, the perceptional memory becomes stronger, but the emotional memory becomes weaker. The reason of this is at each recollection the subject expresses out some of the emotion. So in subsequent recollection, a person feels lesser degree of emotion than the previous one. And after a number of time of recollections, the emotional memory virtually dies out. So after a time, when the subject will remember that incident, only the visual or perceptional memory will recur to him, but the attached emotional memory will fail to evoke any emotional response to him, making that incident emotionally neutral. Though the subject will remember it was a fearful incident as an informational memory, but would not feel 'fear' by recollecting it.

This process of fading off or dying out on repeated recollections (not recurrences) only happens with the emotional memories, where all other types of memories - perceptional memories, intellectual memories, motor memories follow the opposite rule.

But what if repeated recollections are not done? – Perceptional and all other types of memories fade away over time. But in case of emotional memory, complete or incomplete emotional adaptation and subjugation (or upjugation) occur, which ultimately become consolidated into our personality (it has been described later in chapter III). Emotional memories also can die out over time, but reason for that is different. Emotional memories die out over time because of unconscious expressing out of them through our subconscious mind without the awareness of us. Whenever we relax mentally, many of our emotional memories, at least partially, based upon the judgement or discretion of our subconscious mind, get expressed out through the expression of our eyes as well as our bodily expressions. This is the basis of dying out of emotional memories over a long period of time.

For these and for many other reasons, our house of emotion is very different from the other three houses. This book has specifically emphasized on it to deal every aspect of it in different chapters (Ch. I, IV, V, VII).

Another thing that is often less emphasized is degree of potentiation of memories. Along with the duration, the degree of ingrainment or embedding is also important.

Some memories are potentiated very deeply, and we can recall them very easily or they come to our mind instantly. And some memories we have to recall with efforts. Not all the memories, irrespective of repetition, are ingrained in memory with same strength. After an emotionally eventful or traumatic incidence the memories are stored deeply in one's mind and it significantly change his future life. Here not only the memory of the incidence but the severity of emotional experience and how strongly the memory was embedded in memory store – these are significant.

Our retrieval of memory depends also on how strongly the information has been embedded in memory. It is true for all types of memories, including intellectual memories that is the intellectual processes which we have undertaken, emotional memories that is the emotional experiences we have gone through, and motor memories that is the motor skills which we have learned on. But the retrieval process may be hampered or slowed down in physical or mental illnesses, stress, depression, drugs and alcohol abuses, etc. Persons with low MQ usually embed the memories shallow, which is the cause of their forgetting. Again, the persons paying less interest or emotional drive to memorize, will embed the information superficially, rendering them vulnerable to forgetting. A person may learn quickly and soundly if he attaches his area of interest to the materials that is to be memorized. Often jokes, humorous mnemonics, picturaisation, connecting with popular persons or events, anticipation of rewards, wanting to prove superiority in the class help to memorize easily.

Amnesia refers to profound memory deficit due either to loss of what has been already learned (retro-grade amnesia) or inability to form new memories (antero-grade amnesia). The cause of amnesia may be organic due to malfunctioning of the activities of the brain as in certain diseases, or it may be due to major psychological disturbances.

Dementia is loss of memory due to degenerative changes in the brain. But in dementia other mental faculties such as general intelligence, orientations, emotional reactions, behaviour and mood can also be affected. Dementia could be senile dementia which is age related or be due to some underlying pathology in the brain as in Alzheimer's disease (details in Ch.2, Part II).

INPUT OF MEMORY

This is done primarily through our sense organs. There are five senses vision, hearing, smell, taste, and tactile sensations through skin receptors for touch, heat, pain etc. Besides those, there are proprioceptive receptors in joints and internal ear, which bring sensations of balance and spatial orientation.

Through these sense organs and their receptors we get bits of information which are processed with or without emotional charges and stored as memories as reflexive, short-term or long-term as need be.

PERCEPTION

Perception is receival and interpretation of a sensory stimulation. These sensory data come both from the environment and from within the body. But perceiving is selective. At any given moment hundreds of stimuli are impinging on our sense organs; which particular one will be attended that the organism select either consciously or subconsciously.

Our conscious selection of perceiving sensory stimulation depends on (1) Needs (2) Interests (3) Desires (4) Attitude and mental set up.

Our subconscious also follows these principles, but it depends on subconscious' discretion. And I have already said that the subconscious may be quick and wiser than our conscious mind in this regard. In a certain place suddenly one noticed a particular object or a particular person to be untrustworthy or to be avoided. His conscious mind could not explain it. Eventually it went for in favour of his subconscious. Many a time, we experience these type of occurrings. We feel something that our conscious or logical mind fail to explain. Sometimes it is regarded as our sixth sense. But it is nothing but the latent actions of our subconscious, which is too complex to be explicable to our conscious logical mind. But of course, logic is there but beyond our wisdom or capability. From this perspective, man, being a moral animal, lies at a step behind than the other animals who are guided by the animal instincts rather than moral instincts. But as I have already said, our subconscious can be misdirected also, as it happens in case of subjugation and seduction (read following chapters). So, true learning of our proper inside and their processes of activities is more preferential.

Our unconscious selection of perceiving senses are those like severe pain, extreme heat or cold, urgency in micturition or defaecation etc. Here conscious and subconscious mind play little role.

There are two types of perceptional anomalies.
    (1) Illusions and
    (2) Hallucinations

(1) Illusions : An illusion is a misinterpretation of a stimulus, like seeing a rope as a snake. Illusion actually should not be called an anomaly, because it is a normal phenomenon and appear in normal individuals. We call it an illusion because it does not agree with our other perceptions. Illusions could be -

a)   Illusions due to lack of attention and concentration – like overlooking a misprint, interpreting the meaning of something from the general context.

Fig. 3 : You will often overlook the missing-legged horse.

(b) Emotionally determined illusions – In the dark, many people experience a shadow or an indistinct object as human figure or ghost; or any insignificant sound as crying or footsteps made by human. In these cases the mind sets itself emotionally predetermined to experience something.

(c) Illusions driven by expectations or preconceived ideas – there are all categories of illusions like visual, sensory, auditory, tactile, gustatory, that could be generated by expectations or driven by preconceived ideas. Optical illusions lie in its visual sector. Below is an example of optical illusion.

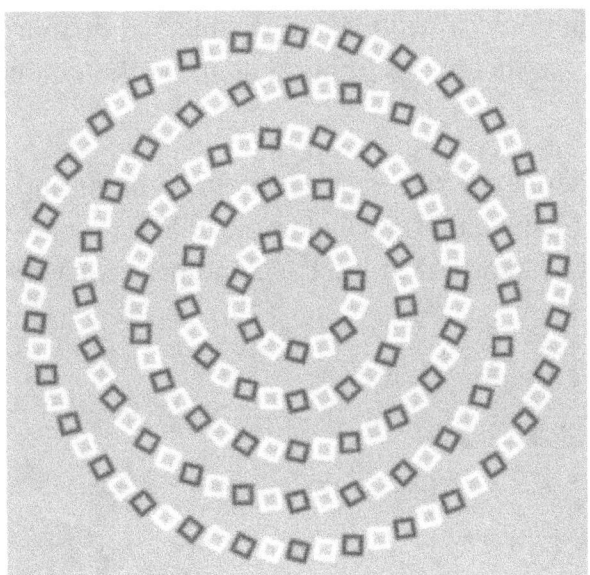

Fig. 4 : Intertwining illusion. The circles appear to be spiraling and intersecting (from Pinna & Gregory, 2002).

Now what are the secrets behind optical illusion?

The secrets behind optical illusion lies within the fact that it, somehow, cheats the associated memory of us. Association of memory refers to the set of memories regarding a particular object, person, or situation. (It has been described later in details under the house of intelligence.) For that, whenever we see a 'cup', we expect or predict to see 'tea' or 'coffee' within it; whenever we look at the sky, we expect or anticipate to see 'stars' or 'clouds' in it. Because they have been embedded in individual sets of associated memories within our brain, the retrieval of which may occur reflexively. In the case of more soundly formed associated memory, we interpret the thing according to the respective set of the associated memory regarding that particular object or situation, though the real thing may not go with this preinstituted memory. And in those cases of discrepancies, optical illusions are formed.

As in Fig. 4, look carefully to the small squares. They would seem to be down-stepping stairs. Now, if we step down, we cannot remain at the same level. So the image is contradicting our embedded and established memories – our knowledge and experience. So the illusion is forming as to be the circles of the stairs being converging.

Our mind also perceives size, shape, colour, contour and depth of the objects from its preabsorbed knowledge and experience. When we observe two objects one in far and another in near, or one in light and another in shadow, our mind takes the

5a   **5b**

Fig. 5a : Ponzo's illusion. The black horizontal line in the distant seems to be longer than the nearer one, though they are the same length (after Italian psychologist Mario Ponzo).
Fig. 5b : Checker shadow illusion. The block A and the block B are of same shades of colour, but the block A appears to be darker than the block B (from Edward H. Adelson).

far object as larger than what it looks, the shadowed object as brighter than what it appears. Look at Fig. 5a and Fig. 5b. In Fig. 5a, two horizontal black lines are of same length, though the distant one seems to be longer. In the Fig. 5b, the block A appears to be darker than the block B, though they are both of same colour. We get illusioned because to us it has been preconceived through our knowledge and experience that the object in distance is larger, or the object in shadow is brighter, than what they actually look like.

Our concept of size, shape, contour and colour partly comes from comparison with the surrounding objects, and dominancy of the overall impression of the image. When two objects of the same size are juxtaposed with two different sized other objects, the one in the proximity of the bigger object seems to be smaller than the one with the smaller accompanied object. When two objects of same colour and shade are imposed on two differently shaded backgrounds, the one with the brighter background looks darker and one with the darker background looks brighter; and when they are proximated with two differently coloured backgrounds, they acquire some effect of the background colour on them, like red looks differently within deep green and yellow. The perception of shape and contour of an object is influenced by the integrated impression or dominant background of the image. In the Fig. 6a (Hering Illusion), the straight lines seem to be curved at the center. Why ? It is due to the fact that the overall impression of the image is divergence particularly at the center. When we look at the center of the image, the mind gets dominated by the idea of divergence. So the straight lines seem to be curved outwards near the center. In the Fig 6b, I have drawn a perfect circle, but because of the wavy nature of the background, which is overpowering the mind, the circle appears to be vertically oval, that is its vertical diameter seems to be greater than its horizontal diameter.

Through binocular vision, from the difference in angles of two images formed in two eyes, we perceive depth of objects. But besides that, we also conceive the depth, contour and three dimensional structure of any object from the knowledge of shades, shadows and contrast, which has already been constituted in our memory since the time of birth. Optical illusions take the route to betray all these firmly pre-embedded knowledge.

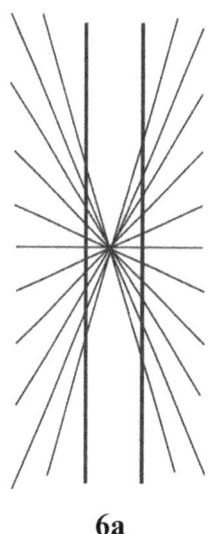

6a   6b

Fig. 6a : Hering illusion. Straight lines appear to be curved outwards near the center (after physiologist Ewald Hering who first described it in 1861).
Fig. 6b : Oval circle.

But some other optical factors also could be involved in creating optical illusions. These are -

(i)   Lateral inhibition : Here in the receptive field of the retina, the photoreceptor cells (rod cells) receiving the lighted part of the image laterally inhibit adjacent photoreceptor cells receiving the darker area of the image. As a result of which, we see increased contrast at the edges of slightly different shades. This constitutes visual acuity or sharpness of the vision. Lateral inhibition also acts in the above example of checker shadow illusion.

(ii) Use of focal point : This is my own conception. When we see an image, we cannot concentrate on every point of it. We usually concentrate on a particular point or focal point of the image both in monocular and binocular vision, and perceive the periphery either through the overall interpretation of the image, or through expectation or anticipation from our already formed assembled associated memories. There are two factors that mind always encounters in perception, 'the possibility' and 'the impossibility'. Our focal vision, where we concentrate, challenges impossibilities; but our peripheral vision does not challenge impossibilities, rather lie between possibilities and impossibilities, if any there.

Below in Fig. 7a, I have drawn an outline of a face, but in the place of eye I drew lips. When you will directly look at the lips, your mind will challenge the impossibility to get new information, new experience. But if you concentrate on the front or lower part of the face, only the impression of an eye will appear to you, the lips will disappear. Our peripheral view of an image is partly formed by our embedded and associated memory. Here I am cheating your embedded associated memory. In the Fig. 7b, when you concentrate on the lower dots, the upper dots will disappear and vice versa happens when you concentrate on the upper dots. You cannot see all of the dots at the same time.

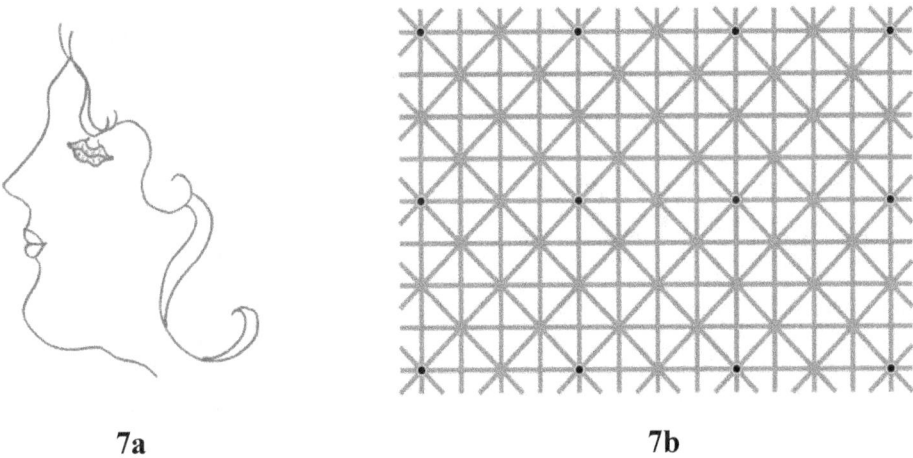

7a   7b

Fig. 7a : Eye-lips illusion. **Fig. 7b** : Disappearing dots. There are 12 black dots at the intersections of the grid. Your mind would not let you see all at a time (from 'Variations on the Hermann grid : an extinction illusion', Jacques Ninio and Kent A Stevens, 2000).

No image is formed at the optic disc (blind spot) of the retina, where the optic nerve with vessels leaves the retina. Usually in binocular vision this deficit is filled up by the image formed in the other eye because the optic disc lies 3mm medial (towards the central axis of the body) to the posterior center of the retina (fovea centralis). But if you close your one eye, you do not see a hole in your vision. How the brain fills up this gap? The brain fills up this gap out of imagination and overall impression of the view.

What we see, partly depends on what we want to see or what we anticipate to see.

(iii) Moving optical illusion : In case of moving optical illusions (Fig.8a & Fig. 8b), the trick is you have to give different shades and lighted areas to the objects of the image. It is not possible when light comes from a fixed direction and objects are stationary. It is only possible when either the light source or the objects are moving. We are usually accustomed to see moving objects rather than moving light source. So the mind perceives that the objects in the image are moving. To create optical illusion whatever you do, your aim would be to betray our firmly embedded associated memory. You can be innovative in creating your own optical illusion yourself.

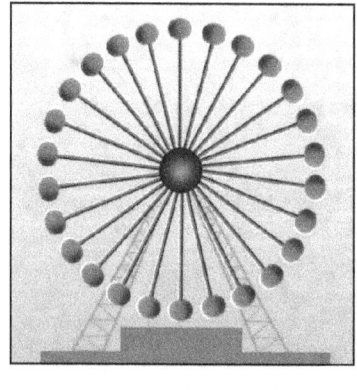

8a

8b

Fig. 8a : Ferris wheel illusion. The wheel seems to be rotating. **Fig. 8b :** Rotating circles : The circles seem to be rotating - inner clockwise, outer anticlockwise.

An interesting proposition was made by professor Mark Changizi. When light strikes the retina, 1/10th of a second goes by before the brain translates it into a visual perception. How does the brain fill up this time to understand the continuity of an event? The brain does it through imagination and prediction. The brain predicts what could be the most possible future in the next 1/10th seconds from its pre-established knowledge and experience, and fills up the time gap to understand the overall continuity of the event.

How fascinating our mind is. Isn't it ?

Hermann Grid optical Illusion :

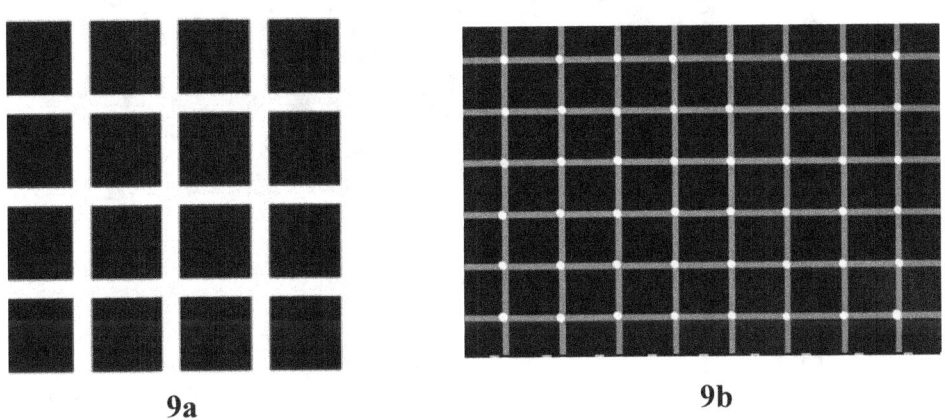

9a   9b

Fig. 9a : Hermann-Grid illusion. Darkness appears at the intersections of the grid which dissipates also along the borders (named after Ludimar Hermann who discovered it, 1870). **Fig. 9b :** Lingelbach illusion. A variation of H. G. illusion. Dark dots appear and disappear at the intersections (after E. Lingelbach, 1994).

Of all optical illusions the most difficult to explain is Hermann-Grid optical illusion (Fig. 9a) and its variation Lingelbach illusion (Fig. 9b). In Hermann grid illusion when we look at the grid, we see blobs of darkness at the intersections of the grids, which dissipate along the border also. In Fig. 9b, in Lingelbach illusion, the dark dots appear and disappear at the intersections only.

Different optical mechanisms, including lateral inhibition, have failed to explain the exact cause which lies behind this illusion. However, to me, it occurs that the exact reason for this illusion does not lie in any aberration of the optical mechanism; but the aberration lies in the process of translation of the optical stimuli to the visual perception in the brain. Because if the shape of the grid is altered, or the grid is tilted at 45 degree, the illusion disappears.

Fig. 10 : Disshaped and Tilted Grid

So what happens there?

We are very accustomed to grided views. Not only looking through the grided windows, but when we walk along the streets, blocks of houses, shops by the sides, with light or darkness coming through them, build our respective impression strong through the absorbed memories of grid views. And this is the reason behind Hermann-Grid optical illusion.

In Hermann-Grid illusion, we challenge 'the possibility' and 'the impossibility'. If the insight light is so bright to make the grid complete white, the darkness beyond the grid could not be as dark as complete black due to reflection and scattering of light. When we look at a bright light source, there appears a hallow around it due to scattering of light by the atmospheric molecules and particles. The darkness around the light source is smudged with same tinge of colour. To watch background as dark as complete black, the insight should be less lighted or the grid should be darkish. So the illusion appears at the peripheral vision which lies between the possibility and the impossibility. In Lingelbach illusion the borders have already been smudged with darkness. So the illusion does not appear at the borders as we are accustomed to see that type of darkness only through that coloured grid.

In the vice versa case, if the background is bright white, bright yellow, bright red or of any bright colour, and the grid is of different colour, the illusion would also appear, because due to scattering of light and reflection of the light from the inside objects including the observer, the grid will have a tinge of that colour.

Why the darkness is more prominent at the intersections? – It is because of the larger area at intersections. Why we do not see the illusion when the grid is tilted at 45 degree or the shape of the grid is changed? – Because we are not accustomed to see those views. We don't see anymore those as usual familiar views, we just see those as a design or a painting that does not challenge our memory.

Fig. 11 : Grid in reality

To check my exposition right or wrong, I did the following simple thing (Fig. 11). I put a black papergrid against the clear day light and photographed it. As I said there was white smudges at the intersections that dissipated along the border also. But when I closely watched the photograph, I got that the white smudges are there, and it is not an illusion in reality. These are due to scattering of light by atmospheric molecules and particles over the dark areas. But here two more factors work – lateral inhibition and contrast colour perception. For that, margins of the grid-border appear completely dark. So in an illusory view of the grid, the mind obviously imagines the peripheral view as it happens in reality as described previously.

The answer is – 'MEMORIES'.

Fig. 12 : Family of birds (by permission from the works of Octavio Ocampio).

Our whole sets of associated memories make our knowledge. It not only includes memories as information, but our intellectual workings, emotional experiences are also assembled properly and stored as memories. All these construct our integrated knowledge, experience, beliefs, ideas; and build the internal shape of our mind. It is obvious to say that it is largely influenced by the family, culture, society and a person's surrounding world.

And our perception is greatly depended on this pre-constituted knowledge and internal model of the mind.

An ambiguous object interpreted differently by two different observers, exposes different structures or shapes of their internal mind. Consider the following image.

One can interpret it reflexively as a woman's face, and another can interpret it as family of birds. What will occur to a person's mind at the first sight of this image that depends on his preinstituted knowledge, the whole organization of his associated and embedded memories. And it exposes one's internal shape of the mind, mental attitude, and way of looking to the outside world.

(2) **Hallucination** : Hallucination is experiencing of a perception although there is no relevant stimulus, like 'seeing a snake though there is no snake' (it is differentiated from illusion by the example 'seeing a rope as a snake'). Like illusions, hallucinations also can occur in any sensory modality like visual, auditory, tactile, olfactory or gustatory. Auditory hallucinations are most common among them. Hallucinations can range from very simple like seeing flashes of light or hearing insignificant sounds to complex and organized form like hear ing running commentary on one's action as in schizophrenia. Besides in normal individuals, hallucinations can occur in a number of mental and physical disorders, and also in cases of psychoactive substance (drugs) usage and withdrawal. The disorders include schizophrenia, delirium, dementia, migraine, epilepsy and mood disorders. Besides alcohol, common hallucinogenic drugs are Phencyclidine (Angel dust), Lysergic acid diethylamide (LSD), Methylenedioxymethamphetamine (MDMA, also called 'Ecstasy'), and natural substances like seeds of I. violacea or T. corymbosa ('Morning glory', active ingredient 'D-Lysergic acid alkaloides'), dried tops of cacti L. williamsii and L. diffusa ('buttons', active ingredient 'mescaline'), dried mushrooms of Psilocybe genus (advertised as 'gold caps' and 'liberty caps', active ingredient 'psilocybin'). Tactile hallucination 'formication', a feeling of bugs crawling over (or under) the skin, may be experienced by the cocaine users. Hypnagogic hallucinations occur at the interface of wakeful state towards sleep

and hypnopompic hallucinations occur when coming out of sleep. They may be normal phenomena. Hallucinations may occur in a setting of clear consciousness as in schizophrenia, or in clouded consciousness as in delirium.

(3) Two other perceptional aberrations are 'Depersonalization' and 'Derealization'. Depersonalization is a feeling that one is not oneself or something has changed within oneself. Derealization is a feeling that one's environment has changed in some strange way that is difficult to describe. [described in Part II, Ch. VII]

Spatial Orientation :

Our spatial orientation is determined by the interpretation of visual images, senses from the inner ear (from semicircular canals, utricle and saccule; collectively called vestibular apparatus which are situated in the internal ear within the petrous part of the temporal bone) and senses from the proprioceptive receptors in joints. There are three semicircular canals in the inner ear situated at right angles to each other. Semicircular canals are responsible for detecting rotational acceleration in a plane of a given semicircular canal. Utricle and saccule respond to linear acceleration. In general, the utricle responds to horizontal acceleration and the saccule to vertical acceleration.

Proprioceptive senses means position senses. There are two types of position senses: (1) Static position sense - which means conscious orientation of the different parts of the body with respect to each other. (2) Positional sense in movement - which is also called kinesthesia or dynamic proprioception.

Knowledge of position, both static and dynamic, depends on degrees of angulation of all joints in all planes and their rates of change. Multiple different types of receptors, known as proprioceptors, are present in and around the joints to help to determine joint angulation. Tactile receptors (touch and pressure) from skin around the joints additionally help in this task. When the joints are in midranges of motion, muscle spindles act as important receptors. When the angle of joint is changing, some muscles are being stretched while others are being loosened.

These stretch information from the muscle spindles through afferent nerves help to determine complex interrelations of joint angulations when the body is moving. All these proprioceptive information are transmitted up in the spinal cord and thence to cerebral cortex. A good deal of input goes to the cerebellum which is accountable for smooth and coordinated movement through necessary feedback correction.

Our self body image is conceived depending upon four major senses - (1) visual images, (2) tactile sensations from the skin, (3) senses from the inner ear or vestibular apparatus, and (4) proprioceptive sensations from the receptors in joints.

All these input are associated and synthesized at a cortical level, creating a continuous perception of an individual's own image and its orientation with respect to space.

There are various medical and psychological diseases where along with other memories, spatial orientation and perception of self body image are disrupted. Spatial orientation can be disrupted in Cerebral strokes, Alzheimer's disease, and different types of Dementia. Distortion and disturbances in self body image occur in Anorexia nervosa, Bullimea nervosa, Body dysmorphic disorders, and cerebral parietal lobe lesions like Gerstman's syndrome. It must be differentiated from somatic delusion where the aberration lies in false belief, rather than perceptional anomaly. These have been discussed in specific chapters in the Part II.

Current knowledge of the anatomical, cellular, and molecular mechanisms of memory

Where primary areas for the senses - e.g. primary visual cortex, primary auditory cortex, primary sensory cortex - are involved in perception of the senses, secondary or associated areas of the senses - e.g. secondary visual cortex (also called visual association area), secondary auditory cortex, secondary sensory cortex - are involved in storing of respective memories.

Besides storing, association of memories of respective senses is also performed in secondary or associated areas. For example, visual images are organized in a comprehensive form in secondary visual area.

Potentiation of memories as short-term or long-term depends, as already said, on two processes – (1) Repetitive Processes and (2) Emotionally Charged Events. Here we should know, giving attention or engaging interest to memorize something means involving our emotion.

Potentiation of received information that involves emotion, in either short-term or long-term memories is done by the hippocampus. And for that emotional charges from other parts of the limbic system such as amygdala, hypothalamus are important.

Now these other structures can directly influence the hippocampus to potentiate the memories. And it is also done via limbic association area in the temporal lobe.

Like when one watching a horror movie, visual images and emotional experience of 'fear' are both being stored in visual association area and limbic association area through primary visual cortex and amygdala respectively. Then both these two series of memories are associated by the hippocampus to be stored in common association area (parieto-occipito-temporal association area) in brain as long-term memories. But amygdala directly influences the hippocampus also in the process.

Bilateral destruction of hippocampus or disease process that destroy its neurons both in human and monkeys, cause striking defect in consolidation of new memories. But recall of the past events remain intact. After bilateral removal of hippocampus (which has been done in cases of epilepsies), it has been found that the person can recall already established memories, but cannot establish new memories (antero-grade amnesia) save those which are learned through repetitive processes. In Alzheimer's disease, the hippocampus is one of the first regions of the brain that suffers damage.

Once long-term memories are formed, they are stored in different parts of the cerebral cortex. Visual, auditory, sensory memories are stored in respective visual, auditory, and sensory association areas of the cerebral cortex. But memories involving all quarters of senses including intellectual processes and emotional experiences are stored in common association areas of the cerebral cortex.

The memories which are stored by repetition and not dependent on emotional drive are not controlled by hippocampus. It explains that ability to learn new technical skills is not hampered in damage of hippocampus as in this case learning does not depend on emotional drive.

Memories of intellectual processes (sequencing and associating - described later) either can be stored directly as long-term memories or may be stored through hippocampus.

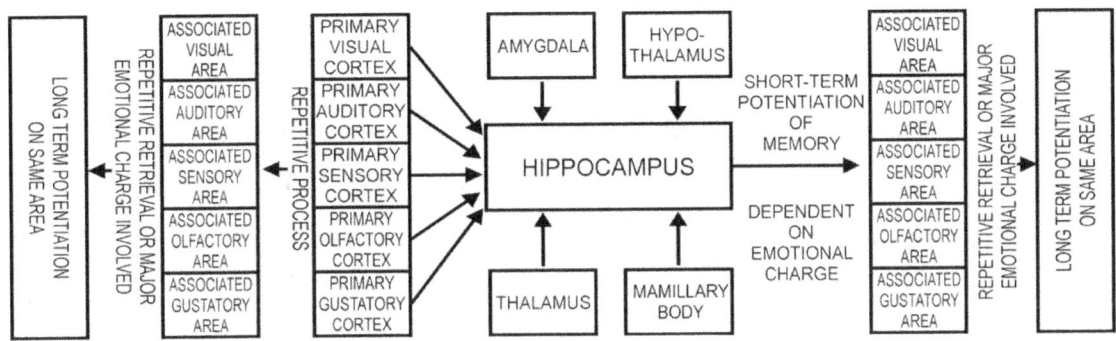

Fig. 13 : Potentiation of Memory

Usually memories, upon their mode of retrieval, has been classified into two groups - (1) Declarative Memory - the memories which we recall consciously. It includes all conscious recollection of facts and events. (2) Procedural Memory - the memories whose retrieval occurs unconsciously, and which come effective without awareness of conscious mind; like riding a bicycle, playing a musical instrument etc.

But there is some misconception about procedural memories.

Procedural memories very often have been linked to those memories which have been learned through repetitive processes. But that is not true.
The true fact is –

(1) Procedural memory is recalled unconsciously or better to say subconsciously. But we can recall it consciously also. When one driving a car he recalls how to drive a car subconsciously. But he can perform the task recalling it consciously also.

(2) Procedural memory does not mean learning only motor skills. When someone is reading a novel he visualizes the facts in it without giving

attention to the language and grammar. The comprehension of language and grammar is being accomplished in his subconscious mind automatically.

(3) The automatic performance of recalling of memories is not only applicable to the memories which has been consolidated by the repetitive processes, but automatic activation is also applicable to the memories which has been consolidated through emotional charges. As learning to drive a car may involve great emotion. It may not be a memory that has been consolidated through repetition. An enthusiastic student may learn it very quickly and then performs the task automatically and subconsciously.

(4) Besides recalling of memory, intellectual processes, emotional adjustments can also be performed automatically. In case of comprehension of language and grammar while reading a novel, there is automatic performance of 'house of intelligence' and 'house of memory'. In case of riding a bicycle, there is automatic performance of 'house of memory' and 'house of physical activity'. As we have already said, our conscious thinking can focus only on one subject at one time, but all other activities of the houses continue in our subconscious mind.

So automatic recalling of memories, which according to the popular notion is known as procedural memory, is nothing but the subconscious activities of any one or more of the houses of our brain initiated by our conscious demand, being effective in a practical way.

As for cellular and molecular mechanisms of memory, studies in snail Aplaysia, has shown mechanisms of habituation and sensitization processes.

Habituation means reduction in response reaction or stoppage of response reaction to a stimulus after being repeatedly charged by it. Sensitization means after a strong stimulus the organism reacts more strongly to a subsequent stimulus, same in nature but weaker in intensity.

In snail Aplaysia study, it has been observed that habituation is due to closure of a number of Ca^{++} channels in the sensory nerve ending, which causes prolongation of action potential with resultant decrease in release of neurotransmitters when stimulation occurs, because release of neurotransmitter is dependent on Ca++ entry.

That means neuronal circuit loses its response to repeated events that are insignificant.

In the case of facilitation, the facilitatory neuron is stimulated at the same time with the sensory neuron and release serotonin at the facilitatory synapse with the pre-synaptic nerve ending. Serotonin through serotonin receptor activates the enzyme adenyl cyclase inside the cell membrane, and form CAMP. This in turn closes K+ channels. Lack of K+ causes prolonged action potential in pre-synaptic terminal of sensory nerve ending and causes prolonged activation of the calcium pores. So when the stimulation comes to the pre-synaptic terminal of nerve ending, there is increased release of neurotransmitters facilitating synaptic transmission.

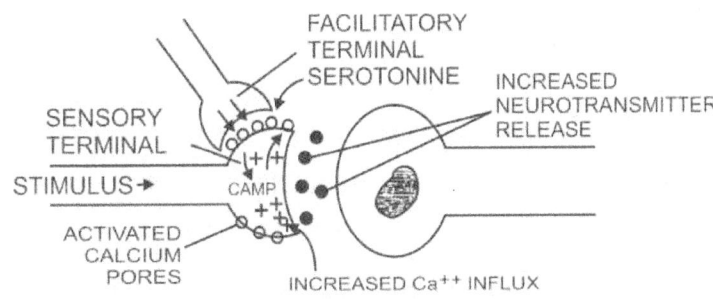

Fig. 14 : Memory System (Habituation and Sensitization) discovered in Snail Aplaysia.

Further studies forwarded protein synthesis hypothesis of memory formation. When stimulation occurs in nerve cells, this activates an intra-cellular transduction cascades. This molecular cascade in turn trigger transcription factors that lead to change in gene expression. New membrane proteins are formed and this finally results in alteration of synaptic proteins as well as in synaptic re-modelling, favoring changes in synaptic transmission.

Recent researches also suggest that microRNA may play an important role in memory formation.

HOUSE OF INTELLIGENCE

Intelligence could be defined as the serialization of received information by our mind in such a sequence that would produce a specific cause and effect.

Let us elaborate it a little further. Primitive man experienced that when two stones are frictioned with each other, give sparks of light and fire. They also experienced that in dry grassy land sometimes from these sparks of fire (which were produced by the friction of the dry plants), fire was caught to the dry plants. And they also experienced when animals were partially burnt in this fire, their flesh tasted good.

So the primitive brain of the man sequenced these three events in following way :– If they can rub two stones before dry leaves and plants, the sparks of fire produced by the friction of stones would catch fire to the woods; then if they put the flesh of the dead animals in that fire so, that those would be partially burnt or roasted; and ultimately they would get more tasteful food.

So they learned cooking.

Our house of intelligence, situated in the frontal lobe of brain, is always doing this thing – is taking information that we have gathered in the house of memory, then doing serializing them in a specific sequence, and finally producing the output, all according to the desire which is being determined by the house of emotion.

Suppose an organism got information that somewhere there is a desired food, and information about different pathways lying before it. The house of intelligence of its mind would serialize the pathways properly to discern by which pathway the food can be achieved easily, and give output to the house of physical activity. Followingly proper action would take place.

Highly intelligent brain can perform this course more efficiently. Difference between high IQ and low IQ is brain with higher IQ can assemble and serialize the bits of information even when they are distantly related, in a comprehensive way to produce excellent result. Brain with lower IQ always jumbles up with the bits of information and cannot reach the desired goal effectively.

The brain with higher IQ is more comprehensive in nature, that means, it can deal with lots of information, even when they are distantly and minutely related, to work with in its intellectual process; whereas low IQ brain takes only limited bits of information and also which are closely related. It is like higher mind can see the things from the top of the mountain, where gradually lower IQ minds reside at gradually lower height.

And this is applicable for both conscious and subconscious minds. The subconscious of a higher IQ person is also definitely more intelligent, as both conscious and subconscious are the activities of the same respective houses, one making aware and another keeping unaware the organism's self.

When we do mathematics, we follow the same rules. Here the already solved processes of mathematics get stored in memory as intellectual memories. In future serialization or solving problems, we use them.

A child of today learns a lot of knowledge and mathematics within 10-12 years of his age. Actually he stores in his memory the already sequenced events done by our earlier men. In the beginning example of 'learning of cooking', experiences and sequencing have not been accomplished in one generation. It took many generations for the primitive brain of the man to achieve experiences and sequence them to get to the ultimate learning of cooking. One intellectual experience has been stored as intellectual memory and been passed to next generation by various ways. Today, in this age of information, this transference is much easier.

Our mind has innovative properties also. That is mind also wants to experiment with the things to get a new result which is desirable. But in this case, it also should be remembered that mind experiments with those things only, which even in a minute way have been stored in its memory or experience. Our mind cannot think or do experiment with the things that have not been stored in its memory, i.e. where there is no bits of information in its memory.

process is absent. Mind intellectualizes it with further investigations after it has been discovered.

Thought : Our whole process of our thinking is just combined actions of the four houses – collecting information, serialising them according to the pressure of different emotions, and producing desired voluntary activities. This process has influence on several other unconscious activities of our brain also, but that is not part of our conscious mind.

And we are doing this continuously as long as we are in awaken state. It makes our thought process and 'I' concept. Even when we do philosophical, scientific, or spiritual thinking, we must know that they are also being driven by our emotional pressure.

By this interpretation, one may think that emotion sets our goals and memory and intelligence become the means.

Broadly speaking, in most of the lower animals this is true. But in man and some other higher animals memory and intelligence also take part in manipulating and setting emotions.

For example, having information that in some place the food can be obtained, and thence intellectual process perceiving the idea that in this way this place can be reached, sets our emotion 'hunger' and 'hope'. By the drive of which subsequent actions take place. But emotional demands always act in the background, to create pressure on the memory and thinking processes.

Suppose I have one dollar and I am very hungry. If I walk two steps there is a bread store from where I can buy a piece of bread with one dollar. But if I walk further two steps there is a store from where I can buy same amount of chicken with one dollar. So to my discretion I will walk four steps. Though I am very hungry I will walk past by the bread store even if it is attainable. Because I know there is better future for me very near. So who is setting my goal ? Of course my emotion 'hunger'. But it is being manipulated by the house of intelligence.

Again, we fight for the betterment of our society sacrificing our emotional needs as it will bring our individual benefits also; even in lower animals, like domesticated dogs are trained to eat when they are ordered, even if there are food before them; – in all these cases memory and intelligence take part in manipulating and directing emotions. Dog may know, if he does not behave properly, he may lose his secured food forever. We sacrifice, because we think it will bring better future to us.

Here the emotional demands always act on the background. The purpose of rationalization is only to serve the emotional demands in a controlled and more achievable way.

Socrates said, "He is the worst of all slaves, who is a slave to his passions." Practically we all are slaves to our passions. Neglecting emotional demands brings nothing but mental catastrophes and other mental instabilities and unhappiness. But being intelligent, we can control and manipulate our emotions in more enjoyable and achievable way.

In philosophy, philosophers forever fluctuated between Hedonism and Rationalism. Truly both are the properties of our mind. We seek pleasure, enjoy being driven by our emotions and also act on our intelligence or rational thinking.

It is a bit mysterious, when someone commits suicide or sacrifices his life for some other reason devoid of any self-interest. Selfish gene does not seem to work here. But these are not usual life phenomenon. In these cases brains are modulated by the severe negative pressure of the surroundings or society. 'Fear' may play a role in dominating the brain.

Another point should be realized, that no organism upon this earth spends its life to become the fittest. Life's only goal is to serve the emotions towards positive scale. 'Survival of the fittest' is an outcome of it.

Again 'survival of the fittest' should be recoined as 'survival of the fittest ecosystem'. Because every organism is dependent on others for its survival in a given ecosystem. Organisms fit in the fittest ecosystem either being master or slave. Nietzsche's 'master and slave' theory is good, but he disregarded the essentiality of slaves. In the fittest ecosystem life surrounds about the fittest organism in its centre. Others have to cope with to become the fittest to fill up the periphery. Or more precisely, organisms live in a symbiotic manner with symbiotic relationships to each other in an ecosystem which is the fittest in the nature.

Innovation in science and imagination in art are similar. When we do artwork we try to imagine something new which should be appreciated as a new and creative work. But in this regard, it must be known that we cannot imagine something that is totally unrelated with what we have experienced in our life; that means, as already said, where there is no bits of information in our memory.

For instance, when someone imagining an animal like Gryphon, he has the experience or knowledge of a lion and a bird.

Leopold Infeld and Albert Einstein, in their book 'The Evolution of Physics', presented a beautiful example regarding why it is hard for us to imagine an extra dimension.

When we watch a movie we see the characters on the screen are moving, talking, playing etc. If those characters were real on the screen and they had existed in a world of their own, it would have been hard for them to imagine there exists an another dimension of depth.

We cannot think that we have not experienced.

Though sometimes mathematical possibilities indicate the chance of existence of many things.

For this, Multiverse theory (existence of many universe), universe with more dimensions and different physical laws, are though very hard for us to imagine, there is no reason from scientific or mathematical angle that they cannot exist.

What we cannot think, does not mean that they cannot exist.

So our intellectual process in a simple phrase is 'serialization of experienced events'. Our prefrontal lobe serializes only whatever information the mind has received throughout the life, to fulfill the need of emotional demand. It does not take or cannot take anything that the mind has not received as a bit of information in its memory or experience. Rene Descartis has said, 'I think therefore I am'. But our own self-realization or self-existence is nothing but ordering or sequencing of all our experiences received through our sense organs throughout the life, according to the demands of emotional pressure, giving a particular shape or model of the mind.

Our thought process serves our emotional demand. The emotions are again set to protect the purpose of the life, that is 'self-preservation and propagation of the species'. It could not have been any otherwise, as the species would have been extinct. So it is self-explanatory. How all the emotions serve our need, has been explained in specific chapter (Ch. V).

Association of Memory

Another important function of Intelligence is association of memory. This associating function is needed in sequencing process also.

Practically this quarter should be regarded as joint property of both house of intelligence and house of memory.

When we see a 'Tree', we simply see a tree. It can be stored as a simple visual image. But there are information which are related with it. That is this tree gives a fruit. That fruit tastes like this. The average life span of these trees is such. These trees are grown on this type of soil or in such areas.

Like ab, bc, ad, de . 'a' is related with 'b' and 'd'; 'b' is related with 'a', 'c'; 'd' is related with 'e'. They are all inter-related with each other in close proximity. So when a person sees an apple tree, immediately he recalls that this tree gives a red fruit, which tastes sweet; these trees are born in these areas or on this soil etc.

Without association of memories, our sorting and retrieval of information would have been a jumbled up process, and often ineffective one.

Dyslexia is a form of disorder, where there is impairment in association of visual memories.

Reading is the most sophisticated form of our association of visual memories.

The sign 'A' or 'J' is related with several associated memories. Not only how they would sound when pronounced or their position in alphabet, but also when they would be grouped with other words in a order, they would produce specific meanings. Association of this vast expanse of memories with a particular visual memory is often disrupted in dyslexia.

So the person sees the word 'A' or 'J', but cannot recall what other great number of items of information are associated with them, particularly when sees them among other letters in words.

The person may not suffer significantly from impairment of other intellectual processes, like sequencing of events, planning for future, goal oriented thinking etc., which are controlled by the prefrontal cortex of brain, if there is no gross disturbance in memory association process.

So if we be more precise, the intelligence has two functions. One is sequencing of information which is required for goal- oriented planning and actions, and is controlled by the frontal area of our brain. And another is association of the received information in memory which is controlled by the different association areas of brain.

Schizophrenia (in general term 'madness') encompasses a group of disorders rather than a single entity. It involves impairment in action of all the four houses, though memory impairment has been less clinically stamped.

Autistic thinking and Loosening of associations are two of the most important features of schizophrenia.

In autistic thinking, the person's thinking is governed by private and illogical rules.

Loosening of association is a pattern of spontaneous speech in which things said in juxtaposition lack meaningful relationship. The speech is often described as being 'disjointed'.

Delusions or false unshakeable beliefs, which are more characteristic of Paranoid Schizophrenia are also formed basing on illogical thinking or reasoning.

Like memory, emotion, the house of intelligence is also divided into three faculties.

Reflexive Intelligence

It is called intuition. The whole intellectual process occurs within a very short period of time, that is within a fraction of a second without awareness of our consciousness.

This reflexive intelligence formation depends on the person's experience of intellectualizations in general as well as in any specific field. As Sir Conan Doyle's famous fictional character used to say, 'Watson if you ask me how I did tell, I will have to think about it. The train of thoughts occurred in my mind in a very quick pace'. In reality it is also true.

Reflexive intelligence can be triggered by reflex emotion, as is in our 'snake and reaction from it' example, or it may occur individually.

Short-term and Long-term Intelligence

Short-term intelligence is that faculty which is exercised in our normal daily activities.

Regarding long-term intelligence, it should be noted that long-term faculty of any of the houses, not only act like storehouse of information as in memory, but also establishes the strength of that particular house. This strength is also expressed through the owner's look, appearance, behavioural expressions.

A man who is wise and much knowledgeable can be distinguished by his demeanour. A man by birth may be intelligent, but who utilises intellectual processes regularly and extensively, expresses it by his intelligent look. An athletic body can be detected by his strong muscles. An emotionally suffered man also can be identified by his look.

These all depends on the long-term faculties or strength of the respective houses, where they experience, become enriched and increase in their strength.

Intelligence's long-term faculty or Intelligence strength is made up on how many times and to maximum extent, one has exercised the process of intellectualisation.

Current knowledge of the anatomical, cellular and molecular mechanisms of intelligence.

As already described, our sequential thoughts, planning and goal-oriented thinking are mediated in the frontal area of our brain, particularly the prefrontal cortex.

It has been found that patients could receive significant relief from severe psychotic depression by severing of the neuronal connections between the prefrontal area of the brain and the remainder of the brain. This is known as prefrontal lobotomy.

This is done by introducing a knife through small openings on both sides of the skull and slicing the brain from top to bottom.

After introduction of this technique by Moniz (he was awarded Nobel prize in 1949 for invention of this technique), this procedure had been practised for a period of time in the past. Discoveries of anti-depressant drugs has ended their necessities.

Subsequent mental changes that had been observed in these patients are :
(1) The patients have lost their ability to solve complex problems.
(2) They became unable to perform stringing sequential tasks to reach specific goals, and in general lost all ambition.

Here separation of prefrontal area relieves the patient from negative thinking which is associated with mood down-gradation or depression (as I have explained in detail in the chapter III, under Mood). But at the same time, the patient has been made deprived of his major intellectual processes, which is very necessary for setting of our goal and future planning.

So these observations have shown the role of prefrontal cortex with the intellectual processes.

Cortical thickness has been related to intelligence in several studies (Narr, K. L et al 2007; Choi, Y. Y et al 2008; Karama S. et al 2009). It has been found that there is a positive co-relation between intelligence and cortical thickness, especially in the prefrontal cortex and temporal lobes.

Association of memories is accomplished in different parts of the cerebral cortex. Association of memories for the different senses are performed in respective higher areas of those senses. Like association of visual images in comprehensive or understandable form are accomplished in secondary or visual association area. So for the auditory, sensory and other senses.

Besides that there are three large association areas. These are (1) Parieto-occipito-temporal association area (2) Frontal association area (3) Limbic association area.

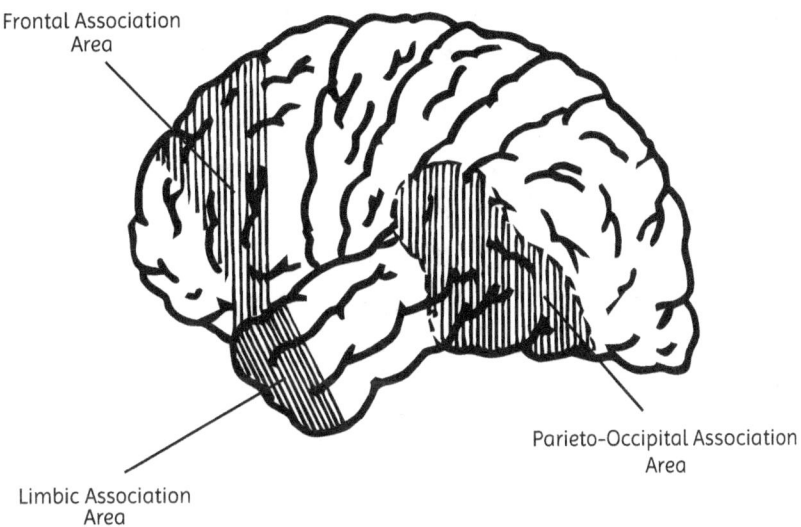

Frontal Association
Area

Parieto-Occipital Association
Area

Limbic Association
Area

Fig. 15 : Major Association Areas of the Brain.

These association areas receive information from multiple regions of the cerebral cortex and even the subcortical structures.

(1) Parieto-occipito-temporal Association Area :

This association area lies in the large cortical space between the somatic sensory cortex anteriorly, the visual cortex posteriorly, and the auditory cortex laterally.

This area also includes Wernicke's area, named after neurologist Carl Wernicke (1848-1905) who first described it. Wernicke's area is the major area for comprehension of language, and lies behind the primary auditory cortex in the posterior part of the superior temporal lobe.

(2) Frontal Association Area :

This area is important for elaboration of thought and planning of motor activities. The intellectual processes that we have already undergone are stored here. This area also receives input from the parieto-occipito-temporal association area through a massive subcortical bundle of fibers. All these input and stored memories are elaborated and associated, which makes our major thought process inducing planning to take proper future actions.

Broca's area, named after Pierre Paul Broca (1824-1880), is situated in inferior frontal gyrus of the frontal lobe immediately in front of the inferior end of the motor cortex. This area is responsible for the speech production and receives input from Wernicke's area through a bundle of nerve fibers known as Arcuate Fasciculus.

(3) Limbic Association Area :

This area is found in the lower portion of the temporal lobe, extending to the limbic system and responsible for association of emotional data.

This area is concerned with the emotions and motivation. The emotional experiences that we have already undergone are stored here. This area has influence on our habit, behaviour and emotional reactions to our surroundings. Secondary or Visual Association

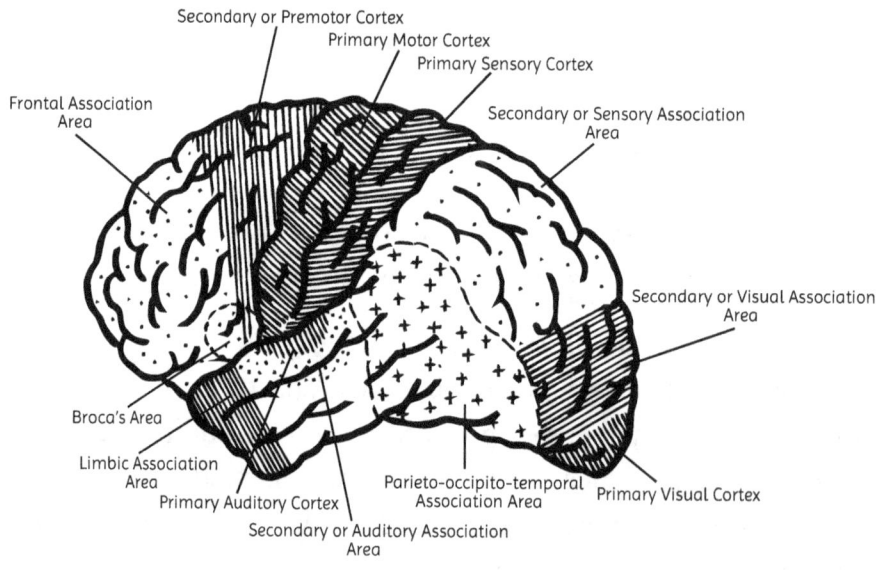

Fig. 16 : Different areas in Cerebral Cortex designated for different functions.

An interesting type of brain abnormality is Prosopagnosia, that is the inability to recognize faces. This abnormality occurs in extensive damage of the ventromedial undersurface of both occipital and temporal lobes

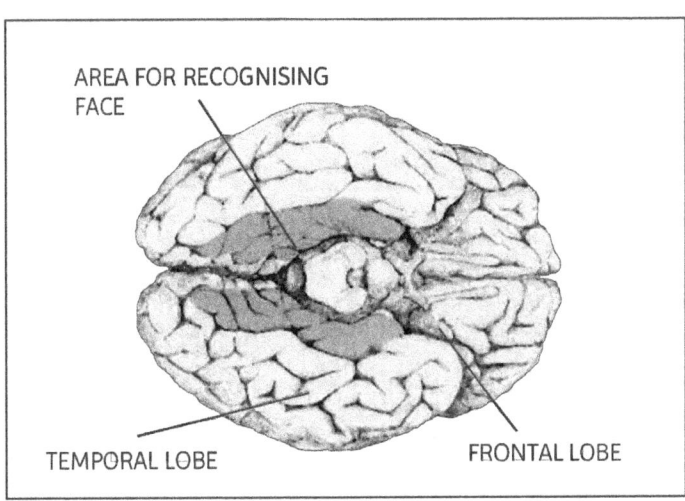

Fig. 17 : Area on the undersurface of the brain responsible for face recognition.

The occipital portion of this area is contiguous with the visual cortex and the temporal portion is closely related with limbic association area that has to do with emotions.

However this abnormality very little interferes with the activities of the other parts of the brain.

Human brain has an average volume of 1200 cm3 and an average weight of 1.2 - 1.4 kg. or 2% of total body weight. Much of its size comes from cerebral cortex which is a thick layer of neural tissue that covers the two cerebral hemispheres, enveloping the surface of all the convolutions of the cerebrum, having a total surface area of about 0.25 square meters.

Human brain is estimated to contain about 86 billion neurons, 20% of which are located in the cerebral cortex. Though whales, elephants and bottle nose dolphins have larger brain than us the ratio between brain weight and body weight of ours far exceeds than those of them.

Besides that, the prominent gross feature in human brain is there has been striking development of frontal lobe and other associatiction areas compared with the brains of their animal relatives.

So the whole mechanisms of recollecting memories, planning and performing tasks can be diagrammed as followingly.

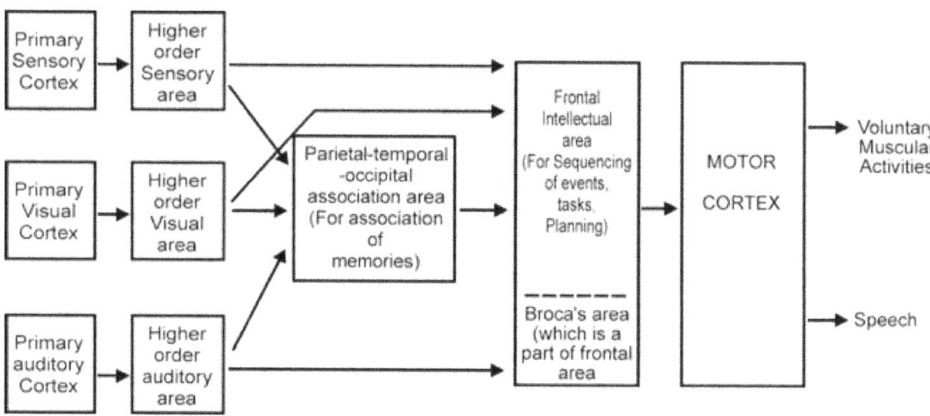

Fig. 18 : Sequential Actions in Brain for Performing Tasks.

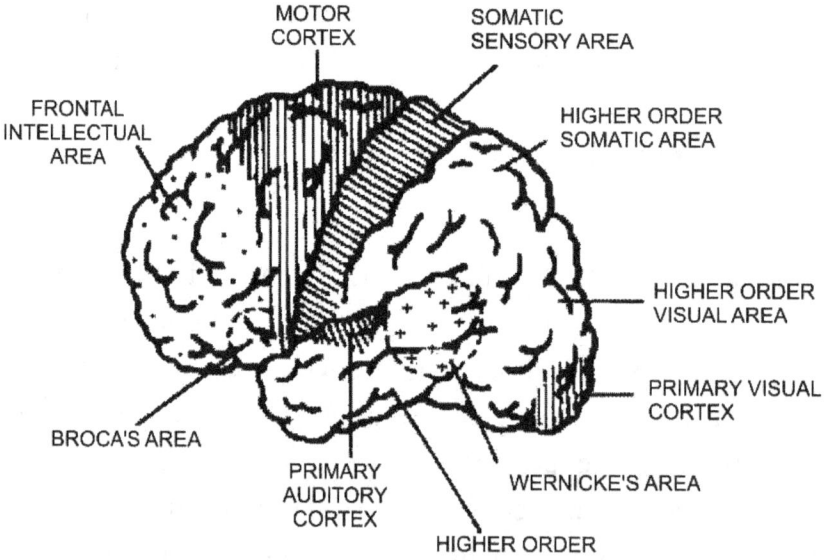

Fig. 19 : Lateral view of cerebral cortex showing specially Wernicke's and Broca's areas responsible for language comprehension and speech.

Regarding the cell-biological processes and molecular mechanisms of intelligence, much is not known at present.

HOUSE OF EMOTION

Psychologist John Watson conducted an experiment on an 11 month old baby, which is known as Little Albert Experiment (1920).

The baby studied by Watson, played with a rat without fear. Subsequently a loud noise was made when he was playing with the rat and the child showed the natural fear reaction to the noise. After the loud sound had been repeated a number of times in the presence of the rat, the baby developed a fear reaction to the rat itself. The child subsequently showed fear reaction not only to rats but to all furry objects.

According to Watson fear for loud sounds, sudden loss of support is unconditioned, present from birth. The fear for rat is conditioned which has been developed by learning.

From his studies on infants, Watson exposited that love, fear, and anger are three primary emotions like primary colours. And other emotions develop through conditioning from these three primary emotions.

First of all, we have to define what emotions are.

Emotions are some feelings or sensations that provide the driving force for all other houses to perform – to produce eventually the desired results.

As said in the earlier lesson, it does not always set the goal, but it is essentially needed as a drive to carry on the subsequent actions. It may set the goal, or it may be manipulated by our intellectual processes to achieve a more desirable result, but without it even our intellectual house would be unable to carry out the whole function.

Now let us examine what sorts of emotions do we usually possess and what are their utilities.

Hunger and Sex are two basic passions. They both have the features of a perception and an emotion. We perceive or feel hungry by internal stimuli aroused by the receptors in hypothalamus owing to fall in glucose and other nutrients level in blood. Again, we feel hungry thinking of food. We get sexual stimulation from different parts of the body. And also we get sexually stimulated by thinking of sexually provoking thoughts. No need to say, how essential are these two passions. They provide us with the energy to maintain our lives and also needed for the process of preservation of the species.

The emotion 'fear' has been developed to protect the species from the harmful effect of something, either living or non-living, which is more powerful than it.

The emotion 'Anger' has been developed to provide killing instinct in the species against something, either living or non-living, which is less powerful than it.

The emotion 'love' has been developed for two purposes.
One is to give some protection to their opposite weaker sex, particularly at times of pregnancy. And another function of it is to protect their weak offspring and provide food for them in initial stages.

Now, these three emotions, 'fear', 'anger' and 'love' are not only confined to the possession of the human being, but a loads of animals are their possessor too.
Animals exhibit a few other emotions also. Curiosity, that is curious nature of the mind is found in many animals. Sadness and joyfulness are visible in lots of animals.

But in human mind, there has been emergence of an array of more finer and sophisticated emotions which are usually not possessed by animals.

Sense of beauty, laughter, shame or embarrassment – these are the emotions, whose only beholder is human mind.
Along with the course of evolution, emotions have also been developed

individually and have been most sophisticated, subtle, and refined in the most advanced and developed mind, that is human mind.

Now there are the points in favour or disfavour of the conception of primary and secondary emotions.

In disfavour :

(1) If primary emotions are also present in the animals, they should show other emotions also. But they don't. Animals cannot laugh.

(2) One emotion works as an inhibitory modulator to another emotion. For example, 'laughter' temporarily makes us forget 'sadness' or 'anger'.
It is as like, touch or cold sensation alleviates the sensation of pain through simultaneous stimulation of touch and thermal receptors in the same area. The sensory nerve unit for one sensation laterally inhibits the nerve units for other sensations. This is known as lateral inhibition and this lessens the feeling of individual sensations.
If emotions were mixed sensations, it would have not been possible.

(3) Our every emotion has specific purpose and they are very distinct. Not only their expressions are different and distinguished from each other, but their expressions help in the purpose of the emotions also (as described in Ch.V). If there were mixing of primary emotions, in both cases, that is in purpose and in expression, there would have been over-lapping. But that does not happen. So it is very contrary to the concept of primary emotions.

In favour :

(1) There are a lot of emotions, whose number is highest in case of human mind. It is a bit awkward to think that our brain has different centers for each emotion.

(2) It is also possible that animals, though possess the primary emotions, but the process of their mixing and further formation of secondary emotions, have not been developed in them.

Now considering all the points, both in favour and disfavour, it could be opined that our emotions have been developed individually by some common mechanism of the neuronal change during the course of the evolution, and the brain maintains individual centers for every emotion, as we already know and have detected different distinct centers in the brain for 'hunger', 'sexual drive', 'fear', and 'anger'.

So the concept of primary and secondary emotions does not exist.

All our learning is conditioned, so the object of emotion is also conditioned.

Our body maintains some mechanisms that do not depend on our conditioned learning. This is called unconditioned action.

When sugar is put on tongue, the sensation of the molecule by the receptors there, automatically secrets saliva from salivary glands.

No conditioning is needed for this action. When some sour object is put on tongue, to maintain the pH and protect the surrounding structure, the saliva is automatically secreted to reduce the effect of acidic pH. It is not to be conditioned.

But when some food carries taste sensation to our brain and that in turn stimulates the salivary gland, that is conditioned.

In Pavlov's experiment, when the dog sees the food, there is increased salivary secretion. Here knowledge of the vision of food in memory stimulates hunger center and that causes increased salivary secretion.

Here it is conditioned.

When food is placed within his mouth, there is both conditioned and unconditioned reflex.

Nutrient particles stimulate the local receptors which directly stimulate the salivary gland - that is unconditioned.

Nutrient particles through taste receptors send taste sensation to the brain to inform it that it is a food, which in turn stimulates hunger center that causes increased salivary gland secretion - that is conditioned. It is mediated through knowledge of taste sensations of food, which is learned after birth.

To explain it a little elaborately, when we put a non-edible object in our mouth, we get the taste of it, but it does not increase our salivary secretion via taste sensation as we know it is not a food. Because the taste of it has not been conditioned in our memory to recognize it to be as a food.

When the food reaches the stomach and thence duodenum, there is secretion of digestive juices after detecting the presence of the food.

It is all unconditioned.

Presence of nutrient particles there stimulates local receptors to secrete particular digestive enzymes. We don't have to learn it.

A child, at sometime after birth, tries to put everything in its mouth. Actually at this stage memory of taste sensations of food is being conditioned in its brain. I must say mechanism is a bit complex. Non-edible objects would not be digested and would give him gastro-intestinal discomfort which would also be recorded and next time the child should avoid it. After proper conditioning, the child would only take the edible objects for food for the rest of his life.

Perception is an input mechanism to our memory. It brings only information to the memory house. But conditioning activities are carried out by one or all of the four houses.

The most commonly exemplified unconditioned reflex is skeletal muscle jerk. Each muscle maintains a specific tone, that is a sustained contraction that would permit the muscle to maintain a length within average range and it is essential for maintaining posture and balance. If a sudden effort is applied to stretch the muscle beyond its average length, the muscle will reflexively contract.

Now what would be the tone of that muscle?

It depends on earth's gravity. Definitely earth's gravity is not recorded in our genetic code. This tone is developed through a conditioning process during the development of the organism. Time of birth is not the demarcating point, because fetus in uterus also feels earth's gravity.

Though neural circuit for the reflex lies in the spinal cord, there is facilitatory and inhibitory influence of higher brain on it, particularly the house of physical activity and between these two influences, facilitatory and inhibitory, the reflexes are set.

If that same subject had been born in another planet with different gravity, the muscle tone would have been different and the force needed to elicit muscle jerk would have been otherwise.

One can fantasize if he goes to the moon, he would be able to jump at a greater length, or his movements would be awkward. Yes, but that for the initial stage. After a time, his muscle tone would be re-conditioned to maintain normal posture and balance. And he would not feel the lesser gravity. Even in the spaceship it has been observed in astronauts who have resided there for a considerable time, spinal cord excitability has been significantly reduced along with decreased muscle reflex response.

So what does conditioning mean? – Our body's mechanisms which have to be adapted with the external environment, and which information are not encoded in the genetic code, are supposed to be conditioned.

On the contrary, the body's those mechanisms that do not need to be adapted with the external environment, and which information are encoded in the genetic code, are not supposed to be conditioned and they are regarded as unconditioned mechanisms.

So are our all emotions. Emotions are there, but the objects of every emotion are to be conditioned.

What to be feared and what not to be feared are all conditioned.

Sometimes we feel fear in unknown desolate place or seeing an unknown animal.

But here it is also conditioned. The knowledge that unknown place may have unknown danger or any animal whose nature is not known may be harmful, conditions our mind to arouse fear.

Fear for loud noise or sudden loss of support are all conditioned.

In case of skeletal muscle reflexes, they could be both conditioned and unconditioned. Some primitive reflexes, like suckling reflex (reflex sucking behaviour of the new born when nipple or any other object is put within its mouth), palmar grasp reflex (grasping behaviour of the new born when some object is put or touched on its palm) are unconditioned, as they have not to be conditioned with the external environment. But the skeletal muscle jerks (knee jerk, ankle jerk, etc.), that have to be conditioned with the earth's gravity, are conditioned reflexes.

Can emotion be evoked voluntarily?

Memory is stored automatically, we can also memorize things by efforts. So is true for emotions and components of all other houses.

Different emotions such as fear, anger, love etc. are evoked in mind by different stimuli or in different situations. We feel them in our everyday life.

But we can evoke emotion voluntarily also. Thinking of food make us hungry. Our sexual feeling and desire depends on our sexually arousing thoughts and other activities. We set a romantic atmosphere to arouse particular of our emotions.

Professional and experienced actors can arouse their emotion in the most difficult settings. Practically, an actor's efficiency depends on it.

So emotion, like memory and output of other houses, can also be educed voluntarily, but for that training of mind and expertise is necessary.

Like memory, intelligence, emotion can also be subcategorized into three faculties (a) reflexive emotion (b) short-term emotion (c) long-term emotion or emotional strength.

Reflexive emotion

Reflex emotions are those, whose arousal do not involve prior consciousness and actions of them last for a very short period of time.

Short-term emotion

In these cases emotions attack us in different situations and are provoked by different factors. Their action stay from some minutes to several days. But their actions are situational. They stay, so long as the provocative factors act on the mind. Once the provocative factor is dissolved, the emotion is also released. But if the provocative factor is not like something that could be dissolved, the displacement of adaptive range in emotion occurs. It has been described in detail in the chapter IV under emotion.

Long term emotion or emotional strength

At certain point of time in one's life, every person possesses a certain strength of emotion. We experience all kinds of emotions since birth. This emotional experiences are also deposited in our memories, being converted into memorigraphic data.

All these, being accumulated, produce an emotional strength or emotional maturity within us as in other houses of memory, intelligence and physical activity.

An emotionally mature man takes the emotions in more controlled and desired manner than an emotionally immature mind, and directs his emotion for specific purposes.

This emotional strength is also expressed along with his knowledge (memory) and intelligence in his disposition, behaviour, and activities.

Current knowledge of the anatomical, cellular and molecular mechanisms of emotion.

It has been described in the Ch. IV under emotion.

HOUSE OF PHYSICAL ACTIVITIES (OR MUSCULAR ACTIVITIES)

Under this house, voluntary muscular activities of ours come within the realm of mind. Muscles are acted under the voluntary commands of the mind and also they act involuntarily like issues of any other of four houses. Some muscles are regulated by autonomic nervous system and they all act only involuntarily, but any of our conscious action of our mind indirectly may have effect on them. Like, increased activities, emotion 'fear' increase the rate and contractility of heart muscles.

Though the muscles are not part of the nervous system, but they are the end mechanisms of our voluntary neural control of activities. Their actions are very integrated and disturbances in function of mind also affect them.

So the area of mind that controls our voluntary muscular or motor activities, constitute the part of the mind defined under this house.

Like other three houses, this house also has same three faculties - that is reflexive, short-term, and long-term.

Reflexive Muscular activities

We are all well acquainted with reflexive muscular activities.

Muscle jerks, reflex removal of hand from any heated object, reflex closure of eye-lids against strong light are examples.

The neural pathway that mediates these reflexes lies in the spinal cord, consisting primarily of an afferent nerve, an intermediary nerve, and an efferent nerve. But there may be involved more nerves and more synapses. And depending upon them, the reflexes could be monosynaptic to polysynaptic reflexes. Though the reflexes do not require sending information to the higher center of the brain, there always act excitatory and inhibitory influences of higher brain on this neural pathway. And within the adaptive range between these two influences, excitatory and inhibitory, the reflexes become set up. So the reflexes of the voluntary muscles are all part of our mind under the house of physical activity, but set through conditioning processes to function automatically without making aware our conscious self, like reflexive faculties of any other of the houses.

Short term faculty

This faculty includes regular muscular activities in our daily life. In majority they comprise muscular activities on demand, which do not depend on specific learned skills.

There are some automatic muscular activities, like walking, chewing of foods, riding a bicycle, and so others. They develop upon learning processes through the life. And they involve procedural memory, which are automatically conducted by our subconscious, as already been described before under the house of memory.

Long term faculty

It develops long-term physical skills and strength. With exercise and repeated specific use, involving either general or a specific group of muscles, long-term physical skills and strength are constructed - like becoming a footballer, being expertised as a pianist, etc. It involves promotion of both muscular strength and efficiency, as in the cases of lifting more weight easily in case of a weight-lifter (increased muscle strength), or running at higher speed in case of a runner (increased muscular efficiency).

Neurons and skeletal muscle cells (responsible for voluntary actions) produce strength either by increased efficiency, or by hypertrophy (increase in the size of the cells), but not by hyperplasia (increase in the number of cells).

Skeletal muscle hyperplasia can take place in rare cases.

Muscle cells or fibers increase its strength by the following mechanisms :

1. Hypertrophy of the muscle fibers (increase in the size of the cells).
2. Increased amount of myoglobin in each muscle fiber to carry oxygen to the mitochondria.

3. Increased numbers of mitochondria to produce increased quantity of ATP.
4. Increased amounts of oxidative enzymes in the mitochondria to cause increased rate of oxidative metabolism, which further increases the production of ATP.
5. Increased growth of capillaries in the muscle itself, so that oxygen and other nutrients can be delivered rapidly and easily during periods of activity.

Along with these, there is also associated changes in the part of the cerebral motor cortex, particular for that group of muscles. But how neuronal efficiency or strength is increased - the exact mechanism is unknown.

One or more of those above mentioned processes, or other operations may be involved.

Hypertrophy has been found to be associated with different regions of the brain controlling intelligence, memory, and emotion.

Pathological 'fear' has been evidenced to be associated with increased volume of Amygdala, a brain region involved in controlling the emotion 'fear' and others, [Tebartz van Elst. et al., 1999; De Bellis et al., 2000; Frodle et al., 2003].

In studies with rat, it has been observed that there is hypertrophy of amygdala neurons under chronic stress, [Vyas, et al. 2003].

Cortical thickness has been related to intelligence in different studies. It has been found that there is a positive co-relation between intelligence and cortical thickness, especially in the prefrontal cortex and temporal lobe, [Narr, K. L. et al., 2007; Choi, Y. Y. et al., 2008; Karama, S. et al. 2009].

In a study, it has been witnessed that supplementation with choline chloride during early stage of development in rats leads to an increase in the size of cell bodies in the basal forebrain, and this change may contribute to long-term improvement in spatial memory, [Williams, C. L. et al., 1998].

Current knowledge of the anatomical, cellular, and molecular mechanisms of voluntary muscle action

Voluntary activities of the muscles are mediated by the primary motor cortex or area 4 in Broadmann's classification in pre-central gyrus (Fig. 16).

It is interesting that more than half of the entire primary motor cortex is concerned with the controlling of hands and muscles of speech.

There is also premotor cortex and supplementary motor area, involved in muscular actions.

Premotor cortex is involved in activities of groups of muscles to perform specific tasks.

The actions of motor cortex are being continuously adjusted by the other centers of the lower brain - these are the basal ganglia, cerebellum, the reticular formation of the brain stem, the vestibular nuclei, and often the red nuclei - to maintain smooth, coordinated, organised, voluntary movement with maintenance of balance and posture. These are collectively known as Extrapyramidal system. Commands for voluntary movement originate in cortical association areas.

So, actions are regulated like following.

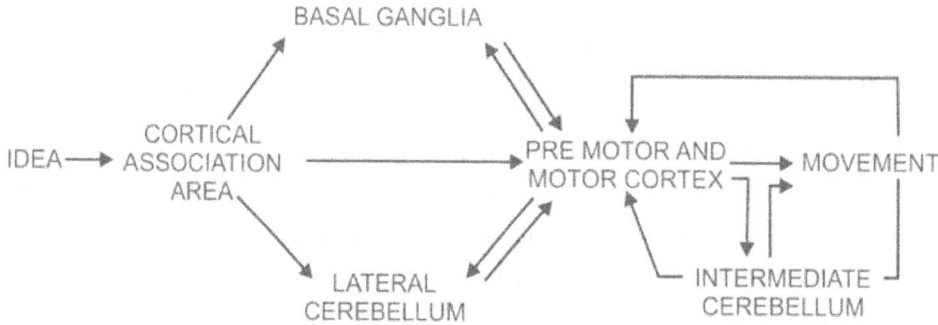

Fig. 20 : Control of voluntary muscle actions by the brain (illustrated after diagram in Ganong's review of medical physiology).

Mechanism of muscle contraction is a well-established knowledge, can be found in any physiology text book, and will not be discussed in this book.

Genetical and Environmental factors controlling the Houses

The person's short-term faculties are mainly dependent on genetics or heredity. And the person's long-term faculties are mainly dependent on environment and the person's activities in life - it means how much he has been subjected to those processes and exercised to maximum abilities.

But as the long-term faculties or strength of the houses have influence on the person's short-term actions and in return, formation of long-term strength is dependent on person's innate abilities, both the faculties have mixed components of genetic and environmental factors.

Same is true regarding the reflexive faculties. But the reflexive faculties are prone to change and are modified and conditioned depending upon the demands of the corresponding environment.

CHAPTER II

IQ, MQ, EQ AND PQ

INTELLIGENCE QUOTIENT

As has been described earlier, Intelligence is the ability to serialize the received information by the brain in such a sequence that would produce specific cause and effect.

There are a number of tests, by which this ability can be measured.

But all these tests measure not only a person's short-term ability to being intelligent, but also, to some extent, person's long-term intelligence strength that depends on his education, experiences of intellectual processes that he has undergone; and culture, environment, society, which promote the mental development of a person favouring rationality.

This is also known as 'g' factor.

Usually children in western countries are grown in such a cultural environment, that the trends of intellectualizing things are promoted in a child's mind. That means, they grow up along with thinking in a more rational way.

Children who are born in a society, where strong religious or cultural beliefs and faith predominate, the exercise of intellectual processes in the child's mind is not that encouraged. That means the children are promoted to think more on faith or cultural beliefs rather than in a rational way. That is, how many times and to maximum extent, a person has exercised the process of intellectualization is an important factor. This promotes development of long-term intelligence strength.

These factors act always as an essential influence in the backdrop, while IQ tests are performed.

But yet these tests can fairly measure the ability of a person's being intelligent.

As IQ measures the person's short-term ability to solve problems, which is also influenced by his long-term faculty or intelligence strength, and as explained earlier both have components of genetical and environmental set up, it could be said that IQ score is dependent on the person's genetical make as well as his long-term experiences and environment he has grown up within.

IQ of the general population follow normal frequency curve (Gaussian Curve), which is bell-shaped.

Most people fall in the center, some score very well, they are marked as highly intelligent people. And some score very poor, they may suffer from some form of mental subnormality.

Usually IQ below 70 is designated as mild mental retardation, IQ below 50 moderate, and IQ below 35 severe mental retardation.

On the other hand, the person possessing IQ over 145, is considered as highly gifted.

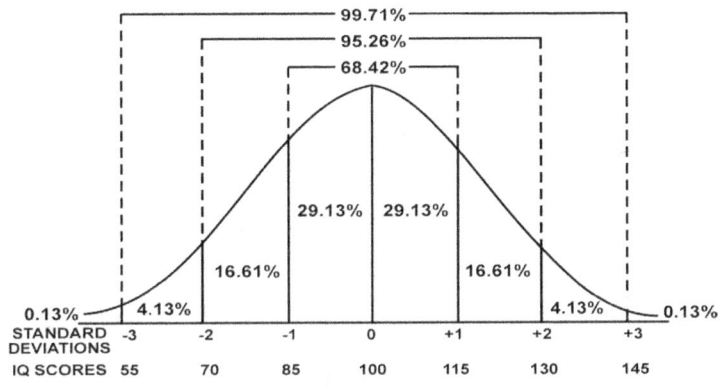

Fig. 21 : Distribution of IQ Scores

Current commonly used IQ tests for measuring IQ are :

(1) Binet type of Test

It was originally improvised by the French psychologist Alfred Binet and was later modified by psychologist Lewis Terman of Stanford University. This test is currently known as Stanford Binet Intelligence Scales.

This test has several revisions, and assays across four areas : Verbal Reasoning, Quantitative Reasoning, Abstract Reasoning, and Short-term Memory.

Stanford-Binet Intelligence Scales, 5th edition (SB-5) is applicable to 2 to 85+ years of age. The test contains 10 individually administered subsets which estimate Verbal IQ, Non-verbal IQ, Brief IQ, and Full-scale IQ.

Some of the sample questions of Stanford-Binet test :

1. Which one of the five is least like the other four?
    a) Bottle
    b) Cup
    c) Tub
    d) Funnel
    e) Bowl

2. Which one of five designs makes the best comparison?

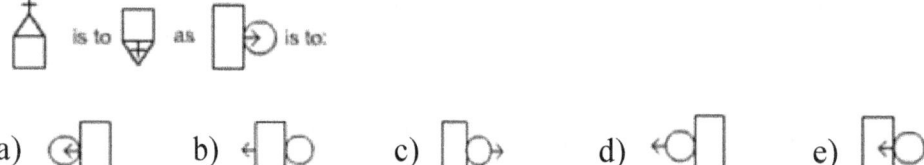

3. Which one of the numbers does not belong in the following series?

   a) 9   b) 7   c) 8   d) 6   e) 7   f) 5   g) 6   h) 3

[correct answers are 1. b, 2. d, 3. h]

The scores of all the tests are put in the following formula, from which Intelligence Quotient or IQ can be derived.

I. Q. = Mental age/ Chronological age x 100

The mental age is determined by the scores, the child obtained in the test. The chronological age is the child's actual age in respect of years and months etc.

So a seven year-old child having normal intelligence or average intelligence would pass all the tasks usually passed by seven year-olds but nothing beyond and would score 100. And in that case, his mental age is the same as his chronological age.

So the score is compared with the intelligence of general population of the same age.

Stanford-Binet Fifth Edition (SB-5): Classification of IQ

IQ range	IQ Classification
145 - 160	Very gifted or highly advanced
130 - 144	Gifted or very advanced
120 - 129	Superior
110 - 119	High average
90 - 109	Average
80 - 89	Low average
70 - 79	Borderline impaired or delayed
55 - 69	Mildly impaired or delayed
40- 54	Moderately impaired or delayed

(2) The Wechsler Intelligence Test

This test was improvised by American psychologist David Wechsler. There are three versions of the test. Wechsler Intelligence Scale for Children (WISC), Wechsler Preschool and Primary Scale (WIPPSI) for children aged 2 to 7, and Wechsler Adult Intelligence Scale (WAIS) for people aged 16 and older.

WAIS-IV contains 10 subsets along with 5 supplemental tests. The test encompasses four major areas : a Verbal Comprehension Index, a Perceptual Reasoning Index, a Working Memory Index, and a Processing Speed Index.

Rather than based on chronological age and mental age, the Wechsler Intelligence test is scored by comparing the testee's score to the scores of others in the sample group of same age.

(3) Raven's Progressive Matrices Test

Ravens's progressive matrices test provides an assessment of non-verbal ability, which is non-dependent on linguistic background and useful for our ethnically diverse population.

The tests are available in three different versions : (1) Standard progressive matrices - designed for general population. The tests get increasingly difficult. (2) Coloured progressive matrices - for children and elderly people. (3) Advanced progressive matrices - this is the advanced form appropriate for adults and adolescents of above-average intelligence.

Each Raven's test has the same format : A 3x3 matrix in which the bottom right entry is missing, and must be selected from 8 alternatives.

An example :

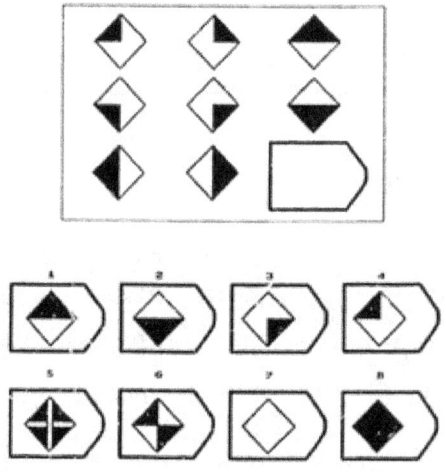

The correct answer is 8.

(4) Woodcock-Johnson Test

This test may be administered to population aged from 2 to 90+ years. The latest version is WJ-IV. WJ-IV includes three independent batteries - 1. Standard Battery, 2. Extended Battery, and 3. Oral Language Battery.

Three batteries can be used independently or in any combination.

The test covers a number of areas - General intellectual ability (GIA), Brief intellectual ability (BIA), Comprehension-Knowledge (Gc), Fluid reasoning (Gf), Short-term working memory (Gwm), Cognitive processing speed (Gs), Auditory processing (Ga), Long-term retrieval (Glr), Visual processing, Quantitative reasoning, Auditory memory span, Perceptual speed, Number facility, and others.

Compositions of those tests contain oral vocabulary, number series, letter-pattern matching, number-pattern matching, story recall, concept formation, visual-auditory learning, picture recognition, memory for words, pair cancellation, sentence repetition etc.

There are also many other tests like Cattell Culture Fair Test, Kaufman Assessment Battery of Children (KABC), Das-Naglieri Cognitive Assessment System (CAS) etc.

But there is no universally accepted intelligence measurement test. Most of the tests are greatly influenced by knowledge, education, culture, language, and regionality. And the standardization of the general population is also not universal.

Another point should be noted here, that as IQ tests provides exercises in the respective house of the mind, these test compositions should not be taken for test and measurement only. Children should also be encouraged to perform this exercises, as this helps to develop the long-term intelligence strength of the child.

MEMORIBILITY AND MEMORIBILITY QUOTIENT (MQ)

The 'Memoribility' means the ability of a person to receive new information, capitalize and store them, and retrieve them when necessary.

Same as in intelligence, 'Memoribility' usually refers the person's short-term ability to remember, but it is influenced by the person's long-term faculty of memory or strength of the knowledge.

As we have discussed in the chapter I, the person has not overall control on the formation of his long-term memories. The formation of long-term memories are dependent on lots of factors. We can help storage of information in long-term memories by repetition process. And our subconscious mind also decides which information are to be stored away; and that depends on information associated with strong emotions, information that significantly modifies one's life, or information which are regarded by our wise subconscious as that have significant future prospects.

From genetical standpoint, short-term memory, although it has an influence of long-term memories' environmental component, is mainly based on person's genetical make up. On the other hand, long-term memory, though dependent on the person's short-term inborn or genetic component of memoribility, is mainly based on person's education and environment.

As like the intelligence tests which measure the person's short-term ability with a background influence of long-term strength, through memoribility tests we also measure the person's short-term ability to memorize which is backed up by his long-term memory strength.

A Memoribility Quotient can be obtained by comparing the scores achieved by the subject with a representative sample of common population in the same age group.

In conventional way MQ has not been differentiated from IQ and all the tests measuring memoribility, also have become part of many standard IQ tests.

So, many in vogue popular tests like Stanford-Binet test, Wechsler Intelligence test, Woodcock-Johnson test have the component measuring short-term memory or in general, memoribility. These tests usually take the following formats :

a) Remembering of words, numbers, pictures, or photos.
b) Remembering of the sequences of words, numbers, and pictures.
c) Remembering of audio-visual presentations.
d) Story recall.
e) Sentence repetition.
f) and others.

Knox's cube test though originally was improvised as an IQ test but it is a simple memoribility test.

Knox's Cube Test

In this test, four 1 inch black cubes are placed 4 inches apart in a series.

The examiner, with a smaller cube, taps these cubes in a particular sequence. The subject has to memorize the sequence and retrieve them.

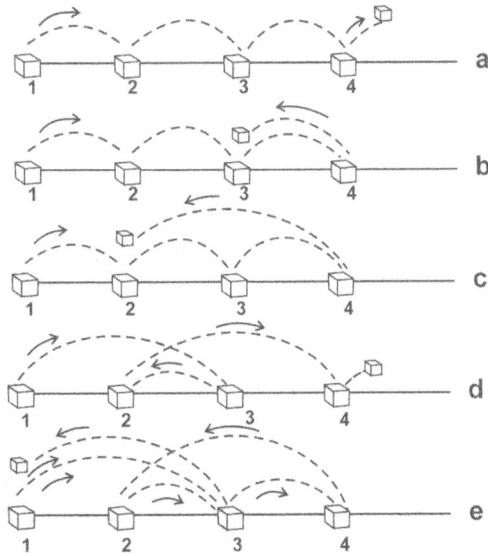

Fig. 22 : Knox's Cube Test

a) 1 - 2 - 3 - 4
b) 1 - 2 - 3 - 4 - 3
c) 1 - 2 - 3 - 4 - 2
d) 1 - 3 - 2 - 4
e) 1 - 3 - 4 - 2 - 3 - 1

According to Knox, a child aged 4 years can recall the sequence a, 5 years b, 6 years c, 8 years d, and 11 years e.

EMOTIONALITY AND EMOTIONALITY QUOTIENT (EQ)

Emotionality means the ability of a person to become emotional to the maximum level in any field of emotion.

Till date, there is no standardized test to measure a person's emotionality, but it is a sine qua non factor for all the achievements of mankind. Without it, there would have not been any difference between a human mind and a computer.

A person however intelligent and memorious he could be, may fail to become successful in life, if he does not have adequate charge of his expansion of emotionality.

As I have explained in the first chapter, the emotion individually does not always set the goal; memory, intelligence can also manipulate emotions. But it creates the driving force for the subsequent actions of the other houses. The role of the other houses in manipulating it, is just to serve the emotions in a more achievable and enjoyable way.

As said in a previous example, receival of information that food can be obtained in some place - evokes the emotion 'hope' and 'hunger', which in turn triggers the house of intelligence which solves out how to reach to that place and achieve the food, and solving this problem, it actuates the house of physical activity, by the order of which further actions take place. Thus, the emotion plays as a driving force for the systematic actions of all four houses to produce the result in an organized manner. And this drive is very much needed for all activities in our life.

There are no standardized test for measurement of a person's emotionality yet. Moreover, it is also a matter of debate whether a person, highly emotional in one field, would be same emotional in other fields also. That is if a person who experiences 'fear' to the maximum level, also would feel 'hope' at the same level.

There has not been any studies so far regarding this. And not all the emotions act from the same centers in the brain.

My supposition is though emotions are not controlled by the same centers in the brain or different emotions have different centers in the brain, a common geneticalsubstage and neuronal efficiency works. So a generalized EQ should be considered.

But if there is variations in the comparative size (which is dependent on neuron numbers) and efficiency (which is dependent on neuronal efficiency) among the emotion centers in different individuals, individual EQ for each emotion should be considered. Such as EfQ (Emotional center fear quotient), EhQ (Emotional center hunger quotient), EsQ (Emotional center sex quotient), ElQ (Emotional center love quotient) etc.

Common neuronal efficiency works also for all four houses. So overall GQ (General Quotient) is a necessary measurement. Again some houses of the brain could be more developed than other houses. So individual quotients for the houses should also be considered. And so is true for each emotion center.

Now till this date, there has not been any attempt to represent a person's emotionality figuratively. To measure emotionality it has to be measured to what maximum extent a person can be emotional with respect to a particular emotion.

Here are some ideas for measurement of emotionality.

(1) `After 24 hrs. fasting, a subject was presented before him some delicious food of his own notion and putting a sensor in his mouth the maximum amount of salivary secretion compared with normal level was measured. It

is because salivary secretion is closely related with 'hunger' emotion, aside from its perceptional part (discussed later in Ch. IV). By this method, we can measure the maximum extent of his hunger emotion.

(2) After 24 hrs. or 48 hrs. of abstinence from emotional exposure (the person should be away from any emotional exposure, mild sedative could be advised for this purpose), A photo-scanning measuring apparatus was attached to the forehead of a person, and he was allowed to watch an intense horror movie, selected upon the person's own notion, alone. And the machine recorded the maximum dilatation of the pupil compared to its normal size. Simultaneously his heart rates, breath rates, body temperature (all the parameters of a 'fear' reaction) were also recorded with attached specific instruments. A hierarchy could also be established with gradually more fearful movies to detect the maximum fear reaction the person can exhibit.

Scores have to be compared with the data of the representative sample of the general population in the same age group.

PHYSICAL ABILITY AND THE QUOTIENT OF PHYSICAL ABILITY (PQ)

An athlete is born with ability and trains himself up to be an athlete.

An athlete's physical ability depends on how fast and powerfully he can actuate his muscular activities - that includes the rate of the muscular contraction as well as the strength of the muscular contraction. Some sports need hand-eye co-ordination or such parameters. This needs quicker activation of muscles after receiving a stimulus in desired manner.

So stronger, faster action of muscles and prompt response of them to a stimulus are all components of physical ability. This ability initially depends on a person's genetical make-up.

But by capitalizing of this ability of him, the person has to train his muscles (in general or a specific set of muscles) through proper training method to be expertised with a particular sport.

Depending upon the exercise and training, strength of the muscles (either general or specific) are increased and an optimum tone of the muscles is maintained.

So an olympic medal winner sprinter has both the component, his athletic ability and the result of his long-term exercise and training processes.

Some sports also favour some specific physical characteristics besides PQ. For example tall physique in basket ball, greater flexibility of the ligaments of bones and joints in gymnastics etc.

Many sports, like football, also demand the person's intellectual ability, that is reflex decision making or intuition and short-term intellectual ability on the field. But those are the part of his IQ, not PQ.

Emotional and memory factors also count in a player's performance.

By PQ tests we usually measure in a child his genetics dependent physical or muscular ability. But in adults, along with the individual's genetic component, his long term exercises and training also counts. So PQ is very much age specific. But in younger age its measurement indicates the person's genetical ability more.

Test scores can be achieved through different tests and should be compared with the data of sample group of people representing general population of same age.

Usually we do not do PQ tests. Because whenever in school, the athletic talents are detected easily. However, to detect PQ, whatever the tests may be, the following four factors must be taken into account when testing PQ.

(1) After receiving a stimulus (visual, auditory, tactile etc.), how quickly the subject can activate his muscle.

(2) How fast he can move a limb, that is the speed of contraction of his muscles in respect of contractions per minute.

(3) The maximum period of time his muscles can contract and relax, that is the muscles can work, within a range of efficiency or contraction rate.

(4) How much power the muscles can generate.

(5) Resting muscle tone. But it measures the long-term strength of the house rather than denoting the subject's PQ. And it can be altered in neurological disorders.

Here are some ideas for measuring PQ:

1) For test type 1 there would be five balls with inside light and a time sensor, placed a little apart from each other. The subject would be ready with a tennis bat or such like thing. Whenever one of the balls would light on, the subject would have to hit the ball as quickly as he can.
The time between the lighting on of the ball and the ball being hit by the subject should be recorded.

(2) For the test type 2 the subject should be allowed to run on a running machine as fast as he can. And it should be recorded on digital radio photographic scanner with timer attached. Then on computer analysis it should be detected the maximum speed of his muscles' contractions and how long his muscles can contract within the range of efficiency speed (that may be from the maximum speed of his muscle contraction to half of that speed). Alternatively a sensor can be attached on the skin of a specific muscle being tested and recording the underlying pressure the speed of muscle contraction can be calculated. Electromyographic (EMG) study also can help to measure this.

(3) For the test type 3, the same procedure should be followed as in (2). But here the subject would be allowed to run within a fixed standardized range of efficiency speed, and the time recorder would record the time how long he can run within this range of speed. This is particularly a test for slow action of muscles without fatigue and it detects the efficiency in sports like marathon running.

(4) For test type four any power measuring apparatus can be used.

I don't know much about sports medicine. But there are a number of available tests and instruments to measure these, that is hand-eye co-ordination measuring instruments, other coordinated muscle reflex measuring instruments, slow and fast acting muscles' efficiency measuring instruments etc.

CHAPTER III

ANALOGY BETWEEN A COMPUTER AND OUR MIND

Computer can do many things, that human mind can do. Knowledge of computer sciences actually helps us to think about many of unknown processes of human mind also.

Yet there are major differences between the mind and computer. The most notable of these is in computer the House of Emotion is absent.

All other three houses are present.

But as I am not too much knowledgeable in computer sciences, I will restrict my attention within the circumference of basic differences between these two.

Computer receives information as digital data, through input devices. Whereas our brain has different sense organs for receiving information. These information are finally converted to memorigraphic data and stored into the neurons of memory regions of the brain as stored information.

Computer has specific storage capacity and it depends upon its built. But it could be enhanced.

Our brain has fixed number of neurons since birth and that do not multiply.

For that reason, our capacity for storage of memory is limited, though a man in his life seldom utilizes his full capacity.

Computer uses outside memory from CD-ROM, DVD-ROM, Floppy, Pen drive etc., and our brain uses it from books, writings etc.

But storing of memory by brain is not like computer storage.

Our storage of memory depends on either emotion, or requirement that is repetitive usage.

Our short-term memory is mainly dependent on requirement, whereas long-term memory mostly needs emotional factors as back up for its being potentiated.

Computer though has RAM memory and Hard disc memory, but mechanisms of action is definitely different.

In some way computer is much speedier than human brain, but that is considering the conscious activities of the human brain. Reflex memory recalling, intuitional activities in human mind, occur in much higher speed, within a fraction of a second.

Computer CPU (Central Processing Unit) can be equated with human intelligence house. Here ALU (Arithmetic Logic Unit) uses different information stored either in RAM, Hard disc, or in external memory stores like floppy, pen drive, CD-ROM etc., and serializes or sequences them to produce definite result as instructed.

Computer output can be delivered through visual, auditory, electro-mechanical (printer etc.) or any other means.

Whereas human mind's output is mediated through the voluntary muscular activities, and involuntary actions like involuntary muscular activities, glandular secretions, etc.

But as in the computer, the House of Emotion is absent, none of its houses can be driven by the computer itself.

For that it needs human mind.

It has no self desire, ambition, or goal.

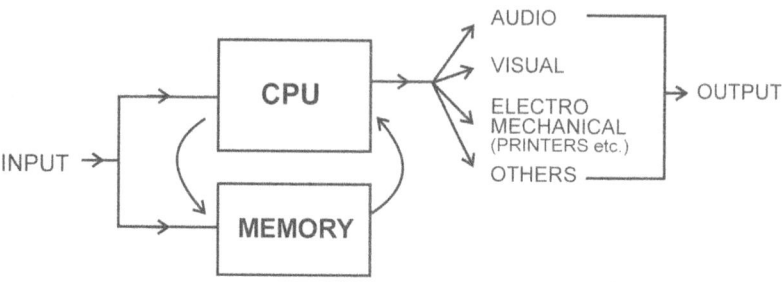

Fig. 23 : Computer Circuitry

Now if we consider the process of storage of memory, in computer information are carried, and stored as digital data. Computer digital data are binary - '0' and '1'; that is, it depends on two modes, one electrical switch 'off' and another 'on'. With permutations and combinations of these two digits all information are constructed, carried through electrical circuitry, and finally stored as digital data. The retrieval follow the reverse process.

In living organism, both external and internal information are carried by the nerve fibers from the sense organs and other receptors located in different parts of the body. The stimulus may be electrical, chemical, or mechanical; but they ultimately are converted into electrical potentials which have to be carried through. But nerve fibers are not "electrical wires". This sensation of the stimulus or electrical impulses is carried through the nerve fibers as action potentials. This is mediated through serial opening and closing of ionic channels across the cell membrane of the nerve fibers, which causes conduction of ions (Na+, K+) through these channels between exterior and interior of the cell membrane, causing serial changes in membrane potentials (electrical potential across the cell membrane) along the nerve fiber; by which, electrical potentials are propagated or carried away through the nerve fibers to their destination. Action potentials follow the ''all or none'' law. That means a certain degree of stimulation or electrical impulse is needed to create or fire an action potential. The minimal intensity of stimulating current to elicit an action potential is known as 'threshold intensity'. The intensity below the threshold intensity would not fire an action potential, and the intensity above the threshold intensity would not augment the intensity of action potential. That means, the action potentials are conducted along the nerve fibers at a constant amplitude.

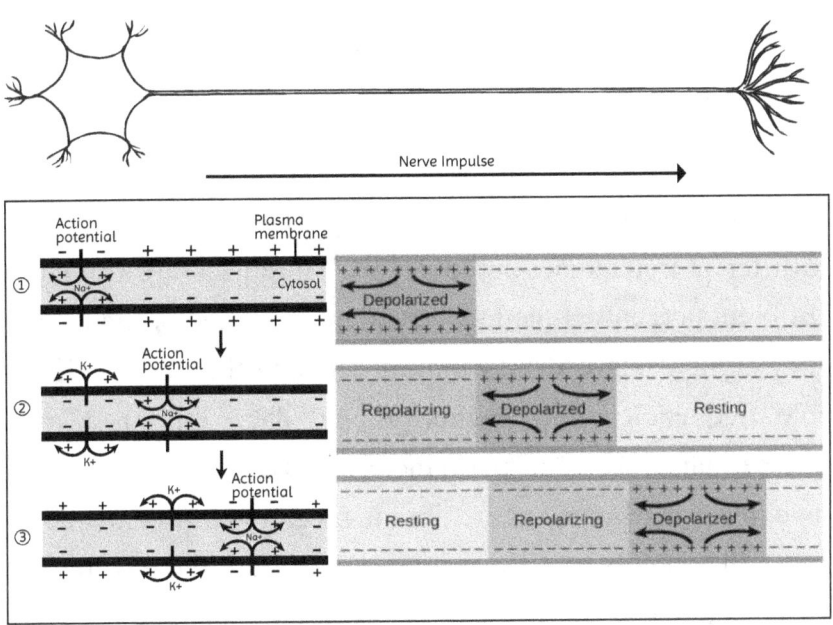

Fig. 24 : Propagation of Action Potential through a Nerve Fiber. (1) When signal comes, first the cell body end of the axon becomes depolarized due to influx of Na+ through openings of the activated voltage gated sodium channels. (2) The depolarization spreads down the axon. Meanwhile, the first part of the membrane repolarizes as Na+ channels are inactivated and additional K+ channels are opened through which K+ ions come out. Membrane comes again to its resting stage. (3) The action potential continues to travel down the axon. (The difference in concentrations of Na+ and K+, created by action potential, later set right by membrane Na+-K+ pump).

But the frequency and conduction velocity of impulses in different types of nerve fibers vary. The conduction velocity depends upon the diameter of the nerve fibers and myelination of them. In general, the greater the diameter of a nerve fiber, the greater is its speed of conduction. The nerve fibers which are covered by non-conducting myelin sheath, ionic conduction occurs only at the junctions between two myelin coverings (the nodes of Ranvier). So impulse conduction through them are much faster. At the termination end, the frequency of action potentials depends on both the speed of conduction and the refractory period of the nerve fibers. The refractory period is the time during which a second action potential cannot be elicited after firing of the first action potential.

Still we are not confirmed, but these variations in frequencies and velocity of conduction of action potentials may do definite job.

As these different frequencies of the electrical impulses, are ultimately converted into either different perceptual feelings, or definite storage or memorigraphic data.

We do not know exactly what changes occur in the nerve cells, that convert these variable frequencies into memorigraphic data, but most probably there happens some permanent or semi-permanent changes either in the structure of the cell membrane (such as changes in membrane receptors or in embedded membrane proteins), or in cell contents (such as changes in intracellular enzymes, intracellular organelles, or changes in gene expression). And that change records the received action potential frequencies, temporarily or for different time-period.

When retrieval is needed, this change again is converted into a certain frequency of action potentials and sends specific desired signal to the targeted parts of the brain.

It is like hundreds of electro-magnetic waves with equal amplitude (as they follow 'all or none' law), but with different frequencies, each representing a different 'bite' or 'bit of information'. In other word, we can say living body's information system is multi-digital.

Nerve fibers with larger diameter are associated with proprioceptive (maintaining balance and posture) sensations, and fibers with smaller diameter are concerned with pain and temperature sensation. Other sensations are carried through different intermediary types of neuronal fibers, with different conduction velocity and different refractory periods.

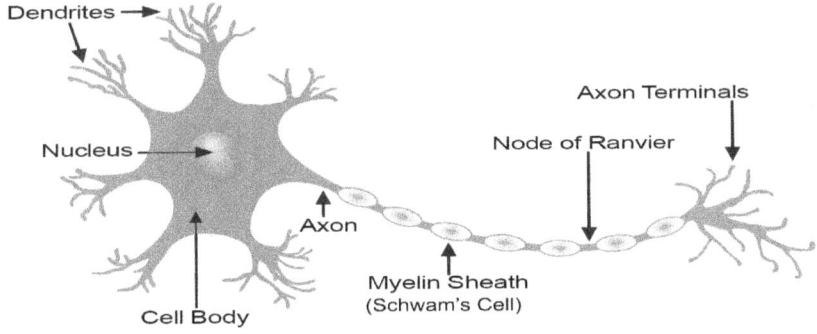

Fig. 25 : A Neuron

Another important factor in memory formation is strengthening of neuronal bond.

For that, when any neuron from hunger center of the hypothalamus fires in the memory neurons of cerebral cortex, only those neurons are activated which have bits of information regarding food.

These bits of information, being summed up, reaches association areas and from there to pre-frontal cortex where further association and sequencing of information take place. And ultimate outcome is transferred to the motor cortex for taking actions.

This strengthening of neural relationship between the specific group of neurons occurs by increase in receptor channels in receiving nerve ending (dendrite), and by increased production of neurotransmitter in the stimulating nerve ending, in the nerve synapses (nerve junctions). Nerve impulse is conducted from one nerve to the next, by the neurochemicals or neurotransmitters like adrenaline, noradrenaline, dopamine, serotonin, and others. These neurochemicals or neurohormones are released from the presynaptic terminals of one nerve ending by emptying of a small number of vesicles into the synapse when action potential comes to that end, and activate the following neuron through membrane receptors of that nerve at the synaptic junctions.

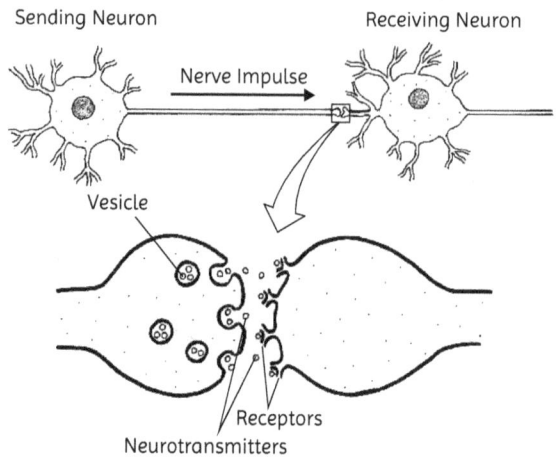

Fig. 26 : Nerve Synapse

Regarding CPU and Human Intelligence House, the ALU (Arithmetic logic unit) of CPU also works by the same sequential process.

Difference is, ALU does sequencing based on binary decision making, that is 'Yes' or 'No'.

But human mind does sequencing on quadrinary decision making process. That is 'Yes', No, Both, and 'I don't know'.

Let us explain it a bit further. Mind has six bits of information 'a', 'b', 'c', 'd', 'e', and 'f'.

Now four tasks are given to it.

    (1) ab = ab
    (2) ab = de
    (3) ab = bc
    (4) xy = yz

Are they related?

In case of (1) the answer would be 'Yes', (2) No, (3) Both, and (4) I don't know.

Sequencing is done – Yes-Both-No – in this manner. 'I don't know' would not come in the sequence.

Our complex intellectual process is based on sequencing information on the quadrinary mode of decision making.

Yet computer could be equivalent to human mind, if emotions are set into it.

As I said earlier, our emotion in simple phrase is "nothing but a goal-oriented drive".

That means putting emotions within a computer is putting a goal within it, when it would not be dependent on external commands.

For all living organisms, this goal is - "self preservation and propagation of the species".

Our emotions are set to pursue that definite goal.

Now if we have to put a goal or any ambition within the computer, the question is – What goal should we put within him?

Definitely, "serving for the mankind".

Robotic teachers, robotic road cleaners, robotic factory workers, robotic personal helpers.

We would create non-biological slaves for us.

We are going to see this very near in our future, may be, before the end of this century.

CHAPTER IV

EMOTION, MOOD AND WAKEFULNESS

We often get confused with these things - emotion, mood, feeling of satisfaction, happiness etc.

But to know them, one should have distinctive ideas about them. In the following paragraphs I have tried to give a clear picture about them and the differentiating features that separate them.

Emotions, mood, and wakefulness are three different entities of the brain.

As described earlier, emotions constitute one of the four major houses of the mind. Mood and wakefulness are not part of major houses, but they are also part of our conscious mind.

And emotions, mood and wakefulness, all are controlled by the different distinctive regions of our brain.

First of all, I will come to the common properties of emotion.

EMOTION

What are emotions?

Emotion is a specific sensation or feeling in the mind that provides driving force to the other four houses of the mind, for their actions to be performed.

There are some general and common properties to all of the emotions.

These are :-

(1) Location

Every emotion has been developed during the course of evolution of the species. And they are controlled by the specific regions of the brain. Grossly almost all of our emotion-controlling areas are located in the limbic system, that means thalamus, hypothalamus, amygdala, hippocampus, part of basal ganglia and septate nuclei.

Every emotion has two different centers, one controlling pleasure or satiety end and another controlling pain or non-satiety end. Complex biochemical reactions by which emotions are controlled are not known. But between these two extreme ends, emotional scale is maintained.

(2) Pleasure and Pain end

As already said, controlled by two mutually distinctive areas, every emotion has two extreme ends on their scale. One negative end or pain end or non-satiety end, and another positive end, or pleasure end, or satiety end.

This is also true for the emotions like fear, anger etc. which are usually considered as negative emotions. 'fear' has other positive end of courage, 'anger' has other positive end of revenge satisfaction. But feeling of their positive sides are less frequent compared to their negative sides as we less encounter situations that evoke positive response of them. Think we go to watch movies, to see the revenge action at the end of the movie, even we pay for it, because for that particular moment, the stylus of stimulus for our 'anger' emotion evokes response towards the positive end. But this feeling is transient.

Other examples are 'joy and sadness', 'love and bereavement', 'curiosity and boredom', etc.

(3) Adaptive Point and Range

In any particular moment, our mind experiences all of our emotions. Yet those do not reach to our conscious awareness, because their stylus of stimulus lie on the adaptive point and moves within the adaptive range (Fig. 23).

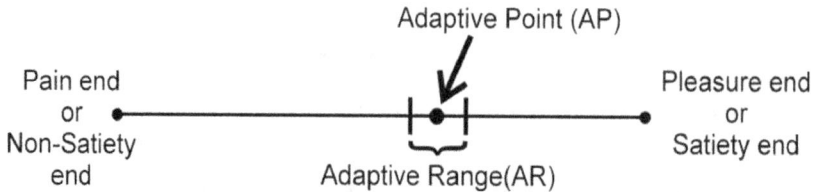

Fig. 27

When the stylus of the stimulus lies within the adaptive range of the scale, it does not bring any conscious sensation to our mind. We feel that particular emotion only when the stylus of stimulus for that emotion moves beyond the adaptive range, or certain event or situation incites emotional response beyond the adaptive range, either towards the positive end or towards the negative end (Fig. 24).

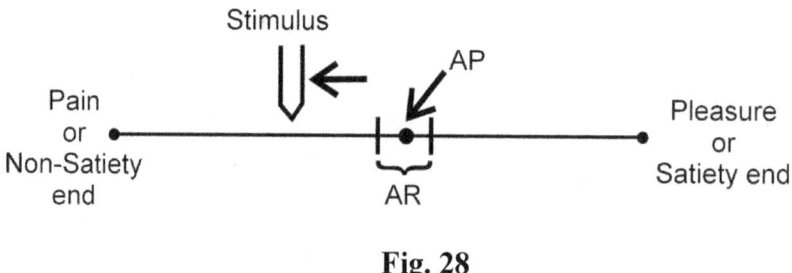

Fig. 28

When a stimulus (an object or a situation upon facing or imagining the memory of it) induces a response on the positive side of the scale from the adaptive point, it brings pleasurable sensation to us. When the stimulus stimulates on the negative side of the scale away from the adaptive point, it brings unpleasurable sensation to us.

[Note : it is the adaptive point, not the midpoint of the emotional scale.]

For this reason, same emotional response can bring different sensation in different persons, and even in same person in different time when adaptive range has been shifted.

Here we must know that emotion scale, adaptive point, adaptive range are all representative figures to represent the mechanisms of biochemical reactions of emotions, and like intelligent co-efficient, emotional co-efficient, experimentally they all could be illustrated and represented figuratively.

Adaptive point and range for every emotion is not fixed in a person during his life. More happier the person is, when the more displacement and fixation of the ARs of emotions occurs towards the pleasure or satiety end.

Now how is this adaptive range formed?

It depends on how much we are compromising with our surroundings.

If a person is put to a situation of fear for some time, he would feel it and would physically and psychologically express 'fear' reactions.

But after a considerable time if the situation still persists, the mind and body of the person gradually become adapted to that situation.

That means, he would no longer feel any sensation of fear, neither he would express any fear reaction through his physique or through his psyche.

Here the adaptive point and range for his 'fear' emotion has been moved towards the negative end on the scale (Fig. 29).

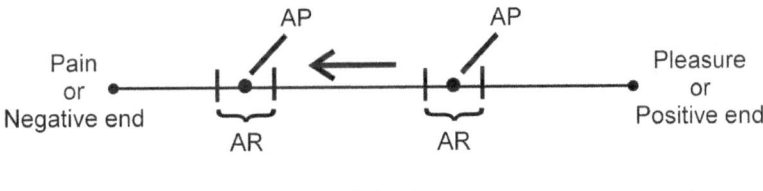

Fig. 29

(4) Positive and Negative Adaptation

When the AR moves from the negative side towards the positive side to be adapted, it is called positive adaptation, and when the AR moves in opposite direction to be adapted, it is termed as negative adaptation. The time for adaptation to be completed varies. It depends on the distance from the evoking stimulus to the adaptive point. The more the distance the more the time is needed for the process of adaptation to have been completed. Usually it is completed within one week if the stimulus remains constantly in its position either in reality or as a memory (that is when the event has happened, and the effect of it working as a memory). But in case of imaginary case, partial adaptation takes place, not complete. In imaginary case, to what extent adaptation will occur that depends on chance of recurrences of the event or the situation.

(5) Emotional Catharsis

Another important feature of emotion is, though in any particular time when we are more or less adapted to all the emotions within their adaptive ranges, yet we sometimes want to exercise any particular or different emotions, moving the stylus of stimulus a bit towards the positive or negative end from the adaptive range.

It is like stretching our legs after sitting for a long time.

This is known as emotional catharsis. The term was first coined by Greek philosopher Aristotle [In Greek catharsis means purification or cleansing]. For that we go to enjoy movie to experience those emotions that we have not exercised for a long time.

These exercise is needed for the other houses of our mind also to keep them on active state.

Now keeping in mind all four above mentioned characteristics of emotions, some common conclusions can be drawn.

(1) In a happy mind, adaptive ranges for the most of the emotions lie towards the positive or pleasure end on the scale.

(2) In a unhappy mind, adaptive ranges for the most of the emotions lie towards the negative or pain end on the scale. But though in unhappy mind, ARs of most of the emotions lie towards the negative end on the scale, yet they create a pressure always on the psyche of the person for the placement of them towards the positive side.

These pressures being aggregated, produce a great directional drive that maximally involves our means, that is our other houses - memory, intelligence, etc.

From this pressure or drive, great creations may come.

A happy mind is hardly creative.

All of our great creations come through the unhappy state of our mind.

(3) Grossly thinking, our life is actually a struggle with the environment in an effort to push our ARs towards the positive end on their scales. As I have already said in the Ch. II, ''No organism upon this earth live to become the fittest, their only goal is to serve their emotions'', in more precise sense, to push their ARs towards positive end.

But in some cases, the displacements of Adaptive ranges of one or more emotions take place to such a negative extent, which the subjects are unable to tackle, may result in their sufferings from various psychoneurotic disorders. Most of the neurotic disorders are caused by the frequent threat of serious negative displacement of ARs on different emotion scales. When there occur marked negative displacement of ARs on a number of emotions, emotional bluntness may follow. Professional's help to grow the subjects' own insight into their problems and suggest the probable ways to come out of those situations may become necessary for them.

Now I would go to deeper in the matter.

For a particular emotion, the adaptive range lies in a particular position on the scale. Different stimuli evoke responses at different points on the scale.

For example, I would take 'fear' as a standard emotional example. The 'fear' is the negative side of the emotion. The opposite side is 'courage' or 'confidence'.

Now the subject has fear of closed space, fear of lightening, and fear of spiders.

Among them, the subject's worst fear is the fear of closed space(claustrophobia).

So, these three fears would evoke responses at three different points on the scale. All of the points are lying away from the AR towards the negative side on the scale. And point for the fear for closed space is lying the furthest towards that end (Fig. 27).

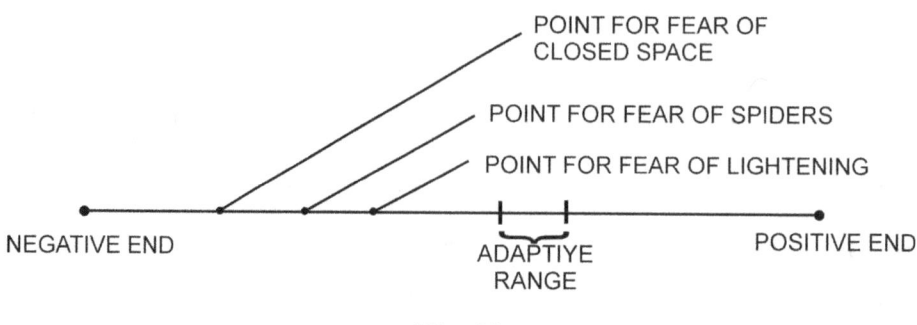

Fig. 30

Now if the adaptation process is undergone for the fear of closed space, that means if the person is gradually compelled to live constantly in closed spaces, his mind will be adapted and he will be able to live in closed space (in this case, we are assuming that he did not win over the fear). And his AR will be shifted towards the negative end and cover the point where the stimulus for closed space was producing fear. But at the same time, as the adaptive range has shifted beyond the point for stimulus of other objects of fear e.g. fear of lightening and fear of spiders, the subject will also cease to fear those objects (Fig. 28).

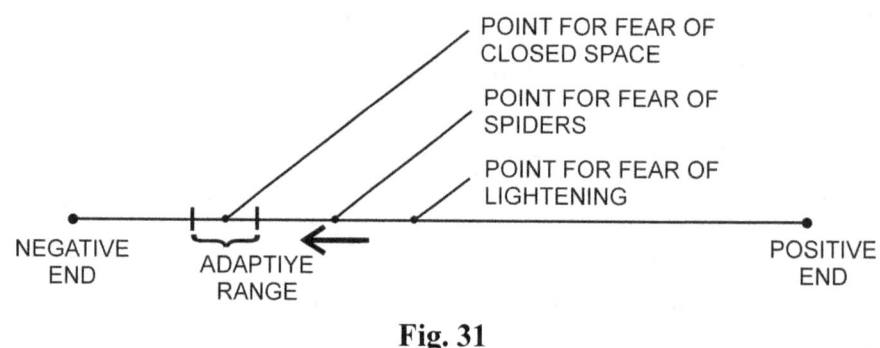

Fig. 31

That means if the subject becomes adapted to co-exist with the object of his worst fear (without winning it - winning means formation of new association of memories and making the stimulus to evoke response up towards the positive side - discussed later), he will lose fear for other objects also.

Or in other words, more the displacement of AR would occur towards the negative side, the more number of objects would lose their recognition as being the objects of fear to a person. Or a person who reaches the tolerance of extreme fear, no objects, previously known to be objects of fear, would seem to him fearsome any more.

Not only that, as the emotional response provoked by the memories of spiders and lightening are lying on the positive side of AR, the person in that adapted condition even may like the sight of them. We all have experienced in a disastrous or worst situation, the sight of our bitter neighbour even brings pleasurable sensation in our mind.

But as already stated, the serious negative displacement of AR creates a great psychic tension of unhappiness or unsatisfaction in a subject's mind. So, although he is co-existing with the object, his mind would always search the route to win over the object, because only in that position his AR may come back to the more desirable position.

It is not an easy job, if the object is truly something to be feared. But it is an achievable goal when the object is truly not something to be feared. That is in case of phobia, where the fear is irrational.

But here we first explain elaborately what winning means. Winning means re-orientation of associated memories. Whenever we see or think of an object, all the associated memories attached with it instantly come to our mind reflexively. These memories can be good or pleasurable, or bad or unpleasurable. If some of these memories bear threatening experiences of the past, the whole associated memory about that object will evoke response on the negative side of the 'fear' scale, that means it will incite 'fear' reaction within us.

Suppose someone was beaten by some person. So whenever he will see that person, the associated memories about him will instigate stimulation on the negative side of the 'fear' scale. But if the associated memories are changed – for example, he retaliated it properly by giving due punishment to him, either by beating him in return or putting him in cell so that it would be hard for him to beat him again – then the associated memories will fail to educe 'fear' response or stimulate on the negative side of the scale. This change of associated memories about that object means winning over the 'fear' reaction evoked by that particular object.

Phobia is irrational fear. Here the object may have not harmed directly the suffering person in the past. But some of the memories which are associated with it bear threatening or unpleasurable experiences suffered in the past. So the whole association of memories regarding that object evoke negative response on the emotion 'fear' or emotion 'disgust' scale. So we may be disgusted to see a spider or cockroach as because there are so many disgusted memories associated with them – such as seen in dirty places, seen frequently spoiling foods, etc.

In the chapter of phobia (Ch. VII), the therapeutic reprocessing of association of memories (TRAM) has been suggested. This therapy (TRAM) is not desensitization and not exactly positive reinforcement. The fear for the object of phobia has been developed when some bad or fearful memories or knowledge has been associated with the object. This can be reverted and phobia for that object can be cured if these group of associated memories are turned to be good by attaching good or pleasurable memories with it, so that number of pleasurable memories associated with the object overweighs the unpleasurable memories attached with it. In that case the associated memories about that object as a whole will fail to incite response on the negative side of the 'fear' or 'disgust' scale.

Now the emotional events that occur in our mind, the mind tries to efface its negative effect by winning over it. Suppose someone gets out in the morning and faced four 'fear' or 'anger' provoking incidents that evoked emotional responses which he did not neutralize on the spot with appropriate actions. By the end of the day when he or she became isolated at home or got away from the incidences, his mind will work upon those. Now which incidence his mind will take first ? If it had been worked out serially, our brain would have been evolutionally backwards. The mind takes them according to their importance, severity and possibilities of facing them again in near future. That means which fear or anger provoking incidence has more severity or has more importance to be neutralized, or which incidence has the possibility of recurring in imminent future (for example, he will have to meet one of those events again in the next morning). The incidence which has the least chance of recurrence or there is no possibility of recurrence of it, the mind can set it aside. But how would he neutralize its emotional effect? The mind does try to neutralize the negative effects of the emotion or prevent replacement of AR from its existing state by expressing the emotion through physique and psyche, or acting out through behaviour, like someone acted out his anger on the spouse or family members. But the fact is actually others are sharing willingly or unwillingly the negative effect of the emotion on themselves. Whatever it is if he does not neutralise the effect, displacement of AR will take place. But he may gradually win over it over a long period of time. All these process occur in our conscious mind as well as in our subconscious mind. But selection of serial of events is conducted automatically mainly by our subconscious mind, switching from one to another, working partially on one, and then shifting to another and then coming back again to the previous one.

Now our mind can consciously put away any emotion provoking incidence, but it is not neutralizing it. So the mind will remain subjugated to that incidence to some extent. Whatever emotional experiences our subconscious mind is setting away, our mind will be subjugated to them also. If that incidence accidentally reoccurs again, the mind will feel the same emotional response with same severity. Not only in the defense mechanism of displacement, even a person with positive pattern of thinking can put aside the negative emotion provoking events to get relief from the distress through positive understanding but he cannot deny the subjugation. So the difference between a person with positive pattern of thinking and a person with negative pattern of thinking is that the positive person would have subjugation only, where the negative person would have subjugation and depression both (more has been cleared next under the heading 'mood').

When the mind is forced to coexist with the emotion provoking agent without neutralizing it, adaptation occurs. Here the displacement of AR takes place. The person can no longer feel any emotional response triggered by that object. But the mind becomes completely subjugated to that object.

Though subjugation reduces the quality of life, but once subjugated it does not bring to the person any mental distress, if it is not too severe. But what effect it implicates on the mind is change in personality. Why do we have different personalities? Different shape or model of our minds ? It is not just associated and embedded memories of information, but the unneutralizedemotional experiences which are also recorded in memorigraphic data. But here along with 'subjugation' positive emotional experiences also share their part. That means some memories which bring happy or pleasurable emotional responses also take part in this process. We can call it upjugation. In every points of life all these memories are acting on our emotional scales, evoking emotional responses, ultimately consolidating into resultant behaviour – making us different persons with different individuality.

It is very interesting to follow that not our neutralized emotional experiences but our unneutralized emotional experiences either positive or negative actually make us, making our personalities.

To these unneutralized emotions, the person may be partially or completely subjugated or upjugated depending upon the degree of adaptation. Partial subjugation or upjugation occurs in case of incomplete adaptation, and complete subjugation or upjugation occurs in case of complete adaptation. When the subject is forced to live with the emotion provoking substance or situation, complete adaptation takes place, in imaginary cases incomplete adaptation occurs based upon the chances of recurrences of them.

It is furthermore interesting that, through the change in our thinking pattern we can combat depression but cannot change our personality if we do not neutralize those unneutralized emotional experiences. But changes in pattern of thinking indirectly may induce a person to neutralize some unneutralized emotional experiences which are responsible for his or her distressing personality and maladaptive behaviour. But it cannot do it directly.

To tell the truth, a person's gross personality changing is difficult. Because one's personality is determined by the thousands of unneutralized emotional experiences that has been stored in his memory since the time of his birth. Alteration or neutralization of all of these is literally impossible. But sometimes it may be possible through expressing out or acting out some of specific emotional experiences which are mainly responsible for the person's distressing behaviour or maladaptation. But in that case a few responsible emotional experiences have to be there. If the experiences are large in number and diffused over a considerable period of one's life, like prolonged ill treatment or abuse throughout the childhood, the personality is less amenable to correction.

But as said in first chapter under 'Memory' unneutralised emotional experiences or emotional memories tend to be faded off over long period of time, if repeated recurrence of the event does not happen. The reason for that is these emotional experiences over time are gradually expressed out by imaginatively repeated thinking of them in the conscious mind, and without the awareness of the subject in the subconscious mind as well. Whenever a person feels relaxed some of his unneutralized emotions get expressed out through his eyes and bodily expressions without the awareness of him. This process ultimately makes the event emotionally neutral memory. But this takes considerable period of time. And it may count for the fact that if some person is completely shifted from one environment or surroundings to another environment or surroundings, being detached from the first one, for a significant length of the time, his behaviour and personality is bound to change and be remodified according to the later one.

Lastly, one point is to be added here that long term strengths of our other houses, such as memory, intelligence and physical activity, are also expressed in our disposition or even in our actions, like an intelligent person would perform a task more intelligently, but they do not take part in formation of the personality of ours.

Perception

Though perception is a receptor mediated sensation that brings information from our external world to the houses of our mind, for being memorized, intellectualized, or emotionalized, it follows some of the features of emotions also, though not all.

They also maintain adaptive point and range.

As we close our eyes in strong light, show reactions to loud sounds, move our limbs from excessive pressure, either crude or fine.

But we do not close our eyes to normally accustomed light, even we do not hear consciously all the sounds within adaptive range. We do not feel the normal barometric pressure.

The adaptive ranges have also been settled in these cases. If we are put to a noisy surroundings, then simultaneously the AR for perception of sound would be displaced. So happens with other perceptions.

But the difference is that, here does not develop psychic pressure for the displacement of the ARs.

We are accustomed to live in normal barometric pressure. And we do not feel any urge to move to any area where this pressure is less.

It is like perceptions are just for adaptations, whereas emotions are for adaptations as well as for progress and evolution.

But extreme of any physical stimulus like extreme heat, extreme light or very loud sound can damage our cells or cell-biological processes.

In my childhood, I have seen Indian yogis lying on bed of pointed iron rods, or walking on the active coals, without showing any feel for the pain.

They actually use, this property of AR. Skin becomes adapted to pointed pressure or heat, and stops giving pain to the conscious mind.

And there may be no harm, if those pointed ends do not prick the skin, or coals do not burn the skin. After a long time practice, there is also skin thickening and callus formation, which provides further protection.

Conscience

In 1923, Sigmund Freud, in his book 'The ego and the Id', divided the mental apparatus into three dynamic parts :

The Id, the Ego, and the Superego.

The Id is the original instinct of our mind.

Superego is our conscience, which is concerned with our moral standards, and develops on the basis of rewards and punishment, through parental and social influences.

And Ego maintains a balance between the Id and the Superego.

According to Freud, the superego is formed between 5-12 years of age.

According to some of the later psychoanalysts like Melanie Klein, this superego develops during the first and second years of a person's life.

Actually the superego or conscience starts to develop from birth or before birth.

And its formation is not fixed or completed at any stage of life.

It can be modified or changed at any stage of life as long as the person lives.

Not only that, displacement of the person from a certain environment to another environment with different ethical values, cultural beliefs can gradually change his conscience or superego to different extent. But the previous imprint, his knowledge and maturity count and act in favour or disfavour of the change.

But first of all we should define what actually 'the conscience' is.

Conscience is nothing but the adaptive ranges of the emotions, acting together subconsciously or consciously to modify one's thoughts and behaviour. The emotion 'Fear' plays a significant role in this case.

In this regard, I cannot check myself from quoting Friedrich Nietzsche - " conscience is internalization of man's instincts which do not find their external expression".

Nietzsche is right.

For example, to a man 'stealing' is a sin or bite to his conscience.

But what would happen to him if he steals?

There is chance of being detected, legal punishment, bad police records, rejection from future jobs, social rejection, displacement from the normal civilian life.

Unless he already has undergone this before, the thinking of all these prospects will make a significant emotional response on the scale of the emotion 'fear' towards the negative or pain end, and will produce fear within his mind.

This fear checks him from the action of stealing. So the adaptive range of fear which remains unconscious or better subconscious and disfavours negative displacement and promotes positive displacement of it, actually makes the conscience.

Had the stimulus remained within the adaptive range on the scale, he would not have to suffer from the bite of conscience.

If he is a convicted thief, he has already suffered these before and there has been displacement of the AR already. In this case his conscience would not prevent him from stealing if he needs to take that action again. Here the unpleasant experience of the previous punishment will only act on his mind to produce fear reaction, if it is really fearsome, but others mentioned above would not. But as I have told in previous lesson that over a long period of time many of unneutralised emotional experiences tend to fade off with the change of environment or if there is no repeated recurrences of the situations that arouse his memories either upon facing, or on imagining of them; and this can be done by active effort also, – the correction of the conscience of a thief may be possible to some extent with complete change of environment, but not wholly.

So 'Rewards and Punishment' theory is partially true, because the person who is already adapted to the punishment, to him fear of punishment would play less role on conscience.

In case of rewards, the conscience favours the displacement of AR towards the positive end. When the AR is already settled on the scale in near proximity of the positive end, there is little place for further displacement of AR towards the positive extremity.

That is, to a man, who has been already rewarded a lot, further any reward would produce less effect on his conscience.

So, the effect or urge of conscience for doing something (with regard to a particular emotion) $\propto$ the distance of the stimulating point of the associated memories, from the adaptive point towards the positive end on the emotion scale.

And, the effect of conscience for not doing something (with regard to a particular emotion) $\propto$ the distance of the stimulation point of the associated memories, from the adaptive point towards the negative end on the emotion scale.

Together, **the effect of conscience (for doing or not doing something) = e x Distance of the stimulation point from the adaptive point.**

(If this distance is towards the positive end from the adaptive point, it would be positive and if towards the negative end, it would be negative).

So, **Total effect of conscience C_T** = Average of aggregation or sum of all the effects of the associated memories on different emotional scale, that is

$$= [C_1 + C_2 + C_3 + \ldots\ldots\ldots + C_n] / n.$$

Here 'e' is a constant, which defines emotional co-efficient, which measures quotient of expansion of the person's emotionality with respect to others or normalized standard population of same age. As said in the second chapter, the emotionality or emotional co-efficient may vary for different emotions (such as $E_A Q$ for anger, $E_L Q$ for love etc.), but there is also a common emotionality or emotional co-efficient (EQ) which is based on common neuronal efficiency. But in calculation, for obtaining better result individual emotional co-efficient should be taken for respective emotions, if possible. Otherwise, common emotional co-efficient can also be taken which will produce a fair result.

So, when the Adaptive point and range lie close to the positive or negative end, the stimulus cannot incite response too far to that respective side, so the distance as well as the effect of the conscience becomes consequently lesser.

So it can be said, that the adaptive ranges of all the emotions - anger, fear, hope, joy, shame, disgust, surprise, laughter, and others, conjointly act together and can be taken as to make our unconscious or better to say subconscious conscience.

Now I will go to another deeper discussion. Our mind holds different beliefs, ideas, faiths including thinking and behavioural pattern in a particular shape developed on this conscience.

Whenever there is significant change of ARs, this shape also needs to be restructured by necessary alterations. This includes changing of these ideas, beliefs, faiths, behavioural and thinking patterns also.

We call it 'defence mechanisms'. Defence mechanisms usually take logical route to make this necessary changes and be adapted with newer situations.

But sometimes it may not be able to do that. In those extreme situations, to cope with the shifted ARs, our structural model of faiths, beliefs etc. even become obliged to take ideas, beliefs that may not follow the logical routes.

This is one of the mechanisms behind the formation of delusions. But not the only mechanism. Delusion may also form when the mind's logical thinking ability is impaired (as in schizophrenia). Again, the criteria for delusion are also questionable. How many of our faiths, beliefs are logically or experimentally justified? So we call our beliefs if normal or delusional according to the fact that whether they are going with the cultural norm or not, irrespective of the fact that whether they are rational or irrational.

Current knowledge of the anatomical, cellular, and molecular mechanisms of emotion.

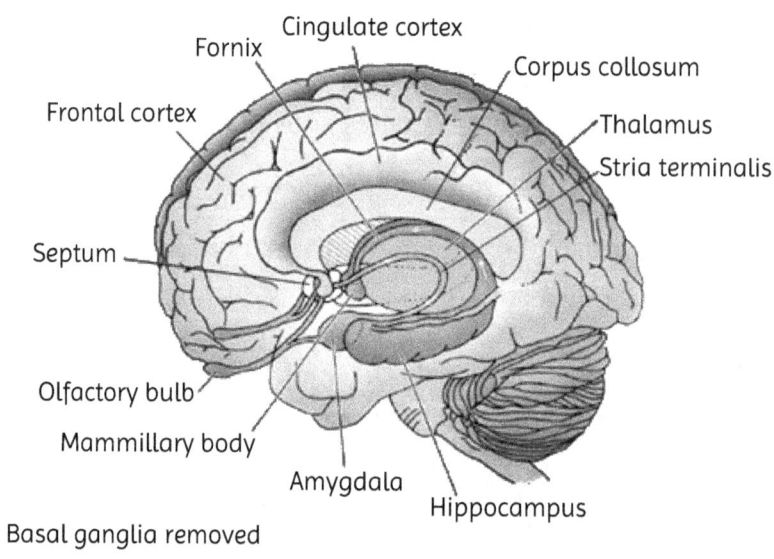

Fig. 32 : Limbic System

Most of our emotions are controlled by the Limbic system, the structures around the basal region of the brain. These structures include the hypothalamus, the amygdala, the anterior nuclei of thalamus, the paraolfactory area, the fornix, the hippocampus, the parahippocampal gyrus, portions of the basal ganglia, the nucleus accumbens, the mammillary bodies, the cingulate gyrus, the orbitofrontal cortex, and the septal nuclei (Fig. 29).

Major neurohumoral system responsible for emotions is dopaminergic system.

The dopaminergic neurons are also present in substantia nigra, a part of basal ganglia, which act in maintaining tone and rigidity of muscles, and are responsible for initiation of voluntary muscle actions (extrapyramidal action).

Antipsychotic drugs block D2 dopamine receptors that are present mainly in the limbic system and also in the extrapyramidal system.

This is the reason why all antipsychotic drugs have extrapyramidal side effects also. Extrapyramidal side effects include muscular rigidity, tremor, hypokinesia (decreased muscle power), mask like facies, bizarre muscle spasms, loss of postural reflexes and disturbances in gait, etc.

Other neurohumoral systems also responsible for emotions are noradrenaline, serotonin, and glutamate system.

Major controlling areas of the brain for our different emotions are as follows :

Hunger and Satiety

Hunger and Sex are two basic passions. They both have the features of a perception and an emotion. We perceive or feel hungry by internal stimuli aroused by the receptors in hypothalamus owing to fall in glucose and other nutrients (amino acids, fatty acids, keto acids etc.) level in blood. Again, we feel hungry by thinking of food. We get sexual stimulation from different parts of the body. And also we get sexually stimulated by thinking of sexually provoking thoughts. It is difficult to say whether the perceptional center and emotional center for both these emotions are the same or different.

But to me, it seems that some other perceptions like vision, hearing, smell, taste also have their respective emotional centers being had attached with. We take pleasure in watching picturesque view, enjoy good music, get enchanted by the scent of a flower and relish the taste of a delicious dish. These are not just receival and perceival of external stimuli.

Stimulation of the lateral hypothalamus causes an animal to eat voraciously, on the other hand stimulation of the ventromedial nuclei of the hypothalamus causes complete satiety. Therefore, we can label this group of lateral nuclei of the hypothalamus as a hunger center, and ventromedial nuclei of the hypothalamus as a satiety center.

Hypothalamus also regulates body water intake by creating the sensation of thirst, which is called the thirst center and located in the lateral hypothalamus.

Sex

Stimulation for sexual arousal could be both perceptional and psychic. Thinking of sexual thoughts, sexual features of the opposite sex, act of intercourse being performed, causes sexual arousal both in male and female.

Alongside, local stimulation, massaging of glans penis in male and glans clitoris in female stimulate sensory nerve end organs, and the sexual sensation is passed through the pudendal nerve and sacral plexus to the cerebrum.

Sexual desire in male is more or less continuous. But in female, desire changes during the sexual month, reaching a peak near the time of ovulation. It is because of the rise of circulating blood estrogen level during preovulatory period.

Higher brain areas controlling sexual feelings and behaviours are not well established. Stimulation along the medial forebrain in neighbouring hypothalamic areas causes penile erection with considerable emotional displays in monkeys.

On the other hand, lesions or damage localized to piriform cortex overlying amygdala cause intensification of sexual activity in monkeys.

Bilateral lesions in or near amygdala has also been reported to cause hypersexuality in men.

Fear

In my book, I have taken 'fear' as a standard emotion to explain different aspects of an emotion. Because this is an emotion which is possessed by almost all the higher animals and many lower animals. It is a pure form of emotion as it has no perceptual component. We do not perceive 'fear' through receptors by external or internal stimuli, but when we do suffer from injury, loss (physical or possessional), events having possibilities of death, we develop fear response in mind regarding the objects or situations responsible for those. And according to the severity of loss, harm and possibilities of consequences, a certain set of associated memory evokes a 'fear' response, upon facing or imagining that object or situation, to a certain degree or intensity. Or it could be said that a set of associated memory instigates 'fear' response on the emotional scale on a particular point upon imagining or facing that object or situation.

Centers for 'fear' reaction lie in Amygdala.

Stimulation of amygdaloid nuclei produces fear reactions in conscious animals.

Bilateral ablation of amygdala (Kluver-Bucy Syndrome) causes complete loss of fear in monkeys.

Rage (anger)

Stimulation of the periventricular zone of the hypothalamus or lateral hypothalamus, causes the animal to produce behaviours, representing rage.

On the other hand, counterbalancing activity is done by the ventro-medial nucleus of the hypothalamus.

Regarding centers for other emotions, much is not known at present.

MOOD

We often get confused with the conception of 'mood' and 'emotion'. Sometimes 'mood' has been described as the sustained emotional response.

Mood is not an emotion at all. Mood is the energetic state of the mind. In a particular time mood defines how much power or energy is being contained or held by the mind at that respective moment.

Elevation of mood is known as elation and degradation of mood is known as depression.

In a certain time, a person can hold only a specific mood between elation and depression. At the same time, the person can enjoy any of other emotions also. So we can astutely disjoin his mood from his emotion, to be recognised separately at any specific moment.

Mood determines quantitatively the amount of energy, the mind is holding on a particular point of time.

An elated mind possesses more power and energy, and a depressed mind possesses less power.

This power can be utilized in all the essential activities of the houses of our mind.

In elated state :-

The person can solve a difficult mathematical problem more easily. (helping intelligence)

The person can memorize a difficult study material more effectively. (helping memory)

The person can play the piano to the best of his ability. (helping emotion)

The person can run a mile to the best of his time. (helping physical ability)

Vice versa occurs in depression.

Normally in our day-to-day life, our mind contains the middle amount of energy with minor variations within acceptable limits, between two extreme ends of elation and depression.

But when there is marked variations of the state of energy of the mind, it causes enough distress. The person when incapable to cope with this, usually seeks medical or other advice.

In a gravely depressed mind, there is a serious lack of energy, that may restrict doing even normal basic daily activities.

In an elated mind, though there is a large amount of energy, by which he can do a lot of works, yet too much excess of this energy may present in some form of distress that is undesirable.

These are –

¤ Euphoria - Increased sense of psychological well-being and happiness not in keeping with the reality.

¤ Increased psychomotor activity, ranging from overactivity to restlessness.
¤ Intense elation with delusion of grandeur.
¤ delirious or stuporous mania.

The person is more talkative than usual. There is marked increase in activity with excessive planning and at times the person tries to do many things at one time. Sleep is reduced and hypersexuality may occur.

Sometimes depression and elation (or mania) occur alternately in cyclical order which is known as manic-depressive psychosis or bipolar mood disorder.

But mild mood elevation and depression within normal range is a natural phenomenon in our everyday life. It is like part of our life.

So variation in mood that causes marked distress which disrupts our normal occupational and social activities, is enlisted in psychological illnesses or diseases.

Hope and elation

There is difference between 'elation' and the emotion 'hope'. Elation is a part of mood, and 'hope' is an emotion. In elated mood one has a lot of power to work, but yet one may not have any definite direction to act. But when emotion 'hope' works, one may not have a lot of power, but there is a definite direction to act.

Now what causes elevation or depression of mood in a normal person, that means if there is no pathology underlying it?

"Positive thinking causes mood elevation or elation, and negative thinking causes mood degradation or depression".

In this regard, person's life-philosophy, educational status, social, cultural and family background, cultural beliefs – every thing is important.

To think positively, every thing mentioned above has significant role.

If a man has a positive attitude towards everything, that is, if he can make his mind think positively in every situation, he can get out of his depression.

But it is not always become possible for everyone on their own. True enlightenment of the mind is that which is most important. Enlightened mind knows to take things, whether good or bad in positive strides, and the person is more stable or static on his mood.

It also follows the rules of evolutionary psychology. When there is negative thinking, that means environment is unfavorable. So the mind as well as mood center get depressed, sending less energy or stimulation to the neurons of cerebral cortex and limbic cortex, reducing their activity. Had it not happened this way, we would have lost mental energy unnecessarily in unfavorable conditions.

Religion plays a very important role to the common people in this regard. Common people often suffer from loss of beloved ones, loss of properties, harm or injuries from any other quarters of life and often fail to cope with these. They suffer from severe negative thinking which causes intractable unbearable depression.

They run to seek relief to their religious leaders in churches, mandir or masjid. They give mental emollient for soothing : have faith in God - everything has a cause and effect - if you have done a sin, it is the atonement for that - if anyone have done harm to you, he will be punished by the laws of God - everything will be amended by the universal law of God – probably there are enough reasons to have faith on it.

But this mental balm of mollification, sets their mind upon thinking on positive scale and makes their mind relieved from the immediate danger of severe depression.

In bipolar disorder, as I have observed in some patients, the patients are very conflicting in nature with regard to their philosophical beliefs, faiths and such other things.

Drugs can do good, acting at molecular level, maintaining serotonin level in neuron endings, but for that the person has to be dependent on drugs. As recurrences are very common after withdrawal of the drugs.

It is rather desirable to posses a true insight which can train the mind to take things in life, either good or bad, in positive manner.

Detachment is another necessary parameter for getting out of depression. Most of our minds are emotionally involved with others in our surrounding societies.

This, not always intentionally - may be unintentionally, may put emotional pressure on the mind that may also set one's mind to think on the negative scale.

For a simple example, someone's father has died. Some close relative of him knew that and when he saw that person, thought inside "Ah! What a poor man, his father has died." and made some words of condolence before him. But the inside negative thinking of the relative, which was also expressed outside through his words, behaviour and attitude, would put an emotional pressure on the mind of the subject and would force his mind to think on the negative scale.

If people think about a person negatively, with whom he is emotionally attached, that also put his mind under severe emotional pressure to think on negative scale, which may cause him severe depression.

For this regard social, cultural, traditional and conventional thinking (community believing in certain beliefs) are so much important to a person.

In schizophrenia patients, depression is an associated factor. Depression may be the initiating factor which arises from such emotional stress and precipitates the symptoms of schizophrenia, in a genetically prone subject.

Attitude of a society towards mental patients (and most particularly to them who are known and recorded by the treatment) is very important.

It has been found that recurrence is less in schizophrenic patients (who have been cured somewhat by drug treatment), when the patients return to mess, hostel, boarding house or such like public residences, rather than return to their families or previous environment.

It is because the patients are more protected from injuries by emotional pressure that he had experienced before.

So relatives of the patients should not think about the patient negatively, even the fact that he is a patient.

In normal life, a person suffering from some normal depression, may get relieved by the process of detachment. Going on a trip, preferably keeping no attachment on phone or such things, not opening even e-mail for some days.

It may improve his mind, if depression comes from surrounding emotional pressure, not from some disequilibrium in his own mind.

It should be also known that, even the disbalanced and restless insight has the higher chance to be set right at the detached state.

We want to go far away, or work in another place, because of the same reason.

Dissociation disorders develop in the same way, but not willfully on the person's own discretion. Here, rupture of the integrity of the person's conscious self occurs due to severe emotional stress coming from the surroundings of the object (read Ch. 5, Part II).

Meditation or such things, help to achieve this detachment state. But I never experienced with them.

Another factor is, in case of bipolar mood disorder, in some cases, I have seen the patient is suffering from ideological conflicts.

A patient, previously known to me, and was attached to some political party with some definite ideology, came to me and was found to be suffering from bipolar mood disorder. At the same time, it was discovered that he is suffering from some major political and ideological conflicts.

I did not say anything about his conflicts but advised him detachment from those activities which were the main source of his conflicts.

He was improved by drug treatment, but did not follow my advice. I made him understand that actual treatment lies in his quarter, and drugs cannot be continued forever. He gradually corrected himself on his own, and there was marked improvement thereafter.

Another supportive fact that BPDs are mostly seen in adolescence or early adulthood. And that is the time in a person's life, when he maximally suffers from ideological conflicts. And the possible cause may be their minds are situational. They do not act on their own sound beliefs, either positive or negative.

But genetical substage obviously works. The persons who have the tendencies of great mood swing, either genetically predetermined or pathologically acquired, mental unsoundness in beliefs plays as a triggering role to precipitate B.P.D in them.

As 'stress' acts as a precipitating factor in case of Schizophrenia, 'confusion' acts as a precipitating or supporting factor in case of mood disorders, particularly B.P.D.

So, the detachment causes the mind's repairment and stabilization in belief in certain form either consciously or subconsciously on its own effort. And that is more important for a person in achieving ideological stability as well as mood stability.

Mood can also be fluctuated by alcohol, different drugs, chemical substances, and melatonin. Disorders of mood have been described in details in the Part II.

Cellular and molecular mechanisms of mood

Mood is controlled by the midline Raphe nuclei in the brain stem.

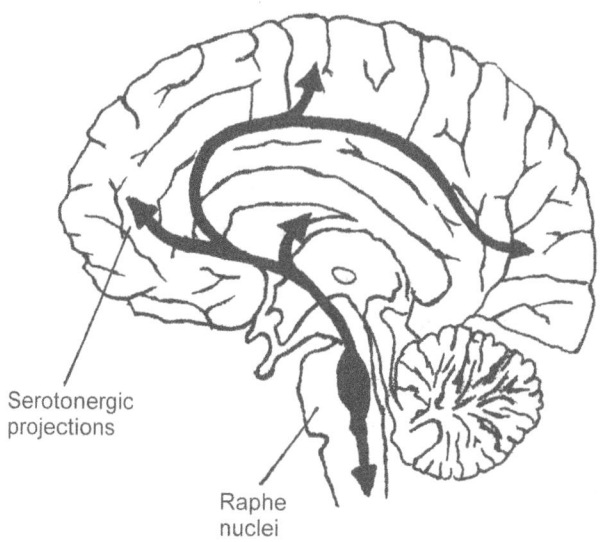

Fig. 33 : Area in brain controlling mood.

From there the nerve fibers go to the hypothalamus, limbic system, cerebral cortex, and spinal cord.

Neurohumoral system responsible for mood is serotonin system.

Serotonin-containing neurons have their cell bodies in these nuclei and from there they project to the above parts of the brain.

3,4-Methylenedioxy-methamphetamine (MDMA), a drug known as 'Ecstasy' was a popular drug of abuse.
It causes elation and euphoria, releasing serotonin at the nerve endings.

Selective-serotonin-reuptake-inhibitors (SSRIs), like fluoxetine, sertraline, citalopram, are used as antidepressant medicine, which inhibit reuptake of serotonin in the nerve endings and maintain higher levels of serotonin at the nerve synapses.

Lithium carbonate is used to treat acute manic episode (elation) and used in bipolar mood disorder. But the mechanism of action of lithium to control mania is still unknown.

SLEEP AND WAKEFULNESS

As mood defines the power of the mind, 'sleep and wakefulness' defines the state of activity of our conscious mind.

So 'sleep and wakefulness' can be compared with the electric switch, voltage between its two points that provides power can be compared with 'mood', and activities that are done with the electricity can be compared with the activities of four 'houses of mind'.

But this switch just does not have an 'off and on' mechanism, but there is a regulator attached with it through which graded power can be supplied.

In sleep, conscious activity of memory, intelligence, and emotional centers are stopped. New information gathering, intellectual efforts, or voluntary muscular activities do not happen in sleep. But though in this stage all activities of our conscious mind stop, our subconscious remains awake. On the contrary, it is the time for the highest activity of our subconscious mind.

Subconscious process of memorization of important information, long term memory potentiation, intellectualization of recent experiences, emotional shuffling and re-shuffling, all run on in sleep.

Subconscious also acts in wakeful state, but it is less active then than in sleep. For that, sleep is so much necessary for higher evolved brain, where a significant factor for survival depends on the higher brain functioning pivoting on experience, knowing and learning.

In sleep, subconscious reframes our mind analysing recent experiences, newer data, etc.

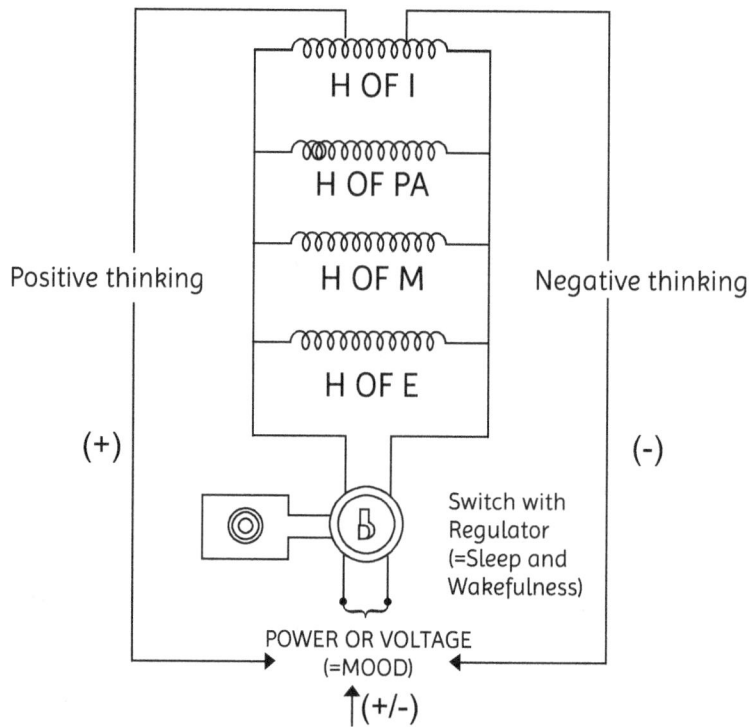

Fig. 34 : Comparison between Electrical Circuit and Brain.
[H=House, I=Intelligence, PA=Physical Ability, M=Memory, E=Emotion]

Dreams occur usually in 'REM' stage of sleep. Though always dreams are not easily interpretable, but they occur in shallow stage of sleep, rather than deep stage. To be precise, they occur just in the previous stage of wakefulness where subconscious merges with the conscious mind to act as a backstage of the conscious mind in the wakeful state. So dreams are actually the projection of subconscious' product, or outcome of works into the awakening conscious mind.

When a person sees a dreadful dream, then he must know that there in his mind are stress factors, which were masked under in his conscious state.

In our conscious life, we are involved in so many activities and attached emotionally with so many relations, that we often forget or be indifferent to many factors that eventually may be harmful for our existence.

A good joke, or buoyant friends or family gathering may obliviate many matters of worry for a time.

But those remain latent in subconscious.

In sleep subconscious resurfaces them, assesses them, judges their gravity on the pretext of the present situation and projects them in dreams, if necessary.

Sometimes we see happy dreams. By that, subconscious makes the conscious mind know that there are possibilities or prospects to become satisfied or happy, and encourages to take activities.

Besides dreams, after a good sleep, we feel fresh with new hope, can think of new possibilities, new ideas and new strategies.

In sleep the subconscious sets the mind on right track, detects and resurfaces masked factors that should be corrected, and give hints for future activities.

In one sentence, subconscious' activity in sleep is essential for higher functioning of the highly developed brain.

Emotions and all other houses as well as mood have feedback influences on centers responsible for sleep and wakefulness (that is primarily RAS or reticular activating system). So when a person's mind is fearful or preoccupied with a thought, it causes prolonged wakefulness. Again, exhaustion from any work involving any of the houses, promotes sleep.

Stages of Sleep

There are two different types of sleep - (1) Rapid eye movement (REM) sleep and non-rapid eye movement (NREM) sleep or slow-wave sleep.

REM sleep is so called, because in this stage, the eyes undergo rapid movements although the person is still asleep.

NREM sleep is again divided into four stages.

EEG recording during the quiet wakeful state with eyes closed shows alpha waves at a frequency of 8-12 cycles/sec. and with an amplitude of about 50 microvolt.

Alert wakefulness with eyes open is characterised by low voltage, high-frequency (18-30 cycles/sec.) beta waves.

When the person falls asleep, first enters NREM stage1. This is characterised by disappearance of alpha waves and emergence of low amplitude, mixed frequency waves, predominantly in the theta range (2-7 cycles/sec.). In next stage, that is NREM stage2, this rhythm is broken periodically by sleep spindles and K complexes. Sleep spindles are bursts of alpha-like, 12-14 cycles/sec., 50 microvolt waves with characteristic waxing-waning amplitude. K complexes are high-amplitude spikes with an upward discharge followed immediately by a downward deflection. In NREM stage 3 and 4, there is progressive slowing of the EEG waves. These high amplitude, slow-waves are known as 'delta' waves. Maximum slowing with large delta waves is seen in stage4.

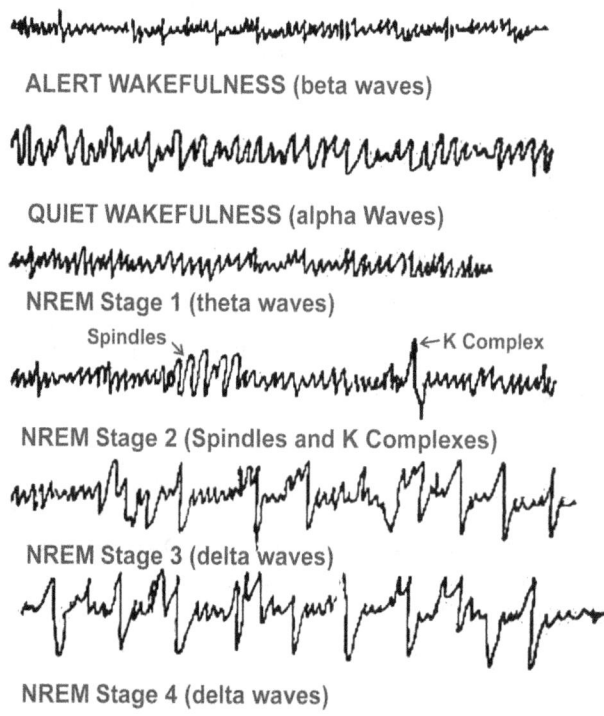

Fig. 35 : Progressive change and characteristics of the brain waves in the different stages of wakefulness and sleep.

NREM sleep is followed by REM sleep. In this stage high amplitude, slow-waves are replaced by low amplitude, mixed frequency waves similar to that of NREM stage1.

Some characteristics of REM sleep are :
1. Active dreaming occurs in REM sleep.
2. Though it is light stage of sleep, the threshold for arousal by sensory stimuli and by stimulation of the reticular formation is elevated.
3. There is marked hypotonia in muscles throughout the body.
4. The heart rate and respiration usually become irregular, which is characteristic of the dreaming state.
5. Despite the extreme inhibition of the peripheral muscles, a few irregular muscle movements occur, which include rapid movements of the eyes.
6. The brain is highly active in REM sleep and the overall brain metabolism may be increased as much as 20 percent.

For these reasons, REM sleep is often termed as paradoxical sleep, because though the person is asleep, there occurs marked activity of the brain in this stage of sleep.

In a typical night of sleep, a young adult first enters NREM sleep, passes through stage 1 and 2, and thence stage 3 and 4. After that sleep lightens and a REM period follows. This cycle is repeated at intervals of 90-110 minutes throughout the night. But there is less stage 3 and stage 4 sleep and more REM sleep towards morning. At all ages, REM sleep constitutes 20-25% of total sleep time. Children have more stage 3 and stage 4 sleep than adults. And stage 1 and stage 2 sleep increase with ages.

Most adults sleep 7-8 hrs. per night. In some cases this is accompanied by a short mid-afternoon nap. While adults of intermediate age tend to have one consolidated episode of sleep per day, infants and elderly show frequent short episodes of sleep.

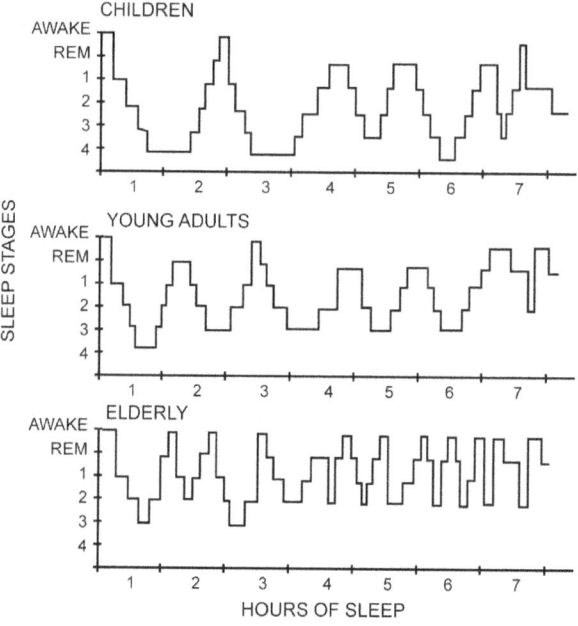

Fig. 36 : Normal sleep cycles at various ages

Sleep Deprivation

Critical period of sleep deprivation is 100 to 120 hours, after which characteristic abnormal mental state develops.

During the first 4 or 5 days without sleep, there appear progressive drowsiness and brief lapses of awareness. There is decreased vigilance with growing sense of fatigue, drowsiness and disinterest, which may be accompanied by feelings of pressure bands on the head, tingling sensations on the skin and noises in the ears.

From the fifth night psychotic syndromes start to develop, which is characterised by break with reality, illusions, hallucinations, intermittent clouding of consciousness and disorientation (in time first, then with place and person). Paranoid ideas are common.

If the sleepless state further continues, frank delirium precipitates. During the day time the picture somewhat resembles paranoid schizophrenia.

Eventually when the person sleeps, there is increase in total sleep duration lasting 12-16 hours, during which dreaming occurs frequently and quickly, as if the person is fulfilling not only his sleep debt but also debt in dreams.

Types of sleep disorders :

Sleep disorders are divided into two categories, (1) Dyssomnias and (2) Parasomnias.

(1) Dyssomnias

These are disorders associated with the amount, quality, and timing of the sleep. This has following subtypes.

(A) Insomnia
(B) Hypersomnia
(C) Disorders of Sleep-Wake Schedule.

A. Insomnia

Insomnia means disorder of initiation and/ or maintenance of sleep as well as poor quality of sleep. Insomnia can be described in terms of the phases of sleep through which it affects the sleep, e. g. sleep onset insomnia, sleep maintenance insomnia (with frequent awakenings during sleep), and early morning awakening. It can also be categorized according to the duration of insomnia, e.g. transient insomnia, short term insomnia and long term or chronic insomnia. Transient insomnia lasts for one or few nights in a single episode dependent on situational stress factors (as before examinations, interviews, and important occasions), or disturbances in sleep wake schedule (as in long journeys). Short term insomnia lasts for few days to few weeks. Long term or chronic insomnia lasts for months or years.

Common causes of Insomnia are :
1. Inadequate sleep hygiene.
2. Any painful or uncomfortable condition or medical illnesses.
3. Old age.

4. Anxiety disorders.

5. Alcohol, drugs or substance use.

6. Brain stem or hypothalamic lesions.

B. Hypersomnia

Hypersomnia is known as disorder of excessive somnolence. It is a serious disorder that affects the subject in work place and may precipitate accident related injuries.

Common causes of hypersomnia are :
1. Narcolepsy
2. Sleep apnea
3. Sleep deprivation
4. Medical Illnesses (Hypothyroidism, Head injury, Encephalitis, Trypanosomiasis etc.)
5. Alcohol, drugs or substance use.

Narcolepsy

Narcolepsy is a disorder of excessive daytime sleepiness with onset of REM sleep either with absence of previous slow-wave sleep, or following reduced span of slow-wave sleep.

In normal individuals, REM sleep almost never occurs without previous slow-wave sleep.

The classical tetrad of narcolepsy features :

(1) Sleep attacks - The person succumbs to irresistible attacks of sleep, anytime during the day. Usually there is a gap of 2-3 hours between two attacks.

(2) Cataplexy - There is abrupt loss of muscle tone in arms, legs or face, precipitated by emotional stimuli such as laughter, anger, sadness etc.

(3) Hypnagogic hallucinations - These are vivid dream-like hallucinations that occur at the onset of the sleep.

(4) Sleep paralysis - This is paralysis of speech and willed movement on waking, when the person is fully alert.

Daytime sleepiness has many causes, but if it occurs with cataplexy, the diagnosis should be narcolepsy, though narcolepsy can occur without cataplexy. Polysomnography studies with reduced sleep latency (10 min. or less); decreased REM sleep latency (20 min. or less) and mean sleep latency (8 min or less); with 2 or more sleep onset with REM period (SOREMP), confirm the doubtful cases.

CSF hypocretin-1 level below 110 pg./ml is also highly specific and sensitive for narcolepsy.

Usual age of onset of the disease is 15-25 yrs. and prevalence rate is 4/10000. 95% of the patients are positive for HLA DR2.

Treatment includes (1) forced short naps at regular intervals in the day. (2) stimulant medications (modafinil, methylphenidate, amphetamines). (3) antidepressants (tricyclic e.g. imipramine, clomipramine; or SSRIs e.g. fluoxetine) to reduce cataplexy, hypnagogic hallucinations and sleep paralysis.

Sleep Apnoea

This disorder is characterised by intermittent closure or collapse of the pharyngeal airway by tongue or other relaxed muscles resulting in apnoeic episodes (cessation of air flow for 10 seconds or longer) during sleep. These are terminated by partial arousal.

Typically the patient is obese, middle aged man or post-menopausal woman.

Other associated features in this disorder are loud snoring during sleep, poor sleep quality, daytime sleepiness, and poor performance due to loss of sleep.

Treatment includes (1) regular exercises and weight reduction, (2) avoidance of tobacco and alcohol, (3) correction of sleeping posture (not to sleep on backs), (4) continuous positive airway pressure (CPAP) through nasal mask during sleep, (5) surgical procedures occasionally.

Non-obstructive sleep apnoea (central sleep apnoea) may occur, where breathing stops with the cessation of respiratory effort.

Aetiology is either unknown, or secondary to effects of different drugs or substances, medical illnesses, or high altitudes.

Treatment is correction of underlying cause, if it is present.

C. Disorders of Sleep-Wake schedule

These are characterised by disturbances in the timing of sleep. The person is not able to sleep when he wishes to, although at other times he is able to sleep.

This is due to mismatch between the person's circadian rhythm and normal sleep-wake schedule.

Common causes are :
1. Jet lag or rapid change in time zone.
2. Work-shift.

(2) Parasomnias

These are disorders associated with episodic events which occur during the sleep.

They occur more frequently in children than in adults with the exception of REM sleep behavior disorder (RSBD), which is more common in men over 50.

Parasomnias are classified basing on in which stage they are occurring. These could be NREM Sleep parasomnias, REM Sleep parasomnias, or miscellaneous (may occur in any stage).

Different parasomnias are :

NREM Sleep Parasomnias :

A. Sleep-Walking (Somnambulism)

This disorder occurs in NREM stage 3 or 4, usually in the first 2 hrs. of the night. The patient carries out automatic motor activities which range from simple to complex. The patient leaves the bed, moves about in the house, or may even leave the house.

Arousal is difficult and accidents may occur in this state.

Though the cause is unknown, the family history of this disorder is positive in roughly one-third cases.

B. Sleep-talking (Somniloquy)

This also occurs in stage 3 or 4 sleep. The person talks in the sleep, but cannot remember anything about it in the morning or when he is aroused. It is usually recognised by the bed partner.

C. Sleep eating

The person takes several courses of eating arising from the bed during the sleep time. But after awakening in the next morning, the subject experiences little or no memory about the night incidences. Left out food confirms the night events.

D. Sleep terrors or night terrors

This disorder primarily occurs in young children usually during the first one third of sleep in NREM stage 3 and stage 4. The child suddenly screams and awakens with fear, associated with the hyperactivity of the autonomic nervous system - sweating, tachycardia and hyperventilation. The subject rarely can recall the episode on awakening in the morning.

E. Bruxism

Bruxism is involuntary, forceful grinding of teeth during sleep. Though the roommates or bed partners report the sounds produced by it, the subject remains completely unaware of the fact when he is awake.

On dental check-up, the destruction of tooth enamel and dentum are seen. In severe cases rubber tooth guard becomes necessary during sleep to prevent disfiguring tooth injury.

F. Sexsomnia

This is a disorder where the person engages himself in different sexual activities during sleep, like masturbation, fondling of sexual body parts either of self or partner and even sexual intercourse, but without conscious awareness. In the next morning he rarely can recall the happenings during the previous night.

REM Sleep Parasomnias :

A. REM sleep behavioral disorder (RSBD)

During REM sleep our muscles become relaxed. This prevents us from acting out our dreams. But sometimes this relaxation mechanism is disturbed. So, enactment of dream (both verbal and motor) occurs. It is characterised by talking, screaming, kicking, running out of bed etc. It predisposes to sleep injuries to both self and bed-partners. Patients suffering from REM sleep behavioral disorder (RSBD) tend to develop Parkinson's disease in later life. Though exact etiology is unknown, but damage or aberrations in the activities of the brain stem areas mediating descending motor inhibition during REM sleep could be a possible reason.

B. Nightmares

Nightmares occur in REM stage of sleep. In contrast to night terrors, which occur in NREM stage3 and 4 (usually during the first one third of sleep), nightmares occur in REM sleep and commonly in last one-third of the night sleep. The person awakens very frightened by fearful dreams, and can remember the dream vividly contrary to the case of night terrors.

Miscellaneous sleep related disorders :

A. Restless leg syndrome

This is an uncomfortable, uneasy sensation, often described as a creepy crawling feeling within the muscles, particularly in lower limbs with an urge to continuously move the limbs when at rest. It resists the person from falling asleep.

This is most probably due to lactic acidosis in muscles owing to incomplete oxidation of nutrient elements, that may result from various medical illnesses like anaemia, chronic obstructive lung disease (COPD), hypothyroidism, diabetes, as well as in normal persons with obesity and sedentary life style.

Treatment of underlying disease is essential. But regular exercises (particularly some specific yogas), avoidance of high protein diet, a short tap of deep hyperventilation before sleep may relieve the symptoms.

B. Periodic limb movement disorder (PLMD)

Periodic limb movement is brief, stereotypic, repetitive, nonepileptiform movements of the limbs, usually legs. It occurs mainly in NREM sleep and involves extension of the big toe. This is frequently associated with brief arousals and disturbances in sleep architecture.

C. Sleep enuresis

This is a disorder in which the subject urinates during sleep in the bed. Bed wetting is normal before the age of 5 to 6 yrs. The condition gradually improves by the age of puberty. If it happens in adulthood, the distinction must be made between the primary and secondary causes. Secondary enuresis is attributed to the cases where the patients were fully continent for previous 6-12 months. Urological abnormalities are more common in primary enuresis. Causes of secondary enuresis are urinary tract infections and acquired malformations, emotional disturbances, cauda equina lesion, epilepsy, sleep apnoea and certain drugs.

D. Nocturnal leg cramps

In this disorder sensations of painful muscular tightness in the calf or the feet during sleep awakens the subject from sleep.

Diagnosis of sleep disorders :

A careful history taking is essential. Information about time, duration and quality of sleep; work times; drugs, alcohol and substance uses; specific types of sleep problems should be recorded. Family members can provide valuable information. Any underlying medical illness should be detected. Many drugs and substances can precipitate parasomnias, particularly those which lighten the sleep. Ingestion of alcohol before sleep triggers parasomnias like sleep-walking. REM sleep behavioral disorder can be provoked or worsened by tricyclic antidepressants (TCAs), monoamine oxidase inhibitors (MAOIs), venlafaxine, selegiline and serotonin agonist.

Polysomnography : Polysomnography is recording of different biophysiological parameters of the body during sleep. Basic polysomnography records electroencephalogram (EEG), electrooculogram (EOG), and surface electromyogram (EMG). Other parameters recorded in related cases (e.g., narcolepsy, sleep apnoea) are nasal-oral air flow, snoring sounds, respiratory effort, arterial oxygen saturation, heart rate and rhythm, and leg movements. Polysomnography is necessary for the diagnosis of specific disorders such as narcolepsy and sleep apnoea, and is of utility in other disorders also.

Multiple sleep latency test (MSLT) is used for diagnosis of narcolepsy. It uses basic polysomnography variables (EEG, EOG and EMG) to assess the degree of day time sleepiness. Five nap opportunities are provided to the patient at two hours intervals across the day. Mean sleep latency (sleep latency is the time between the onset of sleep and appearance of NREM stage II sleep) less than 8 minutes is indicative though not specific for the diagnosis of narcolepsy.

Treatment :

Treatment of underlying cause is the most important intervention in case of sleep disorders.

Sleep hygiene maintenance is essential.

Sleep Hygiene :

- Maintaining regular hours of sleep and arising.
- Controlling of environmental factors such as noise, light, temperature.
- Having a light snack or meal before bed time.
- Avoiding tea, coffee and smoking at least 2 hrs. before bed time.
- Having regular exercises.
- Maintaining cleanliness and comfortability of the sleep place.

Psychotherapy, hypnotherapy, cognitive behaviour therapy, relaxation techniques may be helpful in different sleep disorders.

Drug therapy :

Sedative drugs benzodiazepines either short acting (triazolam, temazepam, lorazepam) or long acting (flurazepam, quazepam) should be prescribed for insomnia in severe cases and on short term basis. Patients develop psychological dependency on the drugs. Their sedative effects also impair generalised alertness, cognitive and psychomotor functioning during day time.

Non-benzodiazepine benzodiazepine receptor agonists (e.g.,zopiclone, eszopiclone, zolpidem) are useful alternative (may be the first line drugs). They have the same side effects as benzodiazepines. Eszopiclone is recommended for relatively long term therapy (say 6 months).

Melatonin receptor agonist ramelteon is used for sleep onset insomnia. It does not seem to cause next day functioning impairment. Suvorexant, an orexin receptor antagonist, is indicated for the treatment of insomnia with difficulties in initiating sleep and/or sleep maintenance. However it also causes next day sleepiness impairing functions which requires full mental alertness.

Sedative antidepressant trazodone is also frequently used to treat insomnia.

Modafinil, an alpha-1 adrenergic receptor agonist is used in narcolepsy to reduce the number of sleep attacks and improve psychomotor functions during day time.

Melatonin is helpful in re-establishing normal sleep cycle in case of circadian sleep cycle disorders e.g. in jet-lag syndrome. Bright light therapy is also being applied to reset the circadian rhythm in shift workers, jet lag syndrome and other circadian rhythm disorders. In case of night-shift workers modafinil is used to keep awakened state, which should be taken one or half an hour before the start of the night shift.

In case of parasomnias, severe, persistent problem may be treated with benzodiazepines, specially clonazepam. Melatonin, Antidepressants (TCAs and SSRIs), antiepileptics, and antiparkinsonian drugs are used in specific cases. Clonazepam has been used successfully to treat REM sleep behaviour disorders (RSBD). Nefazodone, an atypical antidepressant drug, has been reported to provide therapeutic benefit in case of post traumatic stress disorder related nightmares. Dopaminergic agonists pramipexole and ropinirole are the drugs of choice to treat restless leg syndrome and periodic limb movement disorder (PLMD).

A variety of drugs have been used to treat sleep enuresis, such as imipramine, oxybutynin chloride and desmopressin.

Hyperwakefulness

Hyperwakefulness is the opposite phenomenon of hypersomnia. Here sleep is reduced and mind remain alert in too much active state.

A. Anxiety

Anxiety has two components, one the emotion 'fear' and another the state of hyperwakefulness.

Benzodiazepine drugs act as anxiolytic by reducing the hyperwakefulness state.

B. Stress

Stress is also associated with low grade 'fear'. But difference between anxiety and stress is that in stress hyperwakefulness component is less prominent. Another difference is in 'anxiety' everything is uncertain. But in 'stress' the situation to be faced is fixed and escape is almost impossible.

Cellular and molecular mechanisms of sleep and wakefulness

Wakefulness is controlled by the reticular activating system (RAS) in the brain stem reticular formation (a cluster of nuclei situated in the midventral position of the medulla and midbrain).

From there some nerve fibers go downwards to the spinal cord to maintain tone in the antigravity muscles. Most fibers go upwards to synapse in thalamus and distributed form there to all regions of the cerebral cortex. Other ascending fibers bypass thalamus and goes directly to different parts of the cerebral cortex and other subcortical structures.

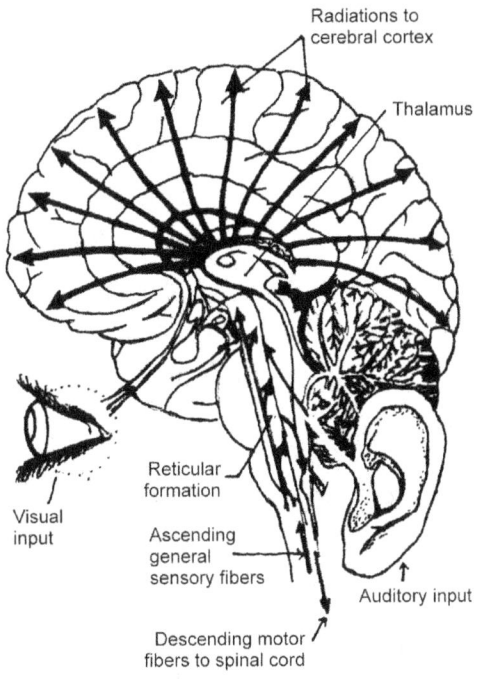

Fig. 37 : Reticular Activating System

Neurons of these alertness areas of the brain send arousal signals to the cerebral cortex as well as inhibit activities of areas of brain that promote sleep, resulting in state of wakefulness.

Recent studies have indicated that there are also other areas, in hypothalamus and basal forebrain, which act as centers promoting wakeful state.

Sleep promoting areas are located in ventrolateral preoptic nucleus (VLPO or VLPN) of the hypothalamus. Neurons from this area promotes sleep by inhibiting activity in areas that maintain wakeful state.

RAS contains both cholinergic and adrenergic nerve fibers which secrete acetylcholine and noradrenaline at their synaptic junctions. Other neurotransmitters involved in sleep and wakefulness are histamine, serotonin, glutamate, orexin (also called hypocretin). Histamine promotes wakefulness, exhibiting high activity during wakeful state. This is why histamine-blocking antihistaminic drugs cause drowsiness.

Serotonin also promotes wakefulness. Orexin is produced by a number of neurons in hypothalamus region. Activation of these neurons, producing orexin, triggers wakefulness, while low levels of orexin induces sleep. Deficiency of orexin produces sleep disorders like narcolepsy.

Ventrolateral preoptic nucleus (VLPO) of hypothalamus produces inhibitory neurotransmitter GABA (gamma amino butyric acid) that inhibits the arousal system during sleep onset.

There is an another mechanism to maintain sleep-wakefulness cycle, which is known as sleep-wake homeostasis. In this mechanism, homeostatic pressure to sleep is largely controlled by a neurotransmitter and neuromodulator called adenosine. Adenosine is built up in the body gradually during the wakeful state and starts to inhibit many of the processes involved in maintaining wakeful state and ultimately promotes sleep. During the night, after a good amount of non-REM sleep, the levels of adenosine gradually decline. And the activities responsible for wakefulness start to take control over sleep again.

Circadian rhythm in 24 hrs. sleep-wake cycle is maintained by the suprachiasmatic nuclei (SCN) in hypothalamus. SCN in turn receives information about outside light through a neural pathway from the ganglion cells of the retina in the eye. Bilateral destruction of these nuclei results in a loss of endogenous circadian rhythm of the sleep.

Another substance, Melatonin, is strongly considered as circadian hormone which causes drowsiness and reduces body temperature. Melatonin is secreted by the pineal gland and secretion of melatonin increases with diminution of light and decreases in bright light.

Sedative drug Benzodiazepines (BZDs) act at RAS by enhancing presynaptic and postsynaptic inhibition through a specific BZD receptor.

This receptor is an integral part of the GABAa receptor-Cl⁻ channel complex. The subunits of this complex form a transmembrane anion channel which is gated by the primary ligand GABA (an inhibitory neurotransmitter) and modulated by secondary ligands like Benzodiazepines.

After binding to the BZD receptor, the drug facilitates the action of GABA and enhances GABA induced hyperpolarization by increasing the frequency of Cl^- channel opening and influx of Cl^- ions into the cell. This decreases firing rate of neurons.

CHAPTER V

EVOLUTION OF EMOTIONS ON THE BIOLOGICAL EVOLUTIONARY PLATFORM

Charles Darwin in his books 'The origin of the Species by means of Natural Selection' (1859), and 'The Expression of the Emotions in Man and Animals' (1872), propounded the theory of evolution and natural selection to both biological evolution of the species and evolution of emotions as a trait of the species.

In his later work (The Expression of the emotions in Man and Animals), Darwin tried to explain how some expressions of the emotion evolved into serviceable habits to man and animals, as he said, ''raising of eyebrows serves to increase the field of vision''.

Some expressions act out in behaviours which are opposite in habits in two different ends. Like, a dog shows joy by elevating and wagging his tail. And inverse occurs when his tail droops in dejection. Darwin called them antithesis.

And there is a third principle, where expression of certain states of mind is the direct result of the constitution of the nervous system, independent of the will of the organism.

First of all, it has to be understood that, almost all of our emotions have survival role in our life and have been developed for our adaptive purposes, and pursue the specific goal "self-preservation and propagation of the species".

And the emotions act as driving force to all the major functions of the brain, either voluntary or involuntary, either directly or indirectly, to make the species pursue that specific goal.

Now the expressions of emotions, through our physical responses, have different objectives. Sometimes, they help us for the best suiting with the concurrent situation. And Sometimes, their habits have been processed to make gestures for intercommunication purposes. Like, wagging of the tail by the dog let others know his happy condition of the mind.

Now first of all, we will come to the facts what different emotions we do possess, and what are their survival roles.

Let us examine one by one.

'Hunger' and 'Sex', two of our basic emotions, which are responsible for maintaining body of the organism and preservation of the species.

'Fear' is essential to avoid things that have overpowering effect against our existence. The 'fear' protects the species from the harmful effect of something, either living or non-living, which is regarded by it as more powerful than it.

'Anger' prepares us to challenge our enemies, with utilizing best of our physical and mental resources - to defeat them. The 'Anger' provides killing instinct in the species against something, either living or non-living, which is regarded by it as less powerful than it.

'Love' is responsible for caring our weak offspring in the initial stage of development, and essential for preservation of the species. It also applies to protect the opposite weaker sex, and to have fellow-feelings towards other members of the group. Because, most of the higher animals including man are gregarious in nature. This gregarious quality helps in chance of survival better. Because, survival against powerful enemies depend partly on co-operative actions of the group members. And 'love', to some extent, helps to form inter-personal bonding of the group members to act jointly.

These above mentioned emotions are primitive and found both in animals and man.

But in case of man, many finer emotions have been developed, all of which have not been evolved in every animal.

Now let us examine them.

The emotion 'Hope' triggers to enhance our organised activities, mental and physical, towards specific goal or goals. Its opposite end is 'Despair'. 'Despair' temporarily stalls or slows our activities. But in this situation, our subconscious mind remain active, involving greatly to find out new routes for achievement.

Our 'sense of beauty', sensitizes us for cleanliness, to adore those things that have positive effects on our health, and also helps us in selection of healthy eligible opposite sex. In its opposite end, it makes us dislike things those are unhealthy in nature. Sometimes we describe something as being 'ugly', though that particular thing does not have deleterious effect on health. But here the view of that, somehow, has been conditioned with some object, living or non-living, which has negative or harmful effect on our health, in the earlier stage of our life.

'Disgust' makes us keep away from living organisms or non-living objects, that either are sticky and creepy in nature, or produces harmful effects on our body or mind. In its opposite extremity, we get informed that the object has beneficial effect on our body or mind, and we get attracted to it. Like being in open nature, sea side, or getting attracted to clean environment.

'Joy' informs us that the situation or surroundings or environment is favourable for us, and encourages us to be involved in maximum activities in that period. In its opposite end 'sadness', the emotion informs us that the environment is unfavourable, and discourages us to take activities, to preserve potentials.

'Laughter' makes us forget temporarily the stress situation. It lightens our serious thinking to get out of the harmful effect of stressful position that we live for that period of time. In its opposite end, we feel urge to involve in serious thinking, when we perceive our surroundings or position on a favourable condition.

'Shame' or 'Embarrassment' informs us that surrounding is unfavorable and un-encouraging for exposing us or doing activities, and so restricts our activities and tries to hide our bodily preserve.

'Surprise' prepares us to adapt with the sudden change in the environment. It is very essential for adaptation in all aspects, physical and mental, when the surroundings suddenly turn to be different.

'Curiosity' urges us to know the unknown. So that, this could prepare us taking challenges from unknown quarters, that yet has not been experienced. Also it helps us to seek prospect of benefit from unknown quarter. Curious nature is seen in many animals also, for the sake of the same reason, either in detecting danger or in searching food.

'Utsaha' or 'Liking to do specific job' – It encourages us to do specific job. It is equivalent with zeal, zest, enthusiasm, or eagerness to do something.

Some of our primitive men, learned to draw realistically, or produce a musical sound by voice or by an inanimate object, that brought pleasurable sensations to human eyes and ears; and discovered that these traits were being appreciated by his other group mates.

Not only that, he soon followed that his this trait was helping him to acquire his basic needs, being supplied by the other members of his group.

So they gradually developed intense liking for that particular job. The human achievements in arts, literature, science, and music followed.

Emotion 'Utsaha' or 'liking to do specific job', is applicable to any work, that directly or indirectly can serve our needs, that is food, shelter, sex, and others. In the other end, we are averse to do some works, which, neither directly nor indirectly, are related to our requirements. Here we sense, consciously or subconsciously, that those works would not bring any benefit to us, or provide for our needs. Sometimes, a person may feel to do some mechanical job, even if it brings money or other benefits to him. In that case, it should be realized that, it does not happen in all the cases. It happens particularly in those cases, when the subject's mind, either conscious or subconscious, informs him that his mind has greater potentiality to achieve better.

Evolution of language

Our most evolved way of communication - that is language - is an outcome of our intellectual process, by the pressing demand of communication.

Man was a gregarious species (where the members of the species live in a group together) in his jungle life like most of the other mammals, till he made an organised society. Whenever a group of people came to live together to serve a common survival need (protecting themselves from enemies, joining in activities in hunting, and fighting with animals physically more stronger than them), there was an increasing demand for an efficient means of transferring received information and giving instructions to others in emergency situations. They first met it with body language, sign language, and poorly illegible sounds. This way of communication was primitive method. But in the course of time, that gradually evolved, and finally developed into an efficient system of communication - that is our language.

Language at first was verbal, making specific sound through the mouth to mean something. But gradually in time, this specific verbal sound was substituted with a drawn picture or drawn sign, where there was difficulty in understanding of verbal sounds.

They also used these signs and pictograms for recording incidences for future reference.

So writing system also evolved.

Finally, this language not only remained as the mode of transferring information and conveying order and instructions, but also became a means of expressing of their inner feelings, that is emotion. Before this, expression of emotions were predominantly through specific physical reactions and voluntary muscular activities - with or without some vocal sounds.

Now here are some examples of how the expression of emotions helps us to take appropriate stance for the best activity in different situations.

Fear	Dilatation of pupil and widening of eyes.	Increases visual field to detect the object of fear.
	Increase in heart rate.	Provides maximum blood supply to brain and muscles to take actions if needed.
	Erection of body hairs.	Produces a larger and fearsome image in the mind of the opponent.
Rage	Strengthening of body muscles.	Helps for taking ready actions against the enemy.
	Showing of canine teeth (in case of animals).	Helps to produce fearsome effect on opponent and also prepares jaw muscles ready to take actions. (It has been modified in man in teeth clenching, because man does not need his teeth to attack his enemy).
	Erection of body hairs.	Same as in fear.
Disgust	Constriction of nasal aperture and oral opening. Decrease in respiratory rate.	Reduces the chance of inhaling noxious and harmful air. (Opposite occurs when we go to open natural space or seaside).
Surprise	Dilatation of pupil and widening of eyes.	Helps in detecting the object which is responsible for sudden change in environment or surroundings.
Shame or Embarrassment	Constriction of the posture to attain a reduced or smaller form.	Hides the vulnerable parts of the body against unfavourable environment.

Joy and Hope	Increase in respiration rate, expansion of chest and increase in lung volume, also free expression of the body.	Takes O2 rich air for maximum activities and activities in organized manner.
Laughter	Repeated forced exhalations of air from lungs.	Purifies our blood from noxious CO2 which had been produced by the stress induced respiratory depression.
Sense of Beauty	Fixes our gaze and promotes slow movements towards the object.	Helps to come in close proximity of the object of beauty.
Curiosity	Widening of gaze and dilatation of pupil.	To detect and find out object unknown.
Love	Clinging the object of love to the breast.	Protects the weak offspring from external assault.

Regardless of all these sciences, human mind is the seat of many other finer and subtle emotions, that cannot be explained all on evolutionary platform.

For example :–

'Nostalgia' which creates a feeling of home-sickness that bars our progress. 'Romantic addiction' to someone of opposite sex, though it is fruitless.

And many others.

In this regard it should be said that, our evolution is not an already finished process. It is an ever-ongoing process as long as life continues to exist upon this earth.

So maybe, our future will exclude many of our emotions from us, and there may be development of new unknown emotions.

CHAPTER VI

HOW TALENT IS DETERMINED GENETICALLY

Before going deeply into the discussion, we should define first what talent is.

Understanding of talent is a little confusing. Talent could be defined as – "a person's any inborn exceptional mental or physical quality compared with normal standardized population, that helps him or her in the survival and prosperity of life, should be regarded as the person's talent". By that definition, we can say higher IQ is a person's talent. Higher the IQ, the better for a person in his life struggle. But if we consider the height of a person - definitely being tall in stature helps a person in different ways, even helps him to become a successful basketball player - but exceptionally tall stature may both be inconvenient for him, and also be taken as socially unacceptable. So a standard height is more desirable to a person for his going through his life. So by that interpretation, we can say not just exceptional feature in some physical or mental quarter could be regarded as a person's talent, but how much that quality is helping him to suit him in his life struggle and leading him in his life's prosperity, is more important.

So, a person with very high IQ which helped him to be a successful scientist, a person's tall stature which helped him to become a successful basket ball player, a girls higher flexibility of pelvic bone ligaments which helped her to win a Olympic medal in gymnastics, a person's higher visual acuity which helped him in some sports like tennis, or even a person's long index finger compared to normal which helped him to grip bat in baseball – all could be regarded as talent.

But as we are here in this book going through our mind, we should restrict our attention to our mental faculties only.

So with respect to our mental apartments we can reiterate the definition as – "Talent is someone's exceptional and favourable inborn ability in any one of the houses of his or her mind compared with that of the normal standardized population".

And by that definition, talent can be categorized as (1) Intellectual talent (2) Memoral talent (3) Emotional talent and (4) Physical talent.

Intellectual Talent

There is no universal concept of what IQ a person should have to be recognised as a talented person.

Usually above 140 IQ is regarded as highly gifted. But what extent of IQ is based on genetics regarding that age, should more importantly be taken into consideration.

That means age specific IQ is more clear indicator of a person's innate or inborn ability.

In earlier years, IQ shows a man's innate ability that means his genetics dependent ability. As he grows up his intellectual power matures by his intellectual exercises. That means his long-term intellectual strength gets increased and starts to influence his ability.

In more advanced age intellectual ability depends much on knowledge, education, and experiences. Of course in very old age all the functionaries of the mental houses are diminished due to age related cerebral atrophy.

Again, in very early stage of life our brain do not exposes fully of its all qualities, that is its maximum ability.

To express the maximum ability of one's mind, it takes time. It comes through the course of development of a child.

So it is very difficult to say exactly in what age the brain's ability would reflect its innate maximum level of ability setting aside the factors of knowledge, experience and others.

Usually like our physique, our mental full-scale, all round development also takes place around the age of puberty.

So the intelligence and other qualities, a child is showing at this age at the maximum level, should be regarded as his innate, genetics dependent maximum ability. After that age, only maturity takes place.

Memoral Talent

Same is true for a child in the field of memory. A child can show his maximum innate ability to memorize around the age of his puberty.

Emotional Talent

In case of emotion, the emotionality or ability to being emotional not only reaches its maximum length at the age of puberty, but during puberty sex-related physical changes, masturbation and menarche also occur. And these changes bring immense impact on a child's mind.

Total psychological emotional set-up in a child gets re-oriented. Hormonal level changes during puberty affects the psyche of a child at great length. Many emotions are evaluated newly.

Both this physical and hormonal changes ultimately converges into a child's transformation into a man.

Along with these incidents, at the same time full scale innate emotionality also become set up.

So the highest EQ a child showing around the age of puberty or just after the age of puberty should be regarded as his or her true inborn potentiality of emotionality.

Physical Talent

A child showing high PQ around the age of puberty also gives the guides to his genetics determined ability, which can be capitalized on through proper training and devoted labour, to his journey to become a successful sportsman.

Here is needed proper guidance. Unlike other quarters (memory, intelligence), sports is much dependent on techniques and proper scientifically established training methods.

So a gifted physical talent, may not find his success in life, if he does not have access to these facilities.

So we see, that showing up or possessing high IQ, EQ, MQ, PQ at the earlier stage of life, particularly around the age of puberty, determines one's genetics dependent innate ability. But to achieve goal the person will have to depend on his efforts and environment factors.

That is how much he can engage himself in the process of success, and how environment supports him, which involves the culture of the surrounding society, place, proper availability of training facilities etc.

Regardless of everything, a person's emotional factor is the vital most important factor for his high achievements. Because it provides the driving force for the actions of other houses also.

A person, at the same time, may possess exceptional ability in more than one quarter.

Consider the following facts : –

- ¤ A person has exceptional IQ and good EQ and MQ.
  - The person is most likely to success in any intellectual field, scientific researches etc.
- ¤ A person has exceptional EQ, and good IQ, MQ.
  - The person is more sure to success in any, not only intellectual but also innovative works. He could be a discoverer or inventor in scientific field. In arts and literature, he can lay significant, permanent impression.
- ¤ A person with exceptional EQ and exceptional IQ.
  - God gifted. Comes in centuries and definitely leaves an everlasting imprint in the history of human achievements.

Same is true in case of sports persons.

¤ A person having exceptional PQ, good IQ and EQ.

- Obviously he is going to be a renowned sportsman, if all the surrounding factors support him, and he also desires to be a sportsman.

¤ A person having exceptional EQ, good PQ and good IQ.

- They are more to make impression as a sportsman.

¤ And a person having exceptional EQ, exceptional PQ and good IQ.

- 'Genius' the term we preserve for them. They are definitely history-maker.

But regardless of these facts, severe adversity, major traumatic experiences in early childhood, lack of proper social support may bar the expression of a person's ability.

A highly emotional man is prone to severe emotional injuries too, compared with other faculties of talent.

So your IQ, MQ, PQ are all of your prides. But the emotionality is like a two-edged sword to you. It can cut you or it may cut for you.

For that reason, psychologist, mentors, guides, are necessary to the child, particularly at the earlier stages of life, until he is becoming experienced and expert enough to deal with these challenges himself alone.

How successful men use the best of their brain resources :

Talent is gifted. It cannot be created. But that does not count on the success of a man in normal life, who has considerably good IQ, EQ, PQ, etc. Having been possessing many an exceptional ability, a man could turn himself into a disaster in life, if other environmental factors do not support him, or he lacks proper direction of motivation. Too many a time, the surroundings misguide a person to waste his talents through mindless unnecessary engagements.

Every successful man, at the very beginning of his life, first has to detect where his strength lies. And he then has to direct his goal accordingly. Parents should know where the most of their child's strength is lying. It could be his IQ, or EQ, or PQ. And they should direct him accordingly.

Once properly set, one should follow that goal earnestly.

The initial choice is very important. Because every person does not possess same IQ, EQ, MQ, or PQ.

A person with high IQ but poor EQ can fail in any field of arts, literature or music. But he can be successful in any intellectual work, computer programming, solution-based scientific research works (innovative thinking requires good EQ).

A person with high EQ, but good to average IQ may choose any branch of arts - literature, music, or painting.

So, one's aim should be dependent on permutation and combination of his abilities in four quarters. And it has to be determined which combination has the highest possibility towards success.

But the motivation and conditioning should start from the early stage of life, that is as early as possible in life.

Now we will go to another discussion.

How can talent be categorized in different fields of activities?

For example, - musical talent, literary talent, artistic talent - are they different?

Or more specifically, have individuals been born with these separate field talents?

Many studies have shown, that in case of musical talents, there has been further development of a particular area of brain, that is mostly localised to the auditory part of the temporal lobe.

Studies have shown that there are hypertrophy of specific areas of brain in musicians, when compared to non-musicians (Schlaug, Jancke& Huang, 1995; Schalaug, 2001; Gaser&Schlaug, 2003; Bangert and Schlaug, 2006).

These areas are located mainly in the auditory cortex and associated area in the dominant cerebral hemisphere. That is in left hemisphere in case of a right handed person.

This structural differentiation has been opined, may be genetical and that one possesses this trait by birth.

Now here comes these questions.

Is this enlargement inborn or acquired? Then, is it related to the differential perceptional sensations of ours?

That means, when one can perceive the frequency of sounds more distinctively compared with other individuals, of course, it can add to one's talent as described at the very beginning of this chapter. And we can assort them, for convenience, within a different quarter of talent - that is perceptual talent (pQ).

For a musician, his pmQ (m = ability to differentiate frequency of sounds) is higher. For an artist his pvcQ (vc = colour vision) is higher. For some sports person his pvaQ (va = visual acuity) is higher.

But for that studies should be conducted from the very early stage of the life. That is if this enlargement is prominent after birth or in earlier stages of life. Only then, we can assert how much perceptual talent count in a musician's performance.

Another thing is, a musician can perceive the frequency of sounds distinctively, but it cannot count on his creativity, which is more important. So how much perceptional ability counts on a musician's talent, that is questionable.

Achieving expertise in dealing with perfect pitch depends on two factors. One is a musician's high mental ability, that is genetical possession of high EQ, IQ etc. It clarifies the prospect that he can extremely involve his high emotionality and intelligence into achieving perfection.

And another is his exercise, his devotion to this work on a long period of time, his longtime arduous training.

We see hypertrophy of a particular group of muscles in a sportsperson in a specific sport. In animal model this imprint also have been found to be associated with hypertrophy of related motor cortex in the brain. But that does not mean this hypertrophy depends on his genetics, and he has achieved this through his birth.

High PQ defines one's physical talent. It depends on neuron number dependent larger development of motor cortex, or neuronal efficiency dependent superiority of the motor cortex. Which particular group of muscles will have to be strengthened for a specific sport that depends on his training process. And associated hypertrophy of the related part of the cerebral motor cortex, is observed with that.

Here emotionality comes as a factor for producing his intense liking for that sport. Otherwise training would have been boring and mechanical, and may be unsuccessful.

Some sports need conditioning of eye-muscle co-ordination (as in car racing), rather than muscle strength. But that is also one component of PQ. And for that also the sportsman has to condition his reflex muscular activity through arduous training.

So a child born with high PQ and good EQ and IQ could be successful in any sports, if other characteristics of physique (e.g. tall physique in basketball, joint ligament flexibility in gymnastics) is not important for that sport.

Likewise, a highly emotional man can contribute his emotionality in the same manner in his different brain activities.

If he uses that for auditory perception and differential understanding of it, and producing perfect pitch through his musical work, his particular area of brain, involved in this activity would also be hypertrophied.

His EQ is gifted. This hypertrophy is not achieved through his birth.

If one argues, a musician is born more in music families – that is because his cultural surroundings is favouring him to engage in this act from the very beginning of his childhood; to make his high EQ be involved in this specific task or stream.

A person with high EQ and IQ can involve his strength into any creative work, artistic work, literature, music, acting, and many others. Nothing is genetically coded. It depends on his choice. And it depends on the environment surrounding him, because a particular environment (family or social) encourages a child to be involved in specific field of activity from the very start of his life.

Our learning is most effective in the earlier stages of our life, particularly before puberty. Particular eye-muscle, or ear-muscle (in case of music) co-ordination reflexes all are conditioned better in the early stages of life.

Relationship of the pre-frontal cortex and temporal association area with intelligence has been observed in different studies.

Positive co-relation between cortical thickness and intelligence, especially in the pre-frontal cortex and temporal lobe has been found in several studies [Narr, K.

L. et al., 2007; Choi, Y. Y. et al., 2008; Karama, S. et al., 2009].

In a study (Shaw, P. et al., 2006), it was found that there is marked developmental shift from predominantly negative co-relation between intelligence and cortical thickness in early childhood, to a positive co-relation in late childhood and beyond.

Additionally it was found that the trajectory of cortical development primarily of the frontal region is implicated in the maturation of intellectual activity.

They divided the subject into three groups, superior, high, and average intelligence. And found that there is a negative co-relation between IQ and cortical thickness (particularly frontal) in the youngest group. And this co-relation reversed in the older age groups.

This all depend on two factors. One mental development pattern of a child, and another the fact that IQ's genetics dependent component is not directly proportional to cortical thickness or hypertrophy of cortex in prefrontal area.

A person's genetical component of IQ depends on either higher proportion of neuronal number dependent brain volume, particularly in the prefrontal and temporal association area, to body size; or greater neuronal efficiency of that part of the brain.

Cortical thickness due to hypertrophy is related to the person's intellectual exercises over a long period of time.

So a person with high intellectual ability may not show increased thickness of prefrontal cortex in the very early stage of his life. But as a person with high intellectual ability usually involves himself in more intellectual processes followingly in life, as a result, there is increased thickening of cerebral cortex in prefrontal area in later stage of life.

And the second factor is a child's mental developmental pattern.

In the beginning of life, the mind is more concentrated to know things first. Upon basing of this knowledge several conditioning processes also take place and are set up in this early stage.

After a certain age of the child, the child starts to take up intellectualizing things. And in this stage more higher intelligence groups involve more intellectualizations and involve more pre-frontal cortex and temporal association area. As a result of which, there is positive co-relation between IQ and cortical thickness in these areas in the later period of life.

So our talent is not dependent on the thickness due to hypertrophy of any part of the brain, if the thickness is not due to increased neuronal number.

It can be dependent on more number of neurons in a particular region of the brain, and proportion of neuron-number dependent brain volume of that part to the body size. Or it may be dependent on higher neuronal efficiency in specific regions of the brain.

Now, perceptual talent may contribute to specific field like music, or certain sports where higher visual acuity or depth perception is needed.

But in many other fields of human activities - arts, literature, acting, imaginative works, perceptual talent does not come in action significantly.

Here mind's EQ and IQ are more important.

A significant number of most admired works of Ludwig van Beethoven came from the last two decades of his life when he was about almost completely deaf.

As I have said in the very beginning of this chapter that any quality or feature, physical or mental, that helps a person in a specific field of success could be regarded as his talent. But high EQ and IQ are most important for success because they denote for creativity and innovation, and being supported by high MQ and PQ, they favour success in specific fields. A person with high EQ and IQ can surpass his other deficiencies also.

So, a great musician could have been equally a great artist also.

CHAPTER VII

NEGATIVE EMOTIONS AND THEIR ENCOUNTERS

As we have discussed already in the chapter on emotion (Ch. IV), no emotion should be regarded as either positive or negative emotion.

Because all emotions have both positive and negative ends.

Yet we regard those emotions as negative which produce most trouble to our social life, and events frequently evoke responses on the negative side of their scale rather than positive side.

Also we refer by negative emotion to the negative extremity of the same emotion. For example, between 'fear' and 'courage', one is negative and another is positive side of the same emotion. We refer 'fear' as the negative emotion.

Among 'joy and sadness', 'anger and revenge satisfaction', 'love and bereavement' we consider the negative ends - sadness, anger, bereavement as negative emotions.

The common emotional sufferings that we go through in our everyday life, are phobia, anger, fear, anxiety, stress, obsession, sadness etc. We will discuss those followingly. But I will recommend, before reading this chapter, to look over the 'chapter IV - Emotion' once again to make the reading easier.

PHOBIA

Phobia is an irrational fear or fear out of proportion to any specific object, situation, or activity.

Here the fear is not based on reason or logic. In most cases the object of phobia brings reflex fear to us.

But it should be differentiated from knowledge-based fears. After watching a snake reflex fear may come to our mind, though the person may not suffer the experience of being bitten by the snake ever.

But the knowledge that it may cause serious damage to us, conditions our mind to fear reflexively to it. Knowledge-based fears are based upon logic and knowledge.

On the other hand, phobia is based on traumatic past experience. Here mind has been conditioned with some associated bad memories with the object. Though that particular object may have not produced any serious harm to the person.

About 5 to 10 percent of the general population suffers from one or more types of phobias. The lifetime prevalence of phobia is about 10 - 20 percent. The rates of specific phobias in women are double than those in men.

Signs and Symptoms of Phobia

From a few signs and symptoms to a full-blown panic attack may occur in phobia.

The signs and symptoms of phobia include :

(1) difficulty in breathing
(2) increase in heart rate and palpitation
(3) trembling or shaking
(4) feeling dizzy or light-headedness
(5) sweating
(6) hot flushes or cold chills
(7) dry mouth
(8) restlessness
(9) numbness or tingling sensations
(10) an intense desire to escape
(11) feeling of powerlessness or loosing control of oneself.

(12) sensing impending doom (dying or passing out)

There are many types of phobia. Common types are :

1. Agoraphobia : irrational fear of surroundings away from the familiar setting of home. Earlier it was thought to be fear of open spaces only. But now it includes any place like shopping malls, movie theaters, railway platforms, crowded places, airplanes, where there is no easy escape or escape is embarrassing. The term is derived from the Greek words 'agora' and 'phobia', meaning the fear of marketplace.

2. Social Phobia : Irrational fear of social interaction. The person is apprehensive to perform any activities in presence of other persons and to interact with others. He feels his activities are being watched by others critically, resulting in his embarrassment and humiliation. The persons with social phobia find difficulties in performing activities in parties and social gatherings, in oral presentations, meeting new people, and even eating and speaking in front of others.

3. Claustrophobia : Fear of enclosed places like elevators, underground trains etc.

4. **Katsaridaphobia :** Fear of cockroaches. This fear is very common, particularly among the women. There are two kinds of feeling towards this insect. One is, intense distaste or disgust towards the insect. That is brought about by the bad look and the fact that it is often found in the kitchen, contaminating the food.

Another is true phobia or fear about it. Regarding fear, one thing should be remembered, when two living subjects confront each other in a non-friendly environment, fear is imposed by the subject who is less fearful, regardless of the fact which one is more powerful.

It is also true for the human society. Often we see, a person who is much smaller but fearless and aggressive, imposing fear upon a much bigger sized fellow.

Psychic factors here much matter. One's fearlessness produces fear upon another mind which is prone to fear.

The typical feature of this insect is fearlessness. They cannot be driven away, even after extreme effort. Instead goes in direction where effort to drive it, is originating. This produces an intense fear on the opponent's mind. This may be their one of the survival trait.

5. Acrophobia : Fear of high places.

6. Zoophobia : Fear of animals.

7. Xenophobia : Fear of strangers.

8. Arachnophobia : Fear of spiders.

9. Haemophobia : Fear of blood.

10. Tetraphobia : Fear of the number 4.

Treatment for Phobia

Currently flooding and systematic desensitization processes are used as psychotherapies for phobia.

(1) Systematic Desensitization

In this treatment the subject is gradually exposed to anxiety provoking object or situation and overcomes his 'fear' by learning through relaxation technique. A hierarchy of feared situations are set and the patient after completely relaxing or experiencing an anxiety-free state in a step, climbs the next step in hierarchy, till he feels total anxiety-free state at the highest or maximum level. Relaxation technique, usually adopted, is Jacobson's progressive relaxation technique where patients are trained to relax different groups of muscles in sequential order.

(2) Flooding

In this treatment, no hierarchy is maintained. The patient is directly exposed to the object of phobia and escape is made impossible. Through prolonged coexistence with the object of phobia along with the therapist's guidance and encouragement, the patient becomes gradually adapted to the situation and his anxiety slowly diminishes.

Both of these processes treat by deconditioning of the past unpleasant experiences associated with the object of phobia.

Phobia is a conditioned phenomenon. Any bitter experience with the object in the past, developed phobia for that particular object.

Any conditioned phenomenon can be unconditioned through deconditioning or adequate reverse conditioning process.

That means neutral or opposite things have to be happened through their experience.

(3) Therapeutic Reprocessing of Association of Memories (TRAM) :

If the object of phobia can bring pleasurable sensations to one, that would not only neutralise or negate the past bitter experiences with the object, but also form positive attitude towards the object, through reverse conditioning process.

So there should be thought about a set-up where the object of fear not only co-exists with the subject without producing any harm, but also it will bring pleasurable sensations to him or her.

Some sweet, attractive smell, beautiful attractive persons either men or women, or many more things that can be improvised are to be associated while one is co-existing with the object of his phobia.

It would associate the memories of the object with the memories of attractive, pleasurable, desirable things.

Gradually when these associated memories will be set in enough amount and strength to nullify the past bitter experiences, and also to promote positive and liking attitude towards the object, it will be able to better manage phobia, if not the object further brings bitter experiences in future.

For example :

A girl is suffering from acrophobia (fear of height).

Put her on high place with her romantic partner, bring her there a bunch of flowers delivering enticing fragrance, bring her there some delicious food there which she likes intensely, or bring her there anything of her intense desire.

Or when treating arachnophobia, while the subject touches the spiders, the room should be scented with an enticing smell, may be sexually erotic. And there should be low music that the person prefers most.

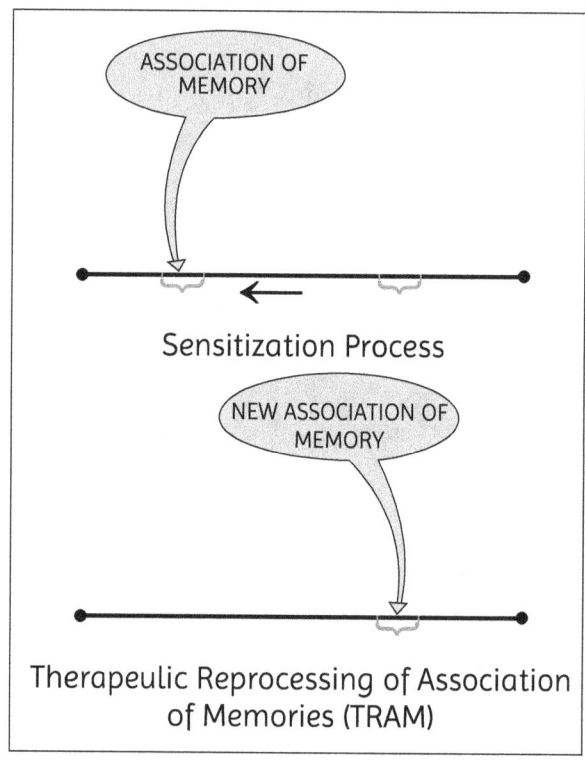

Fig. 38 : Therapeutic Reprocessing of Association of Memories (TRAM).

This should be done on repeated intervals. And gradually new association of memories about that particular object will be formed in the subject's mind. This alteration of association of memories is more important to neutralise the past bitter or fearsome experience.

But the process should start with desensitization. Once the subject is desensitised to a range, the therapeutic reprocessing of memories should start.

The difference between 'systematic desensitization and flooding' and 'TRAM' is, the formers are deconditioning process treated with the presentation of neutral object without any associated harmful or unpleasurable experience. But 'TRAM' is not only a deconditioning process, but also a reverse conditioning process to build a positive attitude towards the object rather than neutral attitude. For that, the effect of it is justifiably better.

TRAM could be applied not only for 'fear' emotion only. It could be applied for any of the emotions, like 'joy and sadness', 'anger and revenge satisfaction', 'disgust and attraction', 'love and bereavement', 'shame', 'embarrassment', 'laughter', 'curiosity' wherever there is an unfavourable responses evoked by the memories of something.

Drug therapy for phobia

Effective drugs in the treatment of phobias include (1) Selective serotonin reuptake inhibitors (SSRIs) - Fluoxetine, Citalopram, Escitalopram; (2) Benzodiazepines - Alprazolam, Clonazepam; (3) Venlafaxine (4) Buspirone (5) Tricyclic antidepressants (TCAs) - Clomipramine, Imipramine; (6) Monoamine oxidase inhibitors (MAOs) - Phenelzine, Moclobemide.

Most clinicians prefer SSRIs as the first line of treatment. The doses of the drugs are to be set as they are used in the treatment of depression. The treatment of social phobia with performance anxiety can be helped by beta-adrenergic blockers - Atenolol or Propranolol, or relatively less sedative benzodiazepine - Alprazolam before exposure (preferentially one hour before the exposure or performance).

Prognosis or Outcome

There is insufficient data regarding the course and prognosis of the phobic disorders, because the people suffering from phobic disorders rarely come for the treatment. In addition sufficient researches have not been carried out on the course of this disorder. It is supposed that once developed the phobic disorders can persist for many years, but waxing and waning may be there depending upon the recurrence of the incidences of facing phobic objects with associated unpleasant experiences. As I have said in the first chapter, the unneutralised emotional memories tend to fade off over period of time, if recurrence of the event does not happen, because attached emotion gradually expresses it out either consciously or subconsciously, making the event emotionally neutral.

ANGER

If someone does misdeed to one, and he cannot neutralise it with counteraction, anger will be produced in his mind, and suffered from that anger adaptive range on the scale of 'anger' emotion will be shifted gradually towards the negative end. And ultimately his mind will be to some extent subjugated to the subject or object of his anger.

What can he do against this? The answer is 'NOTHING'.

Then what is the solution to this problem?

– Time and his intelligent introspection.

The problem lies on the larger infrastructure of our society.

We cannot live on the basis of what you can do or what you cannot do theory, because that would convert our society back into jungle life and we will transform ourselves back into beasts.

If someone does misdeed to one, he cannot do the same misdeed on another else, because that would not solve the problem.

If someone does some misdeed to one cleverly in that way, he cannot take any legal or any possible action, by which he can counter balance it, definitely 'Anger' will be produced in his mind.

His mind will be subjugated to that person and in this subjugated state even addiction to that person may develop (this is also one of the mechanisms of seduction). If one is a fool, he will succumb to it. If he is intelligent, capable of enough introspection, he will think intelligently not on his emotional basis.

He should think intelligently, the person who has done misdeed to him - 'is there any explanation to it?'. If it is there, well and good. But if there is not, he should permanently avoid that person, and should not be emotionally connected with him.

A time will come, when his adaptive range again will move towards the positive end with emotional memory being faded out, and subjugation in his mind will be removed. The person who caused this, will suffer in return, because vice versa will happen in his case.

By this rejection process, ultimately the society will be formed on the basis – 'If one has to win in life, he will have to do it through his true ability - his intelligence, emotionality etc. and his toil. One cannot win by tricks'.

FEAR

Why 'fear' comes to our mind, despite our strong resistance against it?

Because, 'fear' let us know, that we are going to face some object, activity or situation, that had made a defeating effect on our mind in the past.

We fear something that has proven itself more powerful than us in our mind earlier.

Fear for all objects, activity and situations has been developed through conditioning processes. We cannot escape from all these all the time, while living in a society. We have to face them, tackle them, and deal with them.

Now whenever a person meets an object or situation of his fear, there occur three prospects.

(1) He can flee from it. But the environment may be such that it may not allow it.
(2) He can compromise with it and agree to co-exist with it. In that case his adaptive range on 'fear' emotion will be shifted a few points negativewards and his mind will be subjugated to that object of fear to some extent. This is the process of adaptation (negative adaptation on emotion scale - read Ch. IV).
(3) He may win over it. In that case his adaptive range on 'fear' will remain on

previous site. And the object will cease to become an object of fear to him.

But I must say, in the adaptation process, the subject learns to co-exist with the object or situation of fear initially. But that is not the end. Gradually, after some time onwards, his mind may start to win over the thing (winning means either expressing out of the 'fear' emotion associated with the memory of that object, or formation of new association of memories regarding that object).

But we live in a world, where we cannot win over everything. Nobody can. We win, we lose everyday.

Besides, stubbornness or obstinacy to win over everything or every point, makes our behaviour, attitude anxious and sticky over one subject.

So, our strategy should be between win and adjustment.

Again, some fear is useful also to make us civilized, disciplined, and responsible persons.

If we had not feared legal punishment, social rejection or disapproval, our own behaviour would have been out of control, even for ourselves.

Some extent of fear, makes us behave responsibly, aware of fundamental rights of others, and restricts our recklessness.

Fear is useful to manage wicked and idiots also.

Fear also protects us from being exposed to dangerous situations. Without fear we would have been more prone to accidents, harms or injuries to ourselves.

So rational fear is acceptable and that is beneficial even to us.

But unjustified subjugation to any fear should be restricted. Particularly if it comes from the wicked people, who use this to serve their motives.

OBSESSION

In obsession, addiction is formed following incomplete subjugation of the mind by an emotion (most commonly 'fear', but other emotions can also play), to a specific thing - living or non-living, or to any specific situation. So 'obsession' means partial subjugation of the mind to a particular object (living or non-living), activity, or situation on one or different emotion scales. The emotion 'fear' is the most common contributing emotion. Other important emotions, subjugation on which scales commonly develop obsessions, are hunger, sex, love, curiosity, Utsaha etc.

The common obsessive disorders that we see in our usual life, are repeated hand washing, checking things, counting repeatedly etc.

Now take one by one.

Repeated hand washing : it means subjugation of the mind to the 'fear of contamination'.

Now how was this subjugation developed?

Is there any past event of contamination, that seriously damaged one's health? Or is one's body vulnerable to repeated contamination? Or has one been suffering from repeated contaminating diseases? Or is one too much concerned about his or her health or beauty on social background, so that the subject fears that contamination will spoil them?

Somehow the fear of contamination has overpowered his mind and produced subjugation to it. From this subjugation obsessive feelings or habits of excessive cleanliness has been developed.

Repeated checking of things : So is true for repeated checking of the things. Here the subject's mind is always in doubts of security. The subject repetitively checks whether the gas taps, water taps have been turned off, or whether the door has been locked while leaving, and many such things. In this case, the mind has been subjugated to the 'fear of loss or damage to the properties'. And obsessive habits of excessive security checking has been developed on that. Is there any event in the past when the person lost valuable things? Or is there any history when serious damage to the subjects property done (as for in fire)? Or is the subject vulnerable to frequently loosing things or damaging possessions? Sometimes a person in a financial crisis, also suffers from the 'fear of loss and damage to the property'. Proper history taking will reveal the facts.

Besides 'fear' any other emotion can take part in the process of subjugation and can develop obsession.

Seduction is a willful process of forming obsession, and it could be developed by a number of emotions. The most common among them are 'anger', and 'love'. But in this case, there are alternate feeding emotion or emotions. The mind is fed on other emotion or emotions, disproportionate to the subjugation. Feeding emotion could be any emotion, most commonly 'sexual passion'. The emotion 'anger' has been explained earlier. In case of 'love', the emotion has two ends, the feeling of love, and the feeling of 'bereavement'. If an object becomes conditioned as an object of this emotion, and the subject suffers constantly from the threat of losing it, the subject becomes subjugated on the scale of this emotion. In seduction, love is one sided. For that, the subject, speculating the chance of losing his or her object of love, that is being threatened by the chance of suffering from 'bereavement', get emotionally depleted, or subjugated on that emotion scale. So beware of this emotion and its object. Don't let any unwanted thing to be conditioned as the object of this emotion.

A seduced person can hardly realise the fact that he or she is under subjugation and seduction. Practically, in case of any subjugation, we take the object of subjugation as our master, and try to please it. It is an survival instinct. Our primitive men worshiped 'Nature', gave offerings to please it, out of subjugation on 'fear' emotion to its catastrophic power. It is obsession. But, if the object of subjugation has some other emotion satisfying quality, we get seduced by it. Difference between 'obsession' and 'seduction' is 'obsession' develops out of pure 'subjugation', partially not completely, to an object. Why partially ? Because, in case of complete subjugation the subject would fail to sense its effect, which happens when the subject has to co-exist with the object or situation, as explained in 'emotion' chapter. But, in case of 'seduction', the subject gets subjugated on one emotion scale, either partially or completely; and gets satisfied on other emotion scale though much disproportionate to subjugation.

Intense liking to the seducing object may grow in subject in case of seduction, which may not be amenable to persuasion. That means, in this case, even the subject's conscious and subconscious mind will misdirect the subject, failing him or her to realize the situation.

Introspection and psychological exploration will reveal the facts. And counter-conditioning of these emotions would relieve the subject from obsession and seduction.

Counter-conditioning could be done by desensitization process and TRAM (therapeutic reprocessing of association of memories), as has been explained earlier in phobia.

But where object of emotion is not available or willing, there avoidance or complete abstinence along with expressing out emotional memories should be advocated

.

DEPRESSION

Depression is not an emotion. It is one of the extremities of mood.
How to combat depression has been explained in detail in the chapter of mood.

ANXIETY

Anxiety has two components. Hyperwakefulness and the emotion 'fear'.

Hyperwakefulness condition can be treated with mild Benzodiazipines. Alprazolam 0.25/0.5 at bed time can relieve one from this hyperwakeful state.

With regard to 'fear' – the person will have to settle for the matter that is causing worry to him.

It may be a bank problem, a job problem, a family problem or anything.

The person must settle that first.

If it is not possible, sometimes the person may have to accept the fact of loss, instead of endangering his mind.

For example, one owes some money or something like that from someone. But he is unable to obtain it back and it is making him worry.

The person will have to take the fact that he has lost that thing. He should consider that what is more important to him is his time and mental health. So for that if he has to accept some loss sometimes, it is desirable.

But it is a simple example. We have many more complicated things that cause worries or anxieties to us. Escaping from those is not such easy all the time.

In this regard, the person's individual intellectual discretion is necessary.

But he may take help from some professionals in related fields. That means property lawyer, matrimonial counsellor, legal advisor, family counsellor etc.

STRESS

It is also a low graded 'fear' along with hyperwakefulness state. But hyper-wakefulness component is less prominent in case of stress than anxiety. Difference between anxiety and stress is in case of anxiety everything is uncertain. But in case of stress, situations are unavoidable and time to face those are also fixed.

Common stress situations that are seen – examinees before their examinations, players before their games, job seekers before their interviews, or one in a critical financial situation.

Situations are almost unavoidable and time to face them are fixed.

'What would happen if he does not do well in the examination, or perform well in the game or does not get the job?' – this precipitates stress.

Surrounding high expectations from the family and others increase the stress. The relatives and well-wishers should have to consider that they should let the child, or person do well according to their abilities, not to expect something from them that is beyond their capabilities. Encouraging to study before the examination or exercise before the game, is more important than to expect miraculous results from them.

We should try and do as best as we can. What would be the result, is not our concern. Even if the result is not good, we should consider, luck factor is associated with this.

Did we do everything according to the best of our's ability? If the answer is yes, then why should we bother on the result.

Another thing is life's single failure or achievement do not compose our whole life. There are two many chances. Failure in one game does not define one player's ability. It depends on the player's overall performance throughout his life time.

So stress would be reduced, if we widen our views.

SADNESS

Sadness occurs in everyone at several points in the life. Alternatively, we apply the term 'melancholy' to it. But it should be differentiated from depression.

In depression there is severe loss of mental power. It is not a part of emotions.

In sadness, the person feels unpleasurable feelings towards life and environment. It is the opposite end of the emotion 'joy'.

'Joy' brings the information that the environment and surroundings are favourable to life. So it incites us to take maximum activities, that would favour our future existence.

And in case of sadness, which is the opposite end of 'joy', we get intimated with the unfavorability of the situation. Or it may arise from some failure of our directed plan, e.g. failure in exam., loss of someone beloved etc.

It reduces our activities, but at the same time stirs up our higher mental faculties, specifically subconscious, to search out for new avenues to success by changing plans, developing new ideas, or taking new actions. These processes do not occur always in our conscious mind, but subconscious works relentlessly without our conscious intimation, within its realm.

Once we find the solution, or the environment changes for good things, the sadness gradually disappears.

Yet we fail to distinguish it from depression, because in many cases, depression and sadness remain associated together.

And in sadness negative thinking may occur, that leads to depression.

But both can appear in pure form.

Some times, we feel sad. The environment around us seems to us bleak, gloomy and melancholic, though there is no reason for negative thinking. It is pure sadness.

On the other hand pure depression without sadness may occur. Even in a festive, good-weathered, enjoyable surroundings or environment, the negative-thinker will suffer from depression, if he continues to think negatively.

'Sadness' is a feeling, it is a part of the emotion. 'Depression' is loss of mental power. It is the negative extremity of 'mood'. In non-pathological state, what causes mood elevation and mood depression? 'Positive thinking causes mood elevation or elation and negative thinking causes mood degradation or depression'.

Sadness occurs even in a person with all positive attitudes.

Depression occurs predominantly in a person with negative attitudes, at least for that time ongoing.

The persons who have positive attitude in life, just let their sadness pass by. That is the best strategy for tackling sadness - Give some time to it. Any other joyful event will push the stimulus of emotion towards the positive side and will alleviate sadness.

On the other hand, depression occurs in a person, who has negative attitude in life. It cannot be let pass by, if he does not stop negative thinking.

And it may progress to severe condition when the treatment ultimately becomes necessary.

There are also other too many negative emotions, and sexual perversions of different kinds which sometimes incapacitate our life. These should be taken care of.

Subjugation or Depression ?

These are two completely different entities, from which a patient or any person with non-organic psychology (that is without any pathological base) can suffer. A psychologist, psychiatrist or any doctor treating a person in need of psychological help, must differentiate these two distinctive states of the mind. Here I am keeping out of discussion the disorders of the four major houses like schizophrenia, Alzheimer's; or some mood disorders, where there is defect lying in the structural, neurochemical or other mechanisms of activities in brain – either acquired or hereditary. They are diseased process, and have been described in respective chapters.

Subjugation occurs as the adaptive ranges on one or more emotion scales shift towards negative extremity. It may happen on 'fear' scale (which is most common), or on any other emotion scale like 'utsaha', 'joy', anger, love, etc. A person may become subjugated by some fear imposed upon him from some quarter. Again, a person wanted to do something satisfactorily, but it did not become completed according to his will. Here his subjugation occurred on his 'utsaha (= enthusiasm, zeal or zest)' or 'liking to do specific job' scale. A person wanted to build his house nicely. But it did not get finished up according to his expectation. The painter did not do the right colour of his choice, builder did not make some part to go with his vision. So he became frustrated. His mind felt unwell and some kind of bad, that he cannot explain. What is the actual state of his mind? It is certainly not depression. It is subjugation – Subjugation on the scale of 'utsaha' or 'liking to do specific job'. So his mind will not feel good and he may be unable to describe or clarify the actual condition of his mind and may need help for that. Subjugation may occur in any emotion scale. A professional's job is to give the patient a clear insight, so that the patient himself can understand on what emotion scale the subjugation is occurring.

On the opposite hand, depression occurs as there is wrong thinking pattern in mind. Positive thinking causes mood elevation or elation and negative thinking causes mood degradation or depression. Treatment, strategy, and approach to the patients suffering from these two different entities are completely different. It includes psychotherapy as well as the drug treatment. But the psychotherapeutic approach for treating the patients suffering from these two entities are not the same.

Of these two entities, which one is more grave or serious? Definitely the latter. A person can survive in a subjugated state and carry on normal routine works very comfortably and fairly. Domestic animals and animals in captivity all are subjugated, predominantly on 'fear' and 'hunger' scale. But they carry on all the life's basic daily works. In yesteryears, slaves, war prisoners used to live in subjugated state. When an intelligent, creative mind remains subjugated for long time, there is a chance of revolt. The great revolutions and rebellions occurred in this way in our history. To say the truth, all we people in this world including the first man, are subjugated to different extent to different quarters. A man working in his workplace has to be subjugated to higher authorities. But the level of subjugations varies.

However, the fact is that the subjugated person may or may not need the treatment. It depends on the level of subjugations and the acceptability of the person concerned. His willingness is also too important. How much he wants to compromise with things, that depends on him. The professional's job is to give the patient true insight. From that, he can correct himself judging his condition and clarifying his willingness.

Coming over the other entity, the treatment of wrong thinking pattern is rather difficult. It involves his beliefs, faith, culture, family education and many things. It is not easy to set right everything by the psychologist or psychiatrist on a single sitting. Currently drug treatment and ECT are in vogue with fair success. But that is for a definite period of time or as long as the person is on the treatment. ECT has its side effects of amnesia also.

Sometimes mentors or religious teachers are more successful on this field. But one thing is very necessary to be realized, that there cannot be a universal, booked approach to treat depression. It involves the physicians' or mentor's individuality to deal with the case with his astute judgement, and approaching at it improvising new avenues.

Treatment protocol for the two entities :

No drug treatment is advised or legally authorised to treat for the subjugated state. Dopamine re-uptake inhibitors (DRIs) can help in severe subjugation, but they have serious abuse potentials. Many psychoactive substances like cocaine, phencyclidine (PCP), amphetamines act by similar dopaminergic actions. Psychotherapy is the best approach. All I have said so far in this chapter, is about encountering them.

Fortunately, there are a lot of drugs as well as Electroconvulsive therapy (ECT) for the treatment of depression. But yet psychotherapy is to be considered as the definitive therapy. We cannot bring sweet nectar to all. This is all part of our life struggle. But what a professional can do as his part of his job, is to give the patient a clear insight, so that the patient can understand at least what is happening within his mind. And by that approachment, the patient will be able to fight his own problem on his own. At least it would make his life struggle easier. Our knowledge makes us wiser, which is necessary to the most intelligent person also.

SUBJUGATION	DEPRESSION
1. This occurs due to subjugation on one or more emotion scales.	1. This occurs owing to wrong thinking pattern. Positive and negative thinking result in elation and depression respectively.
2. The subjugated person may not need psychological help or treatment.	2. The depressed person often seeks for other's help or professional's help and may need treatment.
3. Though the person may not feel quite satisfied or happy, yet it is not that grave form of mental disorder like depression.	3. If it continues, it may progress to severe form when the person becomes unable to carry out his normal work and the condition eventually may culminate into the individual's committing suicide or being succumbed to alcohol, drugs and other forms of self-abusement.
4. Even in fairly subjugated state the individual can carry out all the routine daily life work.	4. As the depression deepens, it accordingly hampers the individual's ability to do normal daily works. In severe state the person becomes motionless, even forgetting and neglecting eating and other essential works.

5. No drug treatment is advised for the treatment for subjugation. Dopamine re-uptake inhibitors (DRIs), dextroamphetamine may be tried in case of severe uncomfortable subjugation. But they have serious abuse potentials. Sertraline (SDRI, a serotonin-dopamine reuptake inhibitor), having both the properties of blocking serotonin and dopamine, can be used in cases where subjugation and depression are co-existing, like melancholic depression or seductive depression. Pramipexole, a dopamine receptor agonist, combined with antidepressant medication, can also help for this purpose. Sedatives and anxiolytics like benzodiazepines may be helpful to combat with the acute stage of adaptation. But the psychotherapy has a definite role to give the patient clear insight and help with other relevant advice.	5. Fortunately, there is drug treatment for the patients to relieve them from the effects of depression. A number of good antidepressant drugs have been developed during the past few decades. And in severe cases ECT can do good, though there are side effects of amnesia. Psychotherapy is the definitive treatment, but each individual requires individual approach for the treatment basing on the case.

MIND - PART - II
(Psychological Illnesses)

CHAPTER I

SCHIZOPHRENIA

Schizophrenia (in general term madness), enlists a group of disorders, rather than a single entity, affecting all four houses of the mind, that is memory, emotion, intelligence, and motor activity, including sense of perception.

It affects 1% of world population.

Previously it was known as Dementia Precox. Eugen Bleuler (1857-1939) first coined the term Schizophrenia. According to him the four fundamental symptoms of schizophrenia are :

1. Ambivalence : The patient's inability to decide either against or for.
2. Autism : Withdrawal into self.
3. Affect disturbances : For example, flattening of affect (apathy) and inappropriate affect.
4. Association disturbances : Thought disorder, loosening of association.

This are also known as 4 A's of Bleuler.

Later Kurt Schneider (1887-1967) systematically described different clusters of symptoms for schizophrenia, which greatly helped further in clinical diagnosis of schizophrenia. Though any of these symptoms singularly is not diagnostic or specific for schizophrenia, but presence of these symptoms in patients signifies as important indicators to diagnose the disease, and these also helped in the future classification of symptoms for the disease.

These are known as Schneider's first rank symptoms and Schneider's second rank symptoms. Schneider' second rank symptoms are less important.

Schneider's First Rank Symptoms

A. Auditory Hallucinations
- **(a) Audible thoughts** (or thought echo) - hearing thoughts spoken aloud (1st person auditory hallucination).
- **(b) Arguing voices in their head** - two or more voices arguing or discussing the subject in the third person (third person auditory hallucination).
- **(c) Running commentary on one's action** (third person auditory hallucination).

B. Thought Alienation
- **(a) Thought Withdrawal**
- **(b) Thought Insertion**
- **(c) Thought Broadcasting**
  (also called Thought Diffusion)

C. Passivity Experiences
The subject experiences his mind or body being under the influence or control of some kind of external force or agency (delusions of control).
- **(a) Made feelings**
- **(b) Made impulses**
- **(c) Made volition or acts**
- **(d) Somatic passivity** - the subject experiences his bodily sensations, specially sensory symptoms are being imposed on body by some external force.

D. Delusional Perception
The subject links normal perception to a private and illogical meaning.

Symptoms of Schizophrenia

Symptoms of schizophrenia can be grossly divided into either positive or negative symptoms.

Positive symptom means the symptom which has been added to the personality of the patient. For example : Hallucinations, Delusions, Passivity phenomena, Thought Alienation, Movement disorders etc.

On the other hand, negative symptom means what has been taken away from the patient. For example : Emotional bluntness or apathy, Anhedonia (inability to experience pleasure), Social withdrawal, Reduced speech, Poor attention, Loss of motivation, Decreased psychomotor functions (inertia, stupor) etc.

Based on this, schizophrenia has been classified into two types - Type1 (predominated by positive symptoms) and Type2 (predominated by negative symptoms).

Most common positive symptoms of schizophrenia and their approximate percentage are :

- Auditory hallucinations (74%)
- Ideas of reference (70%)
- Delusions of reference (67%)
- Suspiciousness (66%)   Delusional mood (64%)
- Delusions of persecution (64%)
- Thought alienation (52%)
- Thought spoken aloud (50%)

Most common negative symptoms of schizophrenia are :

- Emotional bluntness or apathy (66%)
- Anhedonia (45%)

Negative symptoms of schizophrenia are more troublesome for the patients suffering from the disease for various reasons, such as –

 These symptoms are harder to recognize as part of the disorder and can be mistaken for depression or other mental conditions.

 People with negative symptoms of schizophrenia cannot live independently and manage social situations, contributing to poor functional outcome and quality of life. They neglect personal hygiene and often need help of others or become a trouble to the caretakers.

 Negative symptoms tend to persist longer than positive symptoms and are more difficult to treat. Antipsychotic drugs are more effective against positive symptoms of schizophrenia.

Details of symptoms associated with Schizophrenia

(A) Thought disorders

There are different types of thought disorders. These are :

(i) **Loosening of Associations :** The patient fails to sequence his thoughts and speech. He often jumps from one point to another. And there may be no overall meaningful relationship between all he is saying.

Thought blockage may occur, which is also known as thought deprivation. The patient suddenly stops within his speech, and cannot proceed further.

(ii) **Autistic thinking :** Another important thought disorder is autistic thinking. That is patient's thinking loses logical relationship. His thinking does not follow logical sequencing and are driven by private and illogical rules. An example, I live in the same state where the president lives, so I am also president.

The patient may suffer from poverty of ideas and conceptual thinking, decreased speech production, and in extreme case, complete mutism with no speech production may occur.

Sometimes condensation occurs; a number of different concepts, ideas or words are fused together.

(iii) **Neologism :** The patient may invent new words or phrases to express his thought.

(iv) **Delusions :** Delusions are false beliefs which are not keeping with reality or patient's social, cultural, and educational background and not amenable to persuasion.

Delusion may be primary or secondary. Primary delusions appear de novo, they appear suddenly and not based on other experiences of schizophrenia. Secondary delusions occur on the base of primary delusions or other manifestations of schizophrenia.

Common types of delusions seen in schizophrenia are :

a) Delusion of Persecution : The patient believes some people (people may be particular like police, communists etc. or he may have a vague idea about them) are trying to get after him - trying to kill him, trying to poison him, trying to enter into his room, or trying to do any misdeed upon him.

b) Delusion of reference : The patient feels he is the subject of special reference;

like when he is watching on TV, he considers some TV messages are specially for him. Or when two people are talking, he thinks he is the subject of their conversation.

c) Delusion of grandeur : He thinks he is famous or great. Sometimes delusion of persecution may develop after delusion of grandeur - 'I am so famous that people are after me'.

d) Delusion of control : The patient thinks he is being controlled by outside forces. This force may be known or unknown. He is acting like a robot.

This force may be radiowaves, electricity, or telepathy.

e) Somatic or Hypochondriacal delusion : The patient develops an altered self-image, or false belief about his general health condition (like, he has contacted rabies).

(B) Thought Alienation Phenomena

Thought Withdrawal : The patient thinks his thought is being taken away by external force - like 'the neighbours are stealing my thoughts away'.

Thought Insertion : He thinks, someone is imposing thoughts within him - like 'this is not my idea, he has implanted this thought within me'.

Thought Broadcasting : The patient feels, his thoughts are being escaped from the confines of his self and being broadcasted or transmitted to others.

(C) Disorders of Perception

Perceptional disorders may be of two types.

(1) Hallucination - Perception without stimuli, e.g. seeing something although there is nothing.

(2) Illusion - Wrong perception of an object, e.g. seeing a rope as a snake.

In schizophrenia hallucinations are common. All types of hallucinations may occur; auditory, visual, olfactory, tactile, gustatory. Auditory hallucinations are most common. The patient may hear simple sounds or may hear voices. The voices may come from any part of his body, e.g. heart, stomach, head, limbs; or may come from outside.

The most characteristic of schizophrenia is 'Third person hallucination'. That is voices are talking about the subject in the third person. The voices may make a running commentary on the actions of the patient or may command on the activities of the patient. Sometimes the commanding voices seem so much irritable to the patient that the patient overtly express angry reaction to it. Some patients describe the voices are vague and a lot of nonsense.

Visual hallucinations can also occur, most commonly along with auditory hallucinations.

Other types of hallucinations are less common.

(D) Passivity Phenomena

(1) Made feelings or affect
(2) Made impulses
(3) Made volition or acts

The patient experiences that the feelings, emotions, impulses, are being implanted within him.

And his activities are being regulated by outside forces.

(E) Disorders of Affect

The patient suffers from lack of emotional drive, emotional blunting, lack of interest and enthusiasm (apathy), inability to experience pleasure (anhedonia), or inappropriate emotional reactions.

There is also observed in the patients rapid change of emotions, from one to another. He is happy, angry, sad, afeared, in a quick succession.

Inappropriate emotional reactions vary. Sometimes severe outburst of emotion may occur against trivial stimuli. With slightest provocation or without any apparent provocation, the patient may take violent action.

(F) Disorders of Motor Functions

There may be decrease in psychomotor functions (inertia, stupor) or increase in psychomotor functions (excitement, restlessness).

The patient may show twitching, grimacing, or stereotyped movements of different parts of the body.

Some specific features are :

a) **Echolalia** - repeating the words or phrases which has been told to him.

b) **Echopraxia** - repeating the actions which has been shown to him.

c) **Waxy flexibility** - The patient keeps a definite posture which has been instructed to him for a long time, even if it is uneasy to him. That is if he is told to keep his arms straight above or stand on his one leg, he will maintain this posture for a long time.

d) **Automatic obedience** - The patient follows commands automatically.

e) **Negativism** - He does just the opposite of what he is requested to do.

Types of Schizophrenia

Schizophrenia has been classified into following subtypes.

1. Paranoid Schizophrenia
2. Hebephrenic Schizophrenia
3. Catatonic Schizophrenia
4. Undifferentiated Schizophrenia
5. Post Schizophrenic depression
6. Residual Schizophrenia
7. Simple Schizophrenia

Paranoid Schizophrenia

Paranoid schizophrenia occurs later in life (late 3rd or 4th decade) . This is characterised by the development of delusions.

Most common is delusion of persecution.

Others are delusion of reference, delusion of control, delusion of grandeur, delusion of infidelity (delusion of infidelity when involves the spouse, it is termed as Othello syndrome).

Hebephrenic Schizophrenia

Hebephrenic Schizophrenia is characterised by thought disorders and emotional disturbances.

It occurs in early decade(2nd).

Emotional disturbances include blunt or inappropriate affect, meaningless giggles or self-satisfied smiles. Mannerism may occur (that is stereotyped movement).

Auditory hallucinations are common. There may be marked withdrawal from the society.

Catatonic Schizophrenia

Catatonic Schizophrenia is characterised by marked disturbances in motor functions.

Onset of this type is also early in life, but occasionally may occur later.

Psychomotor functions vary from decreased action (stupor, inertia) to extreme excitement, aggressiveness. Mannerism occurs. Echolalia, Echopraxia, Waxy flexibility, Automatic obedience, Negativism are other features.

Hallucinations, delusions, thought and emotional disorders, are also present but less conspicuous compared to motor behaviour.

Simple Schizophrenia

Its onset is very insidious. That means very gradually it develops.

It is very difficult to determine the time of its onset. And it is also most difficult to diagnose.

Though, it is called simple, its prognosis (outcome) is very poor.

In this type marked social withdrawal, emotional bluntness, apathy (lack of interest) occur. The patient is often found to be associated with poor self-care, poor hygiene-maintenance, and is drifted downwards along the social order - wanders aimlessly as tramps, beggars, destitute persons; women may become prostitute.

Cognitive Impairment in Schizophrenia

It is a widely established fact that the cognitive deficits are core symptoms of schizophrenia. Although these impairments cannot be regarded as diagnostic tools for the disease, but they are strongly related to the functional outcome of the illness.

Working memory deficits are one of the main neurocognitive impairments found in subjects with first episode of schizophrenia and people with established schizophrenia. The severity of working memory deficits that is evident at the first episode of schizophrenia can predict the quality of life at the established stage of the illness. In addition to working memory, impairment in declarative memory, reasoning and problem solving ability, attention, and social cognition have great impact on the subject's vocational functioning. Poor attention, and memory problems affect learning of new work tasks. Verbal and visual memory are also impaired. Impaired executive function seriously affects employment outcomes.

However, the patients with schizophrenia are usually oriented with time, place and person. If such disorientations are present, it should instigate the physician to investigate for the presence of other medical, neurological or brain disorder.

The cognitive impairment of schizophrenia is one of the major areas of pharmacological and psychological experimental researches endeavoured to improve the level of functioning as well as quality of life in people suffering from schizophrenia.

Neurological signs in Schizophrenia

Multiple observations have considerably documented a higher prevalence of neurological signs in patients with schizophrenia (50-60%) compared to healthy normal individuals (5%). Prevalence rates of neurological signs in other psychiatric disorders lie in between these two groups. There is sufficient evidence to opine that these signs are directly related to the disease etiopathology rather than being secondary to other phenomena, such as side effects of antipsychotic drugs. But overlapping and co-occurrence may appear in the case of extrapyramidal syndromes and tardive dyskinesia caused by antipsychotic treatment. Family studies have also found consistently a higher prevalence of neurological signs in relatives of the patients with schizophrenia.

Neurological abnormalities include both 'hard' and 'soft' signs. Hard neurological signs refer to impairment in basic motor, sensory and reflex behaviours; whereas 'soft' neurological signs are described as nonlocalizing neurological abnormalities that cannot be linked to any specific brain region. 'Soft' signs have been found to be more strongly related to the presence of schizophrenia than 'hard' neurological signs.

'Soft' neurological signs include astereognosis (inability to perceive and understand the form and nature of objects by the sense of touch), agraphesthesia (inability to recognize writing on the skin), right-left confusion, intention tremor, dysdiadochokinesis (inability to perform rapidly alternating movements e.g. tapping of fingers on a surface), primitive reflexes (sucking/oral, grasp). 'Hard' neurological signs include synkinesis (an involuntary movement accompanying a volitional movement), dyskinesia (impairment of the power of voluntary movement), gaze impersistence, and cranial nerve abnormalities.

Other abnormal neurological signs include involuntary movements, like twitching, grimacing, tics, stereotyped movements of different body parts, abnormal muscular tone and abnormal gait.

Language and speech disorder though develop as an outcome of thought disorder in schizophrenia patients (e.g. loosening of association), but they may appear as pure neurological signs.

The presence of neurological signs and symptoms in schizophrenia correlates with the increased severity of the illness and indicates a poor prognosis.

Syndromes associated with Schizophrenia :

Capgras Syndrome

This is the delusion of double, commonly found with paranoid schizophrenia.

The patient feels his friends, family members, relations around him has been replaced with doubles who are trying to be imposing as familiar.

This syndrome was first described by French psychiatrist Joseph Capgras after a case of a French woman who had a complain that all 'doubles' had taken the places of her husband and other people around her.

Van Gogh Syndrome

This syndrome is characterised by dramatic self-mutilation which may occur in schizophrenia.

This has been named after the famous painter Vincent Van Gogh, who had cut his ear in the acute stage of this disease.

Late Paraphrenia

This occurs commonly in elderly women - especially unmarried or widowed ones. They form delusional belief that they are being persecuted for being raped, gassed, or people are trying to enter into their rooms to rob them.

Other mental diseases associated with Schizophrenia :

Depression - Depression is commonly associated with schizophrenia. Suicidal attack may occur in schizophrenia patients due to associated major depression and it is the leading cause of premature death in the patients suffering from schizophrenia.

Obsessive Compulsive disorder - This is another comorbid disease that may be associated with schizophrenia. Severe obsessive compulsive disorder may mask an underlying schizophrenic process.

Substance use disorders - Substance use is common in schizophrenia. The schizophrenic patients have an increased prevalence of use of common street drugs. Prevalence of alcohol abuse in schizophrenia is about 40 percent. Alcohol and drug abuse increase the risk of hospitalization and in some patients may increase psychotic symptoms.

Personality disorders - Some personality disorders, like schizotypal, schizoid and borderline personality disorders have some features of schizophrenia, but the symptoms are mild compared to schizophrenia and occur throughout a person's life. But the patients with schizotypal personality disorders may develop frank schizophrenia.

Besides mental diseases, schizophrenia is associated with an increased risk of type II diabetes mellitus, obesity, and chronic obstructive pulmonary disease (COPD).

Diagnosis of Schizophrenia

According to ICD-10 (Internal classification of diseases), there are four major (a-d) and four minor (e-h) groups of symptoms.

For the diagnosis to be made, a minimum of one very clear symptom (two or more if less clear) belonging to the groups (a) to (d); or a minimum of two symptoms belonging to the groups (e) to (h) should have been present for most of the time during a period of one month or more. These are :

a) Thought echo, thought insertion, or withdrawal, or thought broadcasting;

b) Delusion of control, influence or passivity, clearly referred to body or limb movements or specific thoughts, actions, or sensations; Delusional perception;

c) Hallucinatory voices giving a running commentary on the patient's behaviour or discussing the patient among themselves or other types of hallucinatory voices coming from some part of the body;

d) Persistent delusions of other kinds that are culturally inappropriate and completely impossible (e.g. being able to control the weather, or being in communication with aliens from another world);

e) Persistent hallucinations in any modality occurring everyday for at least one month when accompanied by delusions (which may be fleeting or half-formed) or when accompanied by persistent over valued ideas;

f) Neologisms, or interpolation in the train of thought, resulting in incoherence or irrelevant speech;

g) Catatonic behaviour, such as excitement, posturing or waxy flexibility, negativism, mutism, and stupor;

h) 'Negative' symptoms such as marked apathy, paucity of speech, and blunting or incongruity of emotional responses (it must be cleared that these are not due to depression or to neuroleptic medication).

Causes of Schizophrenia

Causes of schizophrenia may be genetical, environmental, and psycho-social.

Genetical factors : Schizophrenia has strong co-relation with hereditary factors. It is seen in 6.5% of first degree relatives of the patients, and 40% in monozygotic twins of affected people.

If one parent has schizophrenia, the chance of the child developing schizophrenia is 13-14%, when both parents are affected, the chance increases to 40-45%.

There seems to be presence of multiple risk genes, several of which the schizophrenic patient may inherit. Aggregated actions of these genes associated with environmental factors lead to the overt expression of the disease.

In a large scale genome-wide association study (GWAS), Schizophrenia Working Group of the Psychiatric Genomics Consortium have identified 128 gene variants associated with schizophrenia.

Strongest candidate genes for schizophrenia are :

¤ Neuregulin (NRG1 located on chromosome 8: 31.64–32.77 Mb) is a growth factor that stimulates neuron development and differentiation. It is supposed to play a role in synaptic plasticity.

¤ Dysbindin (DTNBP1 located on Chr 6: 15.52-15.66 Mb) helps to regulate glutamate release.

¤ Catecholamine O-methyl transferase (COMT located on Chr 22: 19.94–19.97 Mb) - catalyzes O-methylation, a major step in the degradation of catecholamines – including the neurotransmitter dopamine.

¤ Disrupted in Schizophrenia (DISC1 located on Chr 1: 231.63–232.04 Mb) - DISC1 has been shown to participate in the regulation of cell proliferation, differentiation, migration, neuronal axon and dendrite outgrowth, intracellular transport and synaptic transmission.

¤ Regulator of G-Protein Signaling 4 (RGS4 located on Chr 1: 163.07–163.08 Mb) - negatively regulates signaling through G-proteins. G-protein signaling activates second messengers, such as cyclic AMP, which in turn regulate many intracellular processes. RGS4 is involved in neuronal differentiation.

¤ Dopamine- and Cyclic AMP- Regulated Phosphoprotein 32 kDa, also known as protein phosphatase 1 regulatory subunit 1B (PPP1R1B located on Chr 17: 39.63–39.64 Mb) - is an inhibitor of protein phosphatase-1 (PP1) and protein kinase A (PKA).

¤ Metabotropic Glutamate Receptor-3 (GRM3 located on Chr 7: 86.64–86.86 Mb) is a G-protein coupled receptor for glutamate, a major excitatory neurotransmitter. GRM3 also modulates serotonin and dopamine transmission. Several association studies have linked GRM3 polymorphisms to schizophrenia, suggesting functional changes in glutamate transmission in the prefrontal cortex and hippocampus.

Environmental factors : Childhood trauma, parental loss, parental separation, unhappy family atmosphere, social isolation, unemployment, racial discrimination, adversity all may act as precipitating factors in genetically prone patient leading to the causation of the disease.

Psycho-social factors : Stress is a common initiating factor for the disease. Any highly stressful event or situation can play as a trigger on the onset of the disease.

Schizophrenia often occurs in people with introverted personality.

Drugs : Many hallucinogenic drugs like LSD, amphetamine, may cause schizophrenia like syndrome in normal individuals.

Cellular and Molecular mechanisms of Schizophrenia

Pathophysiolpgy of schizophrenia may be both due to reduction in brain volume in specific parts of the brain and due to decrease in neuronal functions (such as metabolic activities) in parts of the brain. But there is no evidence-based conclusion whether this reduction in brain volume is due to decrease in the size of the nerve cells or decrease in the number of the nerve cells. Currently more supported view is that reduction of brain in particular area or areas of brain is due to reduction in inter-neuronal connectives or neuronal arborization. Reduced density of dendrites and synapses are supposed to be the cause for structural deficit in specific zones of the brain of schizophrenia patients.

Studies using multimodal functional brain imaging techniques - such as fMRI (functional magnetic resonance imaging), PET (positron emission tomography), SPECT (single photon emission computed tomography) - have shown that major dysfunctional areas associated with the disease are frontal lobe, temporal lobes, and hippocampus.

Structural neuroimaging studies with CT (computed tomography) and MRI have shown reduction in brain volume preferentially in medial temporal lobe structures (70-80%) that included amygdala, hippocampus, parahippocampal gyrus; and frontal lobe (60-70%) - most notably prefrontal cortex and orbitofrontal cortex.

CT and MRI studies have also consistently shown enlargement of the lateral and third ventricles of the brain in schizophrenia patients.

Other brain regions that have been reported to be involved in different MRI studies are parietal lobe particularly inferior parietal lobule, septum pellucidum, corpus callosum, thalamus, basal ganglia including nucleus accumbens and pallidum (larger volume), and cerebellum. Along with reduction in brain volume, reduced symmetry has also been reported in several brain areas involving temporal, frontal and occipital lobes in schizophrenia patients.

All these studies elucidate the fact that abnormalities in multiple focal regions in the brain are responsible for the development of schizophrenia. But there is variance in the results of the studies regarding whether these changes are static or progressive. Some studies showed that abnormalities do not change from the onset of the disease, while others reported gradual progress of pathological changes during the course of the disease.

Major neurohumoral system associated with this disease is Dopaminergic system. There is excessive activation of dopamine (D2) receptors at the neuronal junctions of dopaminergic neurons which is mainly responsible for producing symptoms.

But whether this aberration in dopaminergic system is a precondition for schizophrenia, or alteration of dopaminergic functions alleviate the disease symptoms is debatable. It has also been suggested that this over activity of dopaminergic system may be due to deficit in functions of another neurohumoral system.

Antipsychotic drugs act by blocking the dopamine D2 receptors in synaptic junctions negating the effect of dopamine on them.

Serotonin may play a role in this disease, as the atypical antipsychotic drugs have functions on both Dopamine (D2) and Serotonin (5-HT) receptors, but sufficient evidence is lacking. The lack of reliable peripheral marker for CNS serotonergic activity believed to be an impediment to 5-HT research in schizophrenia.

Another theory is, glutamate may play a significant role in the causation of the disease.

Glutamate is an excitatory neurotransmitter which act through a group of receptors in the postpsynaptic nerve terminals in many neuronal pathways which are located in hippocampus and many areas of cerebral cortex. Drugs like Phencyclidine (angel dust) that cause blockage of these receptors, particularly NMDA receptors, have been found to produce schizophrenia like symptoms.

It has been postulated that deficiency, or reduced function of NMDA receptors have a significant effect in this disease.

Onset of the Disease

Schizophrenia is a disease that typically begins in early adulthood, that is between the ages of 15 and 25. Men tend to develop schizophrenia a bit earlier than their women counterpart.

The average age of onset in men is 18, and in case of women is 25.

Onset of schizophrenia is quite rare before the age of 10 years and after 50 years.

The age of onset varies in different types of schizophrenia.

Treatment of Schizophrenia

(a) Drug Therapy

Antipsychotic drugs are the mainstay of therapy in schizophrenia patients. Adjuvant treatment with antiderpessive, sedative and anxiolytic drugs may be additionally incorporated.

All antipsychotic drugs have potent dopamine D2 receptor blocking action. Blockade of dopaminergic projections to the prefrontal, temporal cortex, mesocortical areas and limbic system is responsible for their antipsychotic action. Dopaminergic blocked in the basal ganglia causes extrapyramidal side effects.

Treatment should be instituted as soon as diagnosis is made. Hospitalization needed in cases of, i) the patient being a danger to self and others; ii) poor drug compliance or drug response; iii) significant neglect of self-care (neglect of food and water intake); and iv) evidence of taking substances.

Treatment constitutes two phases - (1) Treatment of acute psychosis, (2) Stabilization and maintenance phase.

Acute psychotic phase lasts from 4-8 weeks and associated with severe agitation. The patients in acute stage are treated with antipsychotic and sedative (benzodiazepines) drugs, either orally or through intramuscular injection (in severe form).

In the stabilization and maintenance phase, the treatment is aimed at preventing relapse. Maintenance therapy is usually continued for 6 months to one year for the first episode, more if subsequent relapses occur.

Almost 50% of the patients show complete or near complete recovery.

Antipsychotic drugs are of two types.

1st generation or typical antipsychotics, which have more extrapyramidal side effects, like Chlorpromazine, Trifluoperazine, Fluphenazine, Haloperidol,

Pimozide, Sulpiride etc.

2nd generation or atypical antipsychotics with minimal or absent extrapyramidal side effects like Clozapine, Olanzapine, Quetiapine, Risperidone, Ziprasidone, Paliperidone, Aripiprazole, Amisulpride etc.

Extrapyramidal side effects include tremor, muscular rigidity, hypokinesia, mask like facies, tardive dyskinesia (bizarre muscle spasms - mostly involving linguo-facial muscles), restlessness, feeling of discomfort, agitation etc. One serious side effect among these is tardive dyskinesia. Tardive dyskinesia is repetitive, involuntary, purposeless movements of the tongue and lips. In severe cases, the trunk, limbs and respiratory muscles may also be affected. About 20 to 30 percent of the patients on long-term medication with antipsychotic drugs will develop symptoms of tardive dyskinesia.

Extrapyramidal side effects are treated by adjuvant anticholinergic medicine such as procyclidine, biperidin, benztropine, diphenhydramine, trihexyphenidyl etc. Akathisia (restlessness) may respond to beta-blockers also.

Classification of Antipsychotics

A. First generation antipsychotics

1. Phenothiazines : (a) aliphatic side chain - Chlorpromazine, Triflupromazine; (b) piperidine side chain - Thioridazine; (c) piperazine side chain - Prochlorperazine, Trifluoperazine, Fluphenazine.

2. Thioxanthenes : Chlorprothixene, Thiothixene, Flupenthixol.

3. Butyrophenones : Haloperidol, Trifluperidol.

4. Diphenylbutylpiperdines : Pimozide, Penfluridol.

5. Dihydroindolones : Molindone.

6. Dibenzoxazepines : Loxapine.

B. Second generation atypical antipsychotics

1. Benzo (diaze- or thiaze-) pines : Clozapine, Olanzapine, Quetiapine.

2. Substituted Benzamides : Sulpiride, Amisulpride.

3. Indolones and diones : Aripiprazole, Paliperidone, Risperidone, Ziprasidone.

Usual dosing of some common second generation antipsychotics in Schizophrenia :

Antipsychotic Drugs	Starting Dosage	Maintenance Dosage	Maximum Recommended Dosage	Titration
Aripiprazole	10-15 mg tablet orally once a day	10-30 mg/day; once, or twice in divided doses.	30 mg/day	Increase of the dosage should not be made before 2 weeks.
Clozapine	12.5 mg tablet orally once or twice a day	150-300 mg/day in divided doses or 200 mg as a single dose in the evening	900 mg/day	The dosage should be increased by 25-50 mg/day to a target dose of 300-450 mg/day (administered in divided doses) by the end the second week. Subsequent dosage increments should be made, if necessary, by not more than 100 mg and not more frequent than once or twice weekly.
Olanzapine	5-10 mg tablet orally once a day	10-20 mg once a day	20 mg/day	Dosage adjustment (increment or decrement) by 5 mg/day should be made as required at intervals of at least 1 week.
Paliperidone	3-9 mg extended-release tablet orally once a day	3-6 mg/day	12 mg/day	Dosage increases should be made in increments of 3 mg/day and should occur at intervals of more than 5 days.
Quetiapine	25 mg tablet orally twice a day	150-750 mg/day (as lowest as to prevent remission) in divided doses	750 mg/day	25-50 mg increments divided in 2 or 3 times daily with a goal of achieving a target dosage of 300-400 mg/day (administered in divided doses) by the fourth day. Further dose adjustment should be made by 25-50 mg twice a day at intervals not less than 2 days.

Risperidone	1 mg tablet orally once a day	2-6 mg once a day	16 mg/day	Increase to 2 mg once a day on the second day and 4 mg once a day on the third day. In some patients, a slower titration may be appropriate. Further dosage increments, if necessary, should be made by 1-2 mg/day at intervals not less than 1 week.
Risperidone IM	Start with oral risperidone for 3 weeks	25-50 mg IM injection every 2 weeks	50 mg every 2 weeks	Start from 25 mg IM injection every 2 weeks up to the maintenance dose. Dosage titration should not be made at intervals less than
				4 weeks as release of the drug continues up to 3 weeks after injection.
Ziprasidone	20 mg capsule orally twice a day	20-80 mg twice a day	80 mg twice a day	Increment of dosage should be made on requirement at least at 2 days intervals.
Ziprasidone IM	For acute agitation, 10-20 mg IM injection as required up to a maximum of 40 mg/day	Use beyond 3 consecutive days not applicable	40 mg/day	For acute agitation, dosage of 10 mg may be repeated every 2 hrs. and dosage of 20 mg may be repeated every 4 hrs. up to a maximum dose of 40 mg/day.

Side effects of some common second generation antipsychotics :

Aripiprazole : Most common side effects are sedation or insomnia, dizziness, headache, hypersalivation, weight gain, dyspepsia, nausea, constipation, anxiety, agitation, akathisia (inability to sit or lie quietly, motor restlessness), EPS (+).

Some patients taking aripiprazole may develop muscle movements specially of the face, neck and back that they cannot control. This is more likely to happen in elderly patients. Neuroleptic malignant syndrome (NMS) is a rare but possible fatal syndrome that may be caused by aripiprazole, characterised by fever, confusion and muscular rigidity. Occurrence of NMS is greater in 1st generation antipsychotics particularly high potency drug like haloperidol.

Older adults with dementia (e.g. in Alzheimer's disease) taking antipsychotic medicine, have a higher incidence of strokes and subsequent death. Still antipsychotic drugs have to be prescribed for controlling behavioural agitations in these cases as a last resort or when it is better than no treatment. But there is variance of reports about which antipsychotic is relatively safer than other antipsychotics in this regard. Mostly used antipsychotics are resperidone, aripiprazole and quetiapine, though aripiprazole is not approved by the US FDA to treat mental disorders in patients with dementia.

Clozapine : Sedation, postural hypotension, dizziness, tachycardia, weight gain, nausea, constipation, hypersalivation, fever, seizures, EPS (+/-).

Agranulocytosis occurs in 0.8% of patients. For the first 6 months of treatment, weekly blood WBC count should be carried out. Later the frequency of tests can be reduced if the WBC count is normal. Clozapine should be discontinued if WBC count is less than 3000/cmm or the granulocyte count is less than 1500/cmm. Another infrequent (less than 0.1%) but serious side effect of clozapine is myocarditis which may be fatal. Patients on clozapine should immediately report to the physician if he feels chest pain, fever, dyspnoea or tachypnoea.

Olanzapine : Sedation, hypotension, weight gain, dizziness, headache, dry mouth, constipation, increased appetite, dyspepsia, nausea, akathisia and asthenia (lack or loss of strength and energy), EPS (+/-).

Olanzapine elevates blood glucose, cholesterol and triglycerides level and increases hepatic enzymes (transaminases). Periodic assessment of blood sugar and transaminases are recommended during treatment. Hyperprolactinemia may also occur causing gynaecomastia, galactorrhea, breast pain, breast discomfort.

Paliperidone : Sedation, postural hypotension, tachycardia, headache, dystonia, akathisia, EPS (++).

It may prolong QT interval and should be avoided in combination with other drugs which also cause QT prolongation.

Quetiapine : Sedation, postural hypotension, dizziness, headache, weight gain, dry mouth, constipation, tachycardia. Quetiapine is least likely to cause EPS and hyperprolactinemia is rare. Cataracts have been produced in animal experiments with dogs, though it has not been reported after the start of its clinical use. Yet six monthly opthalmological check-up is advocated while the patients are on quetiapine.

Risperidone : Sedation, weight gain, agitation, anxiety, hypotension, tachycardia, dizziness, nausea, rhinitis, dystonia and muscle spasms, constipation, increased appetite, orgasmic dysfunction, increased skin pigmentation, blurred vision, EPS (+/-). Hyperprolactinemia may occur.

Ziprasidone : Sedation, hypotension, dizziness, headache, nausea, EPS (+). Ziprasidone may cause prolonged QT interval and should not be prescribed with other drugs which also prolong QT interval and in patients with congenital long QT syndrome. Ziprasidone is not recommended in patients younger than 15 years.

Some guidelines for prescribing antipsychotics :

¤ The lowest possible dose should be used.

¤ For majority of patients, the use of a single antipsychotic drug (with or without additional mood stabilizer or sedative) is advocated. Apart from exceptional circumstances (e.g. clozapine augmentation), antipsychotic polypharmacy should be avoided because of the risks of associated QT prolongation and sudden cardiac death. If a person does not respond to the first drug, the drug should be gradually tapered and another drug should be initiated. A second generation antipsychotic needs 4-6 weeks to show its full effectiveness, before that discontinuation of it should be carefully considered. Sometimes benzodiazepines may be needed to augment the effect of antipsychotic in initial stage. Lorazepam 1 or 2 mg orally or IM can be used for acute agitation initially, which can be lowered in dose or tapered off later.

¤ Combination of antipsychotic drugs should only be contemplated where response to a single antipsychotic has clearly been demonstrated to be inadequate.

¤ Response to antipsychotic drug treatment should be documented in patient's records.

¤ Those receiving antipsychotic drugs should undergo close monitoring of pulse, blood pressure, ECG, blood cell count, plasma glucose and lipids concentration, along with specific monitoring related to specific drug.

¤ Safety of antipsychotics in pregnant mothers has not been established, but as the drugs can be excreted in breast milk, they should not be prescribed for breast-feeding mothers.

(b) Electro Convulsive Therapy (ECT)

ECT has been effective in patients with :

i) severe symptoms
ii) treatment resistance
iii) catatonia
iv) severe underlying depression (particularly with suicidal attack).

(c) Transcranial Magnetic Stimulation (TMS)

TMS is application of a rapidly changing magnetic field to the superficial layers of the cerebral cortex, which, as according to the law of electromagnetism, induces small electrical currents to the area applied. TMS devices deliver strong magnetic pulses through an insulated coil held near the scalp. As magnetic field is unburdened of electrical impedance of the skull bones, through TMS more focal and selective area or areas of the brain can be stimulated than ECT.

TMS has been found to be effective in schizophrenia in reducing auditory hallucinations and negative symptoms.

Rare and only serious side effects of TMS are syncope (fainting) and seizures.

(d) Supportive Therapy

(i) Family therapy : Family counselling is done to reduce stress factors and emotional over-involvement or load on the patient.

(ii) Group therapy : Group therapy is aimed at teaching the patient in solving problems, increasing communication skills and in managing stress. Group therapy also helps the patient to establish fellowship sense and prevent from being socially isolated.

(iii) Cognitive behaviour therapy : Cognitive behaviour therapy has been used to correct underlying cognitive distortion and improve cognitive function.

(iv) Individual Psychotherapy : Individual psychotherapy is used as an adjuvant to the mainstay of therapy.

Prognosis or Outcome of the Disease

The prognosis or outcome of schizophrenia is better in developing countries than in developed countries. The outcome is as follows :

After 10 years, of the people diagnosed with schizophrenia

- 25% Completely recover
- 25% Much improved, relatively independent
- 25% Improved, but require extensive support network
- 15% Hospitalized, unimproved
- 10% Dead (mostly suicide).

After 30 years, of the people diagnosed with schizophrenia

- 25% Completely recover
- 35% Much improved, relatively independent
- 15% Improved, but require extensive support network
- 10% Hospitalized, unimproved
- 15% Dead (mostly suicide).

[Source : Surviving Schizophrenia. Ref. 55]

Prognostic factors which have favourable effects in schizophrenia are :

1. Acute onset of illness.

2. Precipitation by environmental or physical factors.
3. Late onset (after 35 years of age).
4. Well-adjusted, stable previous personality.
5. A short duration of the disease (<6 mths).
6. A pyknic (fat) physique.

7. Presence of depression.

8. Catatonic subtype.

9. Predominance of positive symptoms.

10. Good social support.

Poor prognostic indicators are :

1. Gradual onset.

2. Long duration of illness (>2 years).

3. An unstable, ill-adjusted previous personality.

4. Early age of onset.

5. Absence of clear precipitating factors.

6. Asthenic (thin) physique.

7. Hebephrenic or simple subtype.

8. Family history of schizophrenia.

9. Flat or blunted affect.

10. Poor social support or unmarried.

SCHIZOAFFECTIVE DISORDER

This is a mental disorder where the features of schizophrenia and mood disorder (either bipolar disorder or depression) are both present, but do not meet the criteria to be diagnosed as either of them alone. The symptoms of both disorders may be present simultaneously or may follow within few days of each other.

Schizoaffective disorder is estimated to occur in 0.5 to 0.8 percent of people at some point in their life. It is more common in women than men.

Schizoaffective disorder has following subtypes.

(1) Schizoaffective disorder, manic type.

(2) Schizoaffective disorder, depressive type.

(3) Schizoaffective disorder, mixed type.

Common symptoms of psychosis are hallucinations, delusions, and disorganised speech and thought. Symptoms of mood disorder include symptoms of hypomania, mania (manic type); depression (depressive type); and mixed episode (mixed type).

Treatment

Mainstay of treatment is antipsychotics in combination with mood stabilizers or antidepressants or both.

(1) Antipsychotics - There is no single choice for antipsychotics but atypical or second generation antipsychotics should be preferred, because they also have mood stabilizing properties. Antipsychotics used for schizoaffective disorder are paliperidone, risperidone, ziprasidone, olanzapine, clozapine (it causes serious agranulocytosis, so regular blood cell count should be monitored).

Antipsychotics should be prescribed at minimum dose which is necessary to control the symptoms.

(2) Mood stabilizing drugs - These are used for the management of associated bipolar   mood disorder. Lithium, carbamazepine, valproic acid, lamotrigine are the choices.

(3) Antidepressants - These are used for the management of depression. Drugs used are citalopram, escitalopram, fluoxetine etc.

(4) Electroconvulsive therapy (ECT) - ECT should be considered for severe depression or severe psychotic symptoms refractory to medications.

(5) Psychotherapy
   (a) Individual or family counselling.
   (b) group therapy.

The prognosis of schizoaffective disorder is better than that of schizophrenia, but worse than that of mood disorders.

BRIEF PSYCHOTIC DISORDER
OR BRIEF SCHIZOPHRENIA-LIKE PSYCHOSIS

This disorder manifests with variable presentations (confusion and perplexity, formal thought disorder, delusions and hallucinations, disorganised or catatonic behaviour) and resolves within 1-3 months.

This disorder is usually associated with acute stress situation and prognosis is better than in schizophrenia.

Treatment

¤ Benzodiazepines or short term antipsychotics.

¤ Antidepressants or mood stabilizing drugs may be used as adjuvant medication or to prevent relapse.

¤ Supportive psychotherapy.

DELUSIONAL DISORDER

Delusions are false, fixed beliefs which do not keep with the reality or the patient's social and cultural norm, and which are not amenable to persuasion.

Delusions can occur in schizophrenia, mood disorders, somatoform disorder and different other non-psychiatric medical conditions including substance use disorder. But delusional disorder as a single entity is differentiated from schizophrenia by the absence of other psychotic symptoms; from the mood disorders by the absence of associated symptoms of mania, hypomania or depression; and from somatoform disorder by the degree of false belief. In somatoform disorder or hypochondriasis subjects are not fixed in their beliefs. They admit their fear may be groundless.

Prevalence of delusional disorder is 0.2 to 0.3%. It is rarer than schizophrenia (1%) and mood disorders (5%). The delusional disorder can appear at any age ranging from 18 to 90s. The mean age of onset is 40. There is a slight predilection of incidence towards the women's quarter.

Delusions can be grossly categorized into two groups. (1) Nonbizarre delusions and (2) Bizarre delusions.

Nonbizarre delusions - These are delusions which are possible in reality, like the person is being followed, or he has contacted rabies.

Bizarre delusions - These are delusions which are impossible in reality or do not go with the cultural norm. For example, the person walked in the sky at night.

For the diagnosis of delusional disorder the person must exhibit one or more types of delusion for the duration of at least one month, that cannot be attributed to other medical or psychiatric disorders.

Following subtypes of delusions are seen.

a) Delusion of Persecution b) Delusion of reference c) Delusion of control d) Delusion of grandeur e) Somatic or hypochondriacal delusion.
[Already has been discussed under Schizophrenia]

f) Erotomanic delusion : The patient believes that some person is in love with him or her.

g) Delusion of jealousy or infidelity : Marked feelings of jealousy and thoughts of infidelity occur in a person regarding another person in delusional intensity. When this delusion involves the spouse, this is called conjugal paranoia or Othello syndrome.

h) Delusion of guilt : Ungrounded false belief of remorse or guilt in a person, that cannot be persuadable.

i) Nihilistic delusion or cotard syndrome : The person takes delusional negative attitude towards the life and world. He thinks he has lost his strength, hope, energy, possessions; and even may take belief that he does not exist or he has died, the world beyond has been reduced to nothingness.

j) Induced delusion : This is differently termed as shared psychotic disorder, double insanity or folie a deux. This is characterised by transference of delusional belief from one person to another with whom he or she is emotionally attached. But it may involve more persons or an entire family (folie a trois, folie a quatre etc. or folie a famille).

On separation, dependent individuals may give up their delusions and the person with genuine delusion can be treated properly.

Etiology

Exact etiology of delusional disorder is unknown. There is limited evidence suggesting familial pattern of this disorder. And there is insufficient data to suggest that any biological factor is responsible for delusional disorder. This could be suggested that failure of defense mechanisms or logical reasoning to cope with a stressful situation (it may not be generalized stress) make a person take illogical route of cognition to adopt a belief that is incongruent with the reality or the cultural norm.

Treatment

Delusional disorders are difficult to treat. Insight oriented individual psychotherapy, supportive therapy, cognitive behavioural therapy may be effective.

Drug therapy : Antipsychotic drugs (haloperidol, risperidone, olanzapine, pimozide) are the preferred choice. Drugs should be started at low doses. It it fails dose should be increased gradually. Some studies have shown specific response of pimozide in the treatment of delusional disorders, particularly somatic type of delusional disorders.

Prognosis or Outcome

About 50% of patients recover at long-term follow up, 20% show decreased symptoms and 30% show no change.

Good prognostic indicators are earlier onset, acute onset, of short duration (<3 months), female sex, with precipitating stress factors and good social and occupational contacts.

Poor prognostic indicators are late onset, chronic onset, longer duration, male sex, absence of precipitating factors and poor emotional contacts.

CHAPTER II

DEMENTIA AND DELIRIUM

Dementia

Dementia means deterioration in higher mental functioning without any impairment of subject's consciousness.

Memory loss is most common. But any other mental faculties can be affected including general intelligence, orientation, emotional reactions, behaviour, and mood.

Memory loss is most prominent in the learning of new information, but in more severe cases the recall of past learned information may also be affected.

For diagnosis of dementia, symptoms should be present for at least 6 months.

Causes of dementia are various. The most common causes are Alzheimer's disease, Vascular dementia, Lewy body dementia, Parkinson's disease, Fronto-temporal dementia, etc.

Pseudodementia may be associated with depression, but here memory is usually seen intact after careful testing.

Prevalence of Dementia

Prevalence of dementia increases with age. 5%-10% of cases occur in the general population older than 65 years of age, 20% - 40% in the general population older than 85 years of age, 15% - 20% in general medical outpatients, and 50% in chronic care illnesses.

Clinical features of Dementia in general

Dementia may result from cortical disease (e.g. Alzheimer's disease) or from diseases of subcortical structures such as basal ganglia, limbic system, thalamus etc. (e.g. Huntington's disease, Multiple Sclerosis).

Cortical dementia is characterised by loss of cognitive functions such as language, perception, intellectualization, calculation etc. In contrast subcortical dementia is characterised by slowing of cognition and information processing, flattening of the affect, and disturbances in mood.

The following are the principal manifestations of dementia.

(1) Memory Impairment : Recollection of recent events is first affected and the condition becomes progressively worse eventually affecting the remote memories as well.

(2) Impairment in General Intelligence : Impaired judgement and failure to grasp the situation results in reaction to it inappropriately. There is impairment of abstract thinking and problem solving capabilities.

(3) Emotional Instability : Emotional instability is manifested by irritability, impulsive conduct, occasional acts of violence and inappropriate emotional reactions to the situations. In advanced stages, the emotional reactions become blunted and the patient appears to be incapable of responding to emotionally charged events in the environment.

Mood disturbance also occurs in dementia in the form of euphoria or depression.

(4) Other cognitive impairment : Apart from aphasia (speech and language disorder), apraxia and agnosia are common in patients with dementia. Apraxia is inability to carry out learned motor activities even if the motor function is normal, like cooking, washing etc. As the disease progresses patients have difficulties in normal daily activities, like dressing, bathing or feeding.

Agnosia is failure to recognize the import of sensory impressions in spite of other normal sensory functions. Agnosia may be visual, auditory, tactile, olfactory or gustatory. Visual agnosia is failure to identify and recognize familiar objects, familiar faces.

(5) Disorientation : Disorientation in time occurs first. Disorientation in place and person develop in later stages.

(6) Hallucinations and Delusions : 20 to 30 percent of patients with dementia (primarily in Alzheimer's type) have hallucinations and 30 to 40 percent have delusions. The form of delusion is often influenced by the person's previous personality. Paranoid and persecutory delusions are common.

(7) Personal Care : Carelessness in dress and cleanliness occurs. It eventually results in complete disregard for personal cleanliness and hygiene maintenance with appearance of incontinence.

(8) Catastrophic Reaction : There is sudden change in behaviour, with anger and hostility, when the patient fails to cope with a task beyond his intellectual capabilities.

Alzheimer's Disease

This is the most common cause of dementia in the elderly people, accounting for 50% to 60% of all cases of dementia. It is a neurodegenerative type of dementia and characterised by deterioration in memory, cognitive functions and progressive impairment of daily-life activities.

Onset may be sudden or gradual. Usually appears after 60s. Risk increases with the increase in age.

Risk Factors

Defective genes on chromosome 1, 14, 19, 21, and E4 variant of Apoprotein E gene are most important in the pathogenesis of Alzheimer's disease.

Other medical conditions, such as high blood pressure, insulin resistance diabetes, dyslipidaemia, elevated blood homocysteine level, repeated head trauma are associated risk factors.

Neuro-pathological Changes

Flattening of cerebral sulci, brain atrophy, increase in ventricular sizes are found in CT and MRI.

FDG-PET (fluorodeoxyglucose-positron emission tomography) have shown decreased glucose metabolism in the temporal and parietal lobes.

Two important neuropathological findings seen in Alzheimer's disease are neurofibrillary tangles and neuritic plaques.

Neurofibrillary tangles (NFTs) are silver staining neuronal cytoplasmic fibrils composed of abnormally phosphorylated tau protein. Tau binds to and stabilizes microtubules, supporting axonal transport of organelles, glycoproteins, neurotransmitters and other substances throughout the neurons. Once hyperphosphorylated tau can no longer bind to microtubules properly and its functions are disrupted causing resultant loss of nerve functioning.

This is most conspicuous in the regions of hippocampus, parts of temporal lobe and nucleus basalis of Meynert.

Neuritic plaques are composed of insoluble extracellular deposits of beta amyloid protein, a degradation product of larger transmembrane amyloid precursor protein (APP). There are two types of plaques - classical and diffuse. Classical type contains densely aggregated beta amyloid protein around neuronal processes (both axons and dendrites) in intracortical areas, resulting in neuronal degeneration and neuronal cell loss. The diffuse type plaques are amorphous aggregates of beta amyloid protein and not associated with neuronal cell loss.

Both NFTs and neuritic plaques in Alzheimer's disease cause significant loss of neurons and nerve synapses.

Biochemically AD is associated with decrease in neurotransmitters specially acetylcholine and its synthetic enzyme choline acetyltransferase. Reduction in acetylcholine also may be partly due to degeneration of cholinergic neurons in nucleus basalis of Maynert that project throughout the cortex. There is also noradrenergic and serotonergic depletion due to degeneration of brain stem nuclei, such as locus ceruleus and dorsal raphe.

Clinical Features

Disturbances in memory for recent incidents is first to be observed in most cases, which follows changes in other mental activities.

Inability to keep financial tracks, missing appointments, misunderstanding in conversations are usual features. Language becomes impaired - first naming, then comprehension, and finally fluency. Gradually apraxia emerges, that is difficulties in learned sequential motor tasks.

Associated with memory disturbances and impairment of cognitive functions, there appear spatial disorientation, emotional lability, irritability, aggressiveness, apathy, depression, hallucinations and delusions.

In advanced stages of the disease, extrapyramidal signs (muscle rigidity, tremor, slowness of actions) may occur.

Sleep-wake pattern is disorganized. Night time wandering may be disturbing to the household. About 10% of patients with AD develop Capgras syndrome, to think a caretaker has been replaced with an imposter. In end stage of the disease patients become mute, rigid and completely bedridden.

Diagnosis

Diagnosis is based on clinical evaluation and excluding other causes.
The mini mental status examination is a useful screening test for dementia.

On CT, MRI enlargement of ventricles can be demonstrated. PET imaging also helps. But these neuroimaging techniques are not absolutely diagnostic for Alzheimer's disease, particularly in early stages.

However, imaging techniques associated with other laboratory tests should be performed to rule out other diseases causing dementia.

Mini-Mental Status Examination

Orientation	
Name : season/date/month/year	5 (1 for each name)
Name : hospital/floor/town/state/country	5 (1 for each name)
Registration	
Ask patient to identify three objects by name and repeat them	3 (1 for each object)
Attention and calculation	
Serial 7s; subtract from 100 (e.g. 93-86-79-72-65)	5 (1 for each subtraction)
Recall	
Recall the three objects presented earlier	3 (1 for each object)
Language	
Name pencil and watch	2 (1 for each object)
Repeat "No ifs, ands, or buts"	1
Follow a 3-step command (e.g. "take this paper, fold it in half, and place it on the table")	3 (1 for each command)
Write "close your eyes" and ask the patient to obey written command	1
Ask the patient to write a sentence	1
Ask the patient to copy a design (e.g. intersecting pentagons)	1
Total	30

source : Bird TD

A score of less than 24 points (out of 30) indicates a need for more detailed cognitive and physical assessment.

Treatment

There is no definitive treatment for Alzheimer's disease.

Following medications are used to delay the symptoms and modify the course of the disease.

1) Long-acting cholinesterase inhibitors, such as Donepezil, Rivastigmine, Galantamine. They, inhibiting cholinesterase enzymes, potentiate the action of cholinergic neurotransmitters and help in memory function and other cognitive functions. They have minor side effects, such as nausea, diarrhoea and abdominal cramps. Tacrine, used previously, but due to its side effects particularly hepatotoxicity is no longer used.

2) Memantine, an uncompetitive antagonist of NMDA receptors, has shown to

decrease the rate of cognitive impairment functions.

3) Low dose antipsychotics like Risperidone, are used if there is marked behavioural changes. But they should be used with caution due to their side effects, deteriorating the condition of the patient.

4) Antidepressant drugs are used for co-existing depression.

5) Extract of Ginkgo biloba may be helpful to improve cognitive functions.

6) Vaccination with anti-amyloid-beta-protein antibodies are effective, but they developed serious subacute meningoencephalitis. Currently passive immunization with monoclonal antibodies are being evaluated.

Supportive care by the family members and caregivers to the patient is necessary. Patients often benefit from a supportive and educational psychotherapy in which the nature of the illness is explained to them.

Prognosis or Outcome

There is no known cure for Alzheimer's disease.

Supportive care should be provided to the patients suffering from Alzheimer's disease.

Mean survival is 7 years from onset, but it can range from 1 to 25 years. Some courses show gradual declining in pattern and some show a prolonged plateau without major deterioration. Death results from secondary infection, malnutrition, cardiac diseases, and pulmonary complication commonly from aspiration.

Causes of Dementia

(1) <u>Degenerative disorders</u>
Alzheimer's disease, Lewy body dementia, Fronto-temporal dementia, Huntington's disease, Parkinson's disease, Multiple sclerosis, Progressive supranuclear palsy, Multisystem degeneration (Shy-Drager syndrome)
(2) <u>Vascular disorders</u>
Cerebrovascular disease, Cerebral emboli
(3) <u>Normal pressure Hydrocephalus</u>
Primary cause, Secondary to head injury, subarachnoid haemorrhage or meningitis
(4) <u>Trauma</u>
Post-traumatic dementia, Boxer's encephalopathy

(5) Space-occupying lesions in brain
Cerebral tumor (primary or metastatic), Sub-dural haematoma
(6) Infections
AIDS, Cerebral Syphilis, Viral encephalitis, Prion disease (Creutzfeldt-Jakob disease), Papova virus infection (progressive multi-focal leukoencephalopathy), Tuberculosis, Fungal and protozoal infections, Sarcoidosis, Whipple's disease
(7) Endocrine disorders
Hypothyroidism, Hypoglycemia, Adrenal insufficiency and Cushing's syndrome, Hypopituitarism, Hypo and Hyperparathyroidism
(8) Metabolic disorders Liver failure, Renal failure, Remote effects of carcinoma, Wilson's disease, Leukodystrophies.
(9) Toxic disorders
Alcohol intoxication, Chronic barbiturate ingestion, Heavy metals intoxication, Dialysis dementia (aluminium), Psychotropic drugs
(10) Anoxic disorders
Cardiac failure, Heart block, Cardiac arrest, Respiratory failure, Carbon monoxide poisoning
(11) Psychiatric
Depression (pseudodementia), Schizophrenia, Conversion reaction
(12) Vitamin deficiency
Thiamine (B1) deficiency : Wernicke's encephalopathy, B12 deficiency : Pernicious anaemia, Folic acid deficiency, Nicotinic acid deficiency : Pellagra
(13) Others
Acute intermittent porphyria, Recurrent nonconvulsive seizures

Vascular Dementia

It is the second most common cause of dementia accounting for 15-20% of all dementia.

Usual age of onset is 60-70 yrs. of age.

This disease is characterised by stepwise deterioration and presence of cardiovascular risk factors. Three variations can be presented.

(1) Dementia after a single stroke : It results from occlusion or rupture of a

large or medium sized vessel or symptomatic lacunar stroke caused by occlusion of small vessels. The onset is acute. Focal neurological deficit depending upon the site of the infarct is present. Not all strokes result in cognitive impairment. It depends upon the site of the infarct. Post-stroke dementia may remain fixed or may improve partially or completely over time.

(2) Multi-infarct dementia : This is associated with multiple recurrent episodes of cerebral infarction due to occlusion of small and medium sized vessels in brain by atherosclerotic plaques or emboli from distant origins (heart or carotid arteries).

The course of the disease is characterised by alternative periods of improvement and stepwise deterioration due to repeated infarcts (In Alzheimer's disease, there is gradual deterioration in the course).

Focal neurological signs are commonly present. Memory deficits and cognitive impairment occur as in Alzheimer's disease. Behavioural slowing, apathy, emotional lability, dysarthria, dysphagia are common symptoms. Rigidity, hypokinesia, brisk reflexes are associated physical symptoms. Depression and confusion are common. Seizures may occur in few cases.

High blood pressure, previous history of cerebral stroke, transient ischaemic attacks (TIA), atherosclerotic cardiovascular diseases are usual associated findings.

(3) Progressive small-vessel disease (Binswanger's disease) : This is characterised by lypohyalinosis in the small arteries (as in hypertension) in subcortical white matter causing multiple subacute infarcts. CT and MRI scan detects periventricular areas of white matter disruption and gliosis.

This is a subcortical dementia. Early features include confusion, apathy, loss of verbal fluency, slowness of motor functions, and memory deficit. Later cognitive impairment and spatial disorientation develop. As the disease progresses both pyramidal and cerebellar signs appear. Gait disturbance, urinary incontinence, dysarthria, dysphagia, emotional lability are common symptoms. Mood disturbances either elation or depression are not uncommon.

Treatment

In case of vascular dementia what irreversible changes have already done to the brain, that cannot be corrected. The treatment is aimed at to prevent further occurrence of strokes or progress of the disease.

Treatment is done for controlling underlying causes, e.g. hypertension, hyperlipidemia, diabetes, atherosclerotic cardio-vascular diseases, cardiac arrhythmias like atrial fibrillation.

Daily aspirin delay the course of the disease.

Abstinence from smoking; dietary restriction of salt, cholesterol and saturated fat; controlling obesity; mild to moderate exercises improve medical condition and help to prevent further deterioration of the illness.

Lewy Body Dementia

In this disorder, Lewy bodies (an eosinophilic intracytoplasmic neuronal inclusion bodies) are found profusely in brain stem, basal forebrain, hypothalamic nuclei and neocortex. Lewy bodies are identified with antibodies to the presynaptic protein alpha-synuclein. In few cases of LBD, Alzheimer's type neurofibrillary tangles (NFTs) and neuritic plaques appear. However the plaques in Lewy body disease are typically of diffuse type and primarily composed of Ab42 with a paucity or absence of tau positive neurites.

Age of onset is 50-80 years.

Symptoms are fluctuating cognitive loss, loss of alertness, and parkinsonian symptoms (tremor, muscular rigidity, slowness of movement, gait disturbances). Hallucinations and delusions appear, specially visual hallucinations.

On CT, MRI, SPECT scan relative sparing of medial temporal lobe is seen in most cases. ApoE genotyping shows increased frequency of e4 allele.

Treatment

As in Alzheimer's disease, there is no definite cure for Lewy body dementia.

Treatment is aimed at managing symptoms and delaying the progress of the disease.

Following drugs are used :

(1) To help embedding new memories and delaying the course of deterioration.

Cholinesterase inhibitors - Rivastigmine and Donepezil are most commonly used.

(2) To control parkinsonian symptoms.

Levodopa-carbidopa is used to control parkinsonian symptoms.

In Lewy body dementia, there is presence of both psychotic and parkinsonian symptoms, which makes the treatment a bit difficult. Antipsychotic drugs worsen parkinsonian symptoms by their extra-pyramidal side effects. And antiparkinsonian drugs can precipitate delusions, hallucinations.

So, anti-parkinsonian drugs should be used with caution.

(3) To control psychotic symptoms.

Antipsychotic drugs - Quetiapine, Olanzapine, are used to control hallucinations, delusions.

But they should be used cautiously as they worsen parkinsonian symptoms as stated above.

Dementia in Parkinson's Disease

Parkinson's disease is a neurodegenerative disorder that is characterised by motor disturbances, such as tremor, hypokinesia, muscular rigidity and postural instability.

There is no consistent evidence for a clear entity of dementia in Parkinson's disease. However, when dementia develops in an established case of Parkinson's disease with cognitive impairment, it is known as Parkinson's disease dementia (PDD). Features of dementia are similar to Lewy body dementia, with fluctuating attention, executive dysfunction and visuo-spatial disorientation. Visual hallucination can occur. Following the worsening of motor symptoms of Parkinson's disease, the cognitive symptoms of PDD worsen, however the language and learned skills remain stable till the last stage.

Treatment

Various molecules have been tried for PDD, but only a few medications have been helpful. Cholinesterase inhibitors rivastigmine, donepezil improve cognition. Memantine has been found to be effective in ameliorating cognitive impairment. Atypical antipsychotics may be required for psychosis but can worsen extrapyramidal syndromes.

Frontotemporal Dementia

Frontotemporal dementia covers a group of disorders characterised by selective atrophy of frontal and temporal cortex in the brain.

This dementia previously used to be referred as Pick's disease. But now, the term 'Pick's disease' is used for a particular variety of FTD with intraneuronal cytoplasmic argyrophilic inclusion bodies known as Pick bodies.

Usual onset of this dementia is between 4th and 6th decade, but may occur earlier or later.

Though family history of FTD is common, 10%-15% of the patients with FTD have been found to have an autosomal dominant mode of inheritance. The most common autosomal dominant inherited mutations involve MAPT (Microtubule associated protein tau) and GRN (encoding protein Granulin) genes, both on chromosome 17. MAPT is found in the disease with tau positive histopathlogy and GRN is associated with tau negative histopathology. Familial FTD with amyotrophic lateral sclerosis has been linked to chromosome 9.

Histopathologically, there is loss of large cortical nerve cells in frontal and temporal lobes with gliosis and spongiosis of superficial layers.

Accumulation of abnormal tau protein or TDP-43 protein in fronto-temporal region due to defect in tau and TDP-43 gene, and repeat expansion in C9orf72 gene are the major responsible factors causing fronto-temporal degeneration. Limbic system and striatum are seriously damaged.

Three major pathological variants have been observed in FTD cases.

(1) Cellular inclusions containing predominantly phosphorylated tau protein (FTLD-tau).

(2) Cellular inclusions containing tau-negative, TDP-43 positive protein (FTLD-TDP).

(3) Cellular inclusions containing Fused in sarcoma protein (FTLD-FUS).

Both (1) and (2) varieties are equally represented in autopsy, while a substantial minority have FTLD-FUS variety.

Clinical Features

Early manifestations are general impoverishment of mental functions and changes in behaviour and personality.

Some patients develop impairment in language function with difficulty in naming objects and people.

Other changes are :
- significant loss of insight
- loss of empathy
- poor social relationship
- poor impulse control
- inappropriate activities
- decline in personal hygiene
- compulsive behaviours.

Diagnosis is made on impaired frontal lobe functions, with relative sparing of memory, speech and perceptuospatial functions.

On CT, MRI and SPECT scan bilateral abnormalities (asymmetrical) of frontal/temporal lobes are observed. But a significant proportion of patients may show normal structural imaging.

Treatment

There is no cure at present for fronto-temporal dementia. And the progress of the disease cannot be slowed.

Antipsychotics and antidepressants (SSRIs) are used in some cases to control behaviour changes and associated depression.

Supporting the person suffering from the disease is all that is necessary.

Delirium (Acute Confusional State)

Delirium occurs in 5-25% of all hospitalized patients. The incidence is greater with the increased age. About 60 to 70% of patients in intensive care units develop delirium. Delirium is most common in post-operative patients (particularly in cardio-vascular surgery and patients treated for hip fractures), patients with sepsis and chronic obstructive pulmonary disease, and patients on mechanical ventilation. Medications can also cause delirium, specially use of anticholinergic drugs in elderly patients.

The cardinal feature of delirium is clouding of consciousness, which is manifested by impaired alertness, awareness, and attention.

Consciousness is maintained by the reticular activating system (RAS) in the brain stem and thalamic regions. So any space occupying lesion compressing this area (like brain tumors), or pressure from subdural haematoma or hydrocephalus may produce confusional state.

Diffuse brain disease, which grossly involves the neuronal architecture and function, like encephalitis, multiple metastasis, or cerebral concussion injury may present with confusion or clouding of consciousness.

Systemic disease produces confusional state by impairing the nerve functions. This impairment may be due to variety of causes. There may be inadequate supply of oxygen, glucose, and other factors like vitamins and hormones to the brain. This inadequacy may result from hypo-perfusion of the brain, that is decreased blood supply which carries these essentials to the brain.

Hypo-perfusion of brain again may result from cardiogenic shock and cardiac arrhythmias (when the heart is unable to pump adequate blood to the brain), gram negative bacteraemia with endotoxic shock, acute blood loss (both traumatic and post operative), and hypovolemic shock (e.g. in pancreatitis).

Severe anaemia also causes decreased oxygen supply to the brain.

Other factors that impair the neuronal functions are acid-base disturbance, electrolyte imbalance (Na+, Ca++, Mg++), circulating toxins (e.g. ammonia in liver failure). These are known as metabolic encephalopathy.

Drug induced confusional states are caused by the drugs directly affecting nerve conduction process in the neuronal junctions. Acute excited state of delirium after drug withdrawal is caused by reversal of the process.

So, among an endless list for causes of delirium, the most commons can be highlighted as followingly.

Systemic
1. Hypoxia, carbon dioxide narcosis
2. Hypoglycemia
3. Cardiogenic shock
4. Electrolyte imbalance
5. Septicaemia
6. Severe anaemia
7. Hypo and hyper thyroidism
8. Liver failure
9. Renal failure
10. Diabetic ketoacidosis
11. Drug and alcohol intoxication
12. Drug withdrawal
13. Vitamin deficiency (e.g. thiamine in Wernicke's encephalopathy).

Focal
1. Trauma or concussion injury to brain
2. Intracranial and subdural haematoma
3. Subarachnoid haemorrage
4. Multiple infarcts
5. Multiple metastasis
6. Brain tumor

7. Air and fat embolism

8. Hypertensive encephalopathy

9. Meningitis and encephalitis.

Clinical Symptoms

The main feature of delirium is clouding of consciousness with impairment of awareness and attention.

The impairment ranges from mild to moderate, and in severe cases may proceed to coma, if untreated.

Other features associated are –

(1) Disturbance in cognition :
- Impairment of recent memory with relatively intact remote memory.
- Disorientation in time, place, and person.
- Difficulty in performing jobs requiring logic and mathematics.
- Disorganised and disjointed thinking.

(2) Emotional disturbance :
- Blunting of affect or emotional lability.

(3) Psychomotor disturbance :
- Rapid unpredictable hypo or hyper activity
- Increased or decreased flow of speech
- Enhanced startle reaction
- Stereotyped motor behaviour, such as picking at bed sheet or clothing.

(4) Disturbance in sleep and sleep-wake cycle :
- Insomnia or drowsiness
- Worsening of the symptoms at night (sun downing)
- Disturbing dreams or nightmare
- Illusion or hallucination after waking.

(5) Autonomic dysfunction :
- Sweating, tachycardia, dilatation of pupils.

Associated neurological symptoms tremor, asterixis, nystagmus, urinary incontinence may be present in patients with delirium.

Delirium is differentiated from dementia in that, in dementia consciousness remains normal. Sleep-wake cycle is usually not disturbed in dementia, and onset in dementia is usually gradual or insidious. Whereas, in delirium onset occurs usually acutely following some underlying disease.

Diagnosis

Delirium is diagnosed at bed side and is characterised by sudden onset deterioration or alteration of general awareness. Mini mental status examination or confusion assessment method (CAM) can be carried out to detect and assess the cognitive impairment. EEG characteristically shows slowing of activity which may be helpful in differentiating delirium from depression or psychosis.

Intermittent seizures, both focal and generalized seizures follow post-ictal confusion. EEG is essential to differentiate the diagnosis in that case.

Diagnosis of delirium in hospital ward is often overlooked. It is vitally important to recognise it as early as possible. Clinical suspicion and urgent investigations are necessary to determine underlying cause. Any delay in the procedure may result in permanent loss of some neuronal functions.

Complete blood count, arterial blood gas analysis, chest x-ray, blood glucose, urea, creatinine level, liver function tests, electrolyte estimation, blood and urine culture, should be done to detect systemic causes.

CT or MRI is to be done to detect intracranial brain pathology.

ECG should be done for diagnosis of cardiac diseases e.g. myocardial infarction, or cardiac arrhythmias.

Lumber puncture (LP) and cerebrospinal fluid examination is necessary to detect cerebral infection in patients with fever and neck rigidity.

`History should be taken about the drug profile and drug abuse, and blood screening test is to be done in suspicious cases.

Endocrine test (e.g. T3, T4, TSH) and vitamin B12 measurement in blood are indicated in particularly suspected cases.

Treatment

Treatment is correction of the underlying cause.

Peaceful and comfortable surroundings, frequent visit with family persons to maintain home environment, help to prevent development of delirium.

In the severely agitated patients, benzodiazepines or antipsychotics are given on short-term basis. Oral antipsychotics (haloperidol or risperidone) are preferable choice. In acute severe cases parenteral route is preferred. Benzodiazepines should be avoided in hypoxic patients, because it causes respiratory depression further aggravating cerebral ischaemia (suffering from loss of O2) and delirium. Recent trials have focused on sedative dexmedetomidine that is less likely to lead to delirium in critically ill patients.

Parkinson's disease treated with dopaminergic medications can develop a delirium like state that features visual hallucination, fluctuation of consciousness and confusion. Decreasing the doses of the drugs has to be weighed against worsening of motor symptoms. Alternatively antipsychotic agents could be added.

Prognosis or Outcome

The occurrence of delirium is associated with higher mortality rate. The prognosis depends on prompt identification and treatment of reversible causes. Vigilant attention and care of reversible precipitating factors make a patient come out of one episode. Delay in identification may ensue some neurological damage that lay back residue which negatively affects the further and future course of the illness.

3 months mortality rate of patients who have one episode of delirium is estimated at 23% to 33%. The one year mortality rate for the patients who have one episode of delirium could be as high as 50%.

CHAPTER III

MOOD DISORDERS

Mood disorders have two extreme entities, depression and mania (or elation). Depression is by far the commoner. Most patients who have manic symptoms are also prone to depressive episodes, but the reverse does not occur. Sometimes depressive and manic episodes occur in a cyclical manner, which is known as bipolar mood disorder.

Mood is not emotion. It is the powerhouse of the mind. As explained earlier, it provides power for the activities of the four houses of mind, house of intelligence, house of memory, house of emotion and house of physical activities like voltage between two points in electrical circuitry. In elated mood, activities of all four houses are increased and vice versa happens in degraded mood or depression.

Both genetical factors and environmental factors are responsible for mood disorders. Environmental factors are more active in development of depression. Geneticalsubstage with resultant pathology is more responsible for mania or bipolar mood disorder, where mood regulating system is defected. But predisposing geneticalbackwork is multigenomic. Large genome wide association studies (GWAS) have found association of gene for encoding ankyrin 3 (ANK3), alpha subunit of L-type calcium channel (CACNA1C) and enzyme diacylglycerol kinase (DGKH) with bipolar mood disorder.

The plausible candidate genes with which several metaanalystic studies have been done for both unipolar and bipolar disorders are genes for serotonin transporter (SLC6A4), serotonin 2A receptor (5HTR2A), tyrosine hydroxylase(TH), tryptophan hydroxylase 1 (TPH1), catechol-o-methyl transferase (COMT), brain derived neurotropic factor (BDNF), glycogen synthetase kinase 3 (GSK-3B) and others. But no particular gene solely conclusively found to be involved in the development of mood disorders.

Linkage studies have found evidence of linkage regions in chromosome 18, 21q, 22q, 12q, and 4p to be associated with bipolar disorder.

Well known serotonin transporter gene polymorphic region (HTTLPR) which affects the promoter region of serotonin transporter gene, has been found to have modest association with major depression. One study (Casper, et al., 2010) found that the person inheriting this polymorphism only developed depression in definite life stresses. So this can be inferred that environmental factors predilects to disposition of mood disorders in a genetically susceptible patients, where not a single gene but combined mechanisms of several genes are responsible.

According to ICD-10, the mood disorders have been classified as follows :

1. Manic episode
2. Depressive episode
3. Bipolar mood disorder
4. Recurrent depressive disorder
5. Persistent mood disorder
6. Other mood disorders.

Major Depression

It affects 15% of general population at some point in their life.

It may occur at any age, but the peak incidence of the first episode is 25 years. Women are twice vulnerable than their male counterpart.

It may develop over days, weeks, or sometimes over a month and usually resolves spontaneously within 6 to 9 months. There is a high chance of further episode for the patients who already suffered once. About 80% of patients have at least another episode of illness, in their life time.

Some patients follow the chronic repetitive course of the disease.

To diagnose the disease, the symptoms should be present for at least two weeks.

The symptoms of major depression are :

1) Marked loss of interest or pleasure in activities, that are normally pleasurable. Loss of interest results in social withdrawal, decreased involvement in occupational and interpersonal activities. The mood depression is encountered most of the day, nearly every day.

2) Lack of emotional responses to emotionally charged events that normally produce emotional response.

3) Insomnia or hypersomnia.

4) Fatigue or loss of energy.

5) Decrease or increase in appetite.

6) Significant weight loss or gain (more than 5% of the body weight in a month).

7) Psychomotor agitation or retardation. Retardation is more common in younger patients characterised by slowed thinking and activity, while agitation is commoner in elderly patients exhibited by restlessness, uneasiness, pacing, hand-wringing, picking at body parts or other objects.

8) Diminished ability to think or concentrate, or indecisiveness.

9) Pessimism, feeling of worthlessness, self-reproach and excessive guilt feelings.

10) Recurrent thoughts of death or suicide; suicidal ideation without a specific plan, or a suicide attempt, or a specific plan for committing suicide.

Somatic symptoms of Depression :

¤ Sleep disturbance (insomnia or hypersomnia, and early morning waking - 2 hours or more before the usual time).

¤ Worsening of depression in the morning.

¤ Marked loss of appetite.

¤Weight loss (5% or more of body weight in the past month).

¤ Loss of interest and emotional response to pleasurable stimuli.

¤ Reduced libido.

¤ Fatigue.

¤ Headache.

¤ Vague pains (e.g. chest pain, abdominal pain).

¤ Constipation.

¤ Psychomotor agitation or retardation.

Severe depression with psychotic symptoms :

Psychotic symptoms include delusions, hallucinations, and depressive stupor.

Delusions may be mood-congruent, which is logical with the depressed mood (e.g. nihilistic delusions, delusion of guilt) or mood-incongruent, which cannot be related with the depressed mood (e.g. delusion of control).

In no situation, psychotic symptoms should last for as long as two weeks in the absence of prominent mood symptoms (that is, before the mood symptoms developed or after they have remitted).

To establish the diagnosis, it should also be noted that the symptoms are not associated with bereavement reaction (due to death or loss of a loved one), organic lesion or other psychotic disorders.

Depression should also be differentiated from sadness or melancholia. Sadness is an emotion lying on the negative part of the emotion 'joy and sadness'. Like any other emotion its feeling is very subjective and does not depend on thinking pattern. Sadness may be associated with depression or may not be. It is not related or precipitated by environmental stress situation but environment has definite part to act as a stimulus to evoke this emotional response as are the stimuli of all other emotions.

Etiology

Both genetical factors and environmental factors are responsible for depression. Comparing the concordance rates in monozygotic and dizygotic twins, the heritability of major depression has been estimated at 38% (Kendler, et al., 2006).

Three most consistently important environmental factors that increase the likelihood of depression are loss of parent in childhood, lack of social support and recent adverse life events.

Major neurohumoral system responsible for depression is serotonergic system.

Deficiency of serotonin in the neuronal junctions or synapses is the factor for causing depression. Selective serotonin reuptake inhibitors (SSRIs) block serotonin reuptake by the nerve endings and increase the concentration of it in nerve synapses. Multiple serotonin receptors have been identified to develop more specific treatment for depression.

Other neurotransmitters also responsible are noradrenaline and dopamine. Association between downregulation or decreased sensitivity of beta adrenergic receptors and depression suggest involvement of noradrenergic system in depression. The efficacy of venlafaxine, a serotonin-noradrenaline reuptake inhibitor in the treatment of depression, also supports some role of noradrenaline in depression.

The role of dopamine deficiency in depression has been suggested by the increased frequency of depression in Parkinson's disease, a dopamine deficient disorder. The drugs that reduce dopamine concentration, like reserpine, are associated with depressive symptoms and drugs that increase dopamine concentration, like amphetamine, bupropion, diminish the symptoms of depression.

Decreased inhibitory feedback action of serotonergic neurons on hypothalamus causes increase in corticotrophin releasing hormone (CRH) secretion from hypothalamus and induces hypothalamus-pituitary-adrenal (HPA) axis. As a result of which plasma cortisol level is elevated. Cortisol, with other functions, impair hippocampal functions by direct damage to hippocampus. This accounts for structural changes in brain and reduced volume of hippocampus that have been found in patients suffering with depression.

The activity of the gene coding for brain derived neurotrophic growth factor (BDNF) is reduced in stress. BDNF is crucial for process of neurogenesis, axonal growth and maintaining functional status of neurons. Deficiency of BDNF halts neurogenesis and reduces functional status of neurons and even causes cell death. Stress induced damage to hippocampus and other limbic regions is also partly mediated by deficiency of BDNF and other growth factors and cytokines.

Neuroanatomical considerations

Four major areas that have been found to be associated with depression are

(1) Prefrontal cortex (2) Hippocampus (3) Amygdala (4) Anterior Cingulate. Prefrontal cortex constitutes the house of intelligence. As I have described in my previous chapter that besides other pathology and action of different chemical substances either endogenous or exogenous such as alcohol, melatonin, different drugs on mood regulating serotonergic nuclei, positive thinking causes mood upgradation or elation and negative thinking causes mood downgradation or depression. So the role of house of intelligence or prefrontal cortex is the foremost factor in the development of depression. Prefrontal cortex is responsible for our logical, sequential thinking and goal-oriented activities.

Hippocampus is involved , as explained in first chapter, in emotionally conditioned learning. And it is linked with amygdala, hypothalamus, thalamus, mammillary body for emotional feedback. Among these amygdala plays the major role, because it is the site for 'fear' emotion and may be many other emotions that still have not been identified. This conditioned emotional learning give feedback to the prefrontal cortex or house of intelligence to make further goals and future activities in life. This explain involvement of these structures in depression.

The role of anterior cingulate is supposed to be that it mediates between the emotionally conditioned experiences stored in limbic and temporal cortex and ongoing thinking processes in prefrontal cortex and integrates the actions of both of them.

Sleep studies

Polysomnographic studies of sleep has shown approximately 60% of patients with major depressive disorder have shortened time period between the onset of sleep and the first rapid eye movement (REM) sleep (decreased REM latency). This results in decrease in deep slow wave NREM sleep and increased nocturnal awakenings.

Also REM sleep density (measured by number of eye movements) and duration increases and REM activity more occurs at the earlier part of the night.

Treatment

(1) Psychotherapy

Three modalities of psychotherapies are currently followed.

(a) Supportive Psychotherapy

(b) Interpersonal Psychotherapy : Interpersonal therapy focuses on exploring interpersonal problems rooted either in earlier dysfunctional interpersonal relationships or current interpersonal relationships, and by assessing their role in precipitating or perpetuating the current depressive symptoms and solving specific area or areas of problems to reduce the patient's symptoms. The program consists of 12 to 16 weekly sessions. This is effective in the treatment of depression, particularly where problems are arising from interpersonal problems.

(c) Cognitive behaviour therapy : Cognitive behaviour therapy was developed for the treatment of depression and was later extended to anxiety disorder, phobias and other psychological disorders. The cognitive approach of psychotherapy maintains that irrational beliefs and distorted cognition or attitude towards self, environment and future perpetuate depressive trends in the person and these can be reverted through cognitive behaviour therapy.

Besides these, family and marital therapy, behaviour therapy are suggested in specific cases.

(2) Drugs

Antidepressant drugs are the mainstay of therapy. The goal of the therapy is remission of the symptoms, rather than reduction of the symptoms. The patients having residual symptoms after treatment are inclined to develop relapse and recurrence in future course.

a) Tricyclic antidepressants (TCAs) : Amitriptyline, Nortriptyline, Doxepin, Desipramine, Imipramine, Trimipramine etc.

Tricyclic antidepressant drugs have anti-cholinergic side effects, e.g. dry mouth, drowsiness, fine tremor, mild constipation. But most serious side effects are cardiac conduction abnormality and postural hypotension.

So drugs should be used cautiously. ECG should be done to rule out any pre-existing cardiac conduction defects, and regular monitoring is necessary.

b) Mono amine oxidase inhibitors (MAOIs) : Phenelzine, Tranylcypromine,

Isocarboxazid, Selegiline etc.

MAO inhibitors are effective but because of 'drug-food' and 'drug-drug' interactions they are considered as second line of medications. However, MAOIs seem to be particularly effective in atypical depression. Other side effects of MAO inhibitors are hepatotoxicity, insomnia, appetite reduction, weight gain, postural hypotension, ankle edema, and sexual dysfunction.

c) Selective Serotonin Reuptake Inhibitors (SSRIs) : Fluoxetine, Paroxetine, Sertraline, Citalopram, Escitalopram, Fluvoxamine.

SSRIs have less side effects, with no anti-cholinergic side effects and cardiac conduction defects.

Usual side effects of these drugs are nausea, headache, agitation, insomnia, diarrhoea, weight loss, hyposexuality, which may range from mild to moderate.

But symptoms may improve over time.

Other antidepressant drugs are Serotonin noradrenergic reuptake inhibitors (SNRIs) - venlafaxine, duloxetine; Serotonin antagonist/reuptake inhibitors (SARIs) - Nefazodone, trazodone; Noradrenergic and specific serotonergic antidepressant (NaSSA) - mirtazapine; Noradrenline reuptake inhibitor (NARI) - reboxetine; Melatonin agonist and specific serotonin antagonist (MaSSA) - agomelatine; Norepinephrine-dopamine reuptake inhibitor (NDRI) - bupropion.

The efficacy of mirtazapine and nefazodone is similar to tricyclic antidepressants and SSRIs, and they are less likely to have sexual dysfunction.

Drugs should be chosen on patient's medical history, previous response or family history of positive response to a particular antidepressant, side effect profile of the drugs and possible corollaries to patient's comorbid illness.

The antidepressant drugs should be continued for 9-12 months (at least 6 months), and their dose should be gradually tapered before withdrawal.

If there is recurrent episodes of depression (period between episodes is less than 3yrs), or severe depression with high suicidal risk, prophylactic treatment should be continued for at least 5yrs (risk of relapse if medication stopped is 70-

90% within 5yrs).

If initial treatment fails with a particular drug, either switching to an alternative drug or augmenting the treatment with the first drug is needed. Generally switching to another drug is preferred. But augmenting may be considered in those cases where the initial treatment has brought about some considerable benefits to the patient. Lithium is a first line augmenting agent. Lamotrigine is an effective augmenting agent for patients who do adequately respond to fluoxetine. Thyroid hormone supplements is another option for enhancing the antidepressant action of the drug even in euthyroid state.

In depression with psychotic symptoms, antipsychotics (olanzapine, haloperidol) are added.

Antipsychotic side effects may mask improvement in depressive symptoms and combination of antidepressants and antipsychotics worsen side effects common to both (e.g. sedation, anticholinergic effects etc.). So lowest effective dose of antipsychotics should be prescribed.

(3) Electro Convulsive Therapy (ECT)

This is specially effective in severe depression with suicidal risk, depression with psychotic features, and depression refractory to medications.

The response is good.

A convulsion, or seizure, occurs when a large percentage of neurons fire in unison. In ECT seizures are triggered in normal neurons by application of electrical current through the scalp, and the current is carefully controlled to generate a seizure of a particular duration over the entire brain. It exerts effects on the neurophysiological activities of the nerve cells of the brain. And ECT itself acts as an anticonvulsant, by this process increasing the seizure threshold in neurons. The possible mechanism of action of ECT which has been hypothesized is ECT, by increasing seizure threshold, delta activity, and activity of inhibitory neurotransmitters (e.g. GABA and opioids), causes reduction in functional activity in specific brain regions. Decreased cerebral blood flow (rCBF) and glucose metabolism, causing reduction in functions of anterior frontal region after application of ECT, is associated with better outcomes. Neurochemical studies have shown ECT causes downregulation of postsynaptic beta adrenergic receptors, the same receptor change that found in antidepressant drug treatment.

ECT could be direct or modified type. Direct ECT is given in the absence of muscle relaxants or general anaesthesia. Now it is rarely used.

Modified ECT is given under general anaesthesia with drug induced muscle relaxation, so that the patient cannot feel the impulse of the shock.

The electrodes are placed bitemporally (bilateral) or both on the non-dominant hemisphere (unilateral).

Two types of current are used, a sinusoidal current (where current flows continuously in sinusoidal waveform) and a pulse current (where current is delivered in short pulses). Pulse current is newer, safer and is used in modern ECT therapy.

An electric current is applied to produce a seizure lasting not less than 25-30 seconds. This is detected by observing EEG recording during ECT (in modified ECT).

Usual dosage for an adequate seizure is 70-150 volts (avg. 110 volts) for 0.1 to 1 seconds (avg. 0.6 seconds) and usual amount of current passed is 200 to 1600 mA.

In brief pulse devices, pulse width, frequency and total time duration has also to be set.

However individual machines have different specifications. It should be understood before application.

The patient needs usually 6-12 applications, not more than 3 in a week.

Concurrent therapy with antidepressant drugs is usually continued. But other medications have specific recommendations.

Common side effects are confusion, disorientation, and memory loss. Both retrograde (loss of learned memories) and anterograde (inability to learn new information) amnesia are caused by ECT.

Side effects are temporary. Some degree of memory loss could be persistent.

Memory impairment is less with unilateral ECT, but it has less effectiveness compared with bilateral ECT.

(4) Transcranial Magnetic Stimulation (TMS)

It uses very short pulses of magnetic energy to stimulate the brain nerve cells. It is a 40 minute outpatient procedure and the patient do not need sedation or anaesthesia. The procedure is done on daily basis for 4 to 6 weeks. No cognitive impairment is reported. The most common side effect of the treatment is that the patient may complain mild scalp pain. It has promising aspect for the future treatment in depression.

(5) Vagus nerve stimulation (VNS)

Stimulation of vagus nerve, during experimental studies in the treatment of epilepsy, chanced to have found that it elevated the patient's mood. Afterwards it has been studied on patients with major depression with recurrence, which showed its efficacy in the treatment. Though details about its degree of efficacy is still in experimental phase. Exact mechanism of action is not known. It has been postulated that stimulation of vagus nerve releases some peptides that act as neurotransmitters.

Another treatment Deep Brain Stimulation (DBS) is currently under interest and being used experimentally in treatment resistant cases of depression.

(6) Neurosurgery

Neurosurgery is rarely used in exceptional cases when all modalities of treatment has failed. Stereotactic limbic leucotomy, anterior cingulotomy, stereotactic subcaudatetractotomy are the choices.

Prognosis or outcome

An untreated depressive episode lasts for 6 to 13 months; most treated episodes last about 3 months. Some patients develop chronic, repetitive course of the disease. In these cases, with the progress of the disease the episodes become more frequent and last longer. The incidence of relapses is lower in patients who continue prophylactic psycho-pharmacological treatment.

It is a major cause of committing suicide. Approximately 15% of patients suffering from chronic recurrent major depressive illness die by suicide.

There is high rate of alcohol and drug abuse associated with major depression.

Bipolar Mood Disorder

Also known as Manic-depressive-psychosis. The disorder is characterised by recurrent episodes of mania (elation) and depression in a cyclical way.

1-2% of population are affected. Incidence is higher in upper social class.

Most commonly first episode occurs in adolescence and early adulthood, with peak age at 19 years.

The episodes of bipolar disorder can occur in any sequence. Men have more manic than depressive episodes, women have more depressive episodes.

As the age advances, the interval between two episodes shortens and frequency of the episodes increases.

Symptoms that appear in Manic episodes are :

1) Increased physical activity and restlessness.
2) Increased talkativeness.
3) Reduced sleep.
4) Sexual hyperactivity and sexual indiscretion.
5) Inflated self-esteem or grandiosity.
6) Increased sociability or over-familiarity.
7) Reckless behaviour like, buying sprees or reckless driving.
8) Poor concentration and distractibility. The subject may repeatedly change plans and activities; or want to do many jobs on single time.

Mania with psychotic symptoms :

Associated with above features, there are :-

1) Delusion of persecution, delusion of grandeur.
Sometimes delusion of grandeur is imposed on delusion of persecution (like, 'I am so famous that people are after me).
2) Auditory hallucinations.

In depressive episode symptoms occur as stated in major depression.

Mean duration of manic episode is 4 months. Depressive episode stays a little longer with mean duration of 6 months. In the intermediate stage the subject remains otherwise well, as complete recovery from the episode occurs.

Bipolar disorder again subtyped in bipolar I and bipolar II. Bipolar I is characterised by episodes of severe mania and severe depression, and bipolar II is characterised by episodes of hypomania (less severe form of mania, not requiring hospitalization) and severe depression.
A small subgroup of patients manifest very rapid cycles of episodes, which range from 4 episode a year to 24 hrs. every episode.
Rapid cyclers more commonly(70-80%) are women. Impaired thyroid function, previous treatment with tricyclic antidepressants have been suggested to have a relationship in rapid cyclers.

Cause

There is a strong association of genetical factors with bipolar disorder. First degree relatives have 10-15% higher chance of developing the disease compared to general population.
But genetical factors alone are insufficient to cause the disease without environmental co-activity. Any stressful situation, internal conflicts, ideological ambiguities may precipitate the disease in genetically susceptible subjects.
Before treatment, other causes of mania, like substance use, schizoaffective disorder, space occupying lesion in brain should be ruled out.

Treatment

1) Psychotherapy

The aim of psychotherapy is educating patients about their illness, strategies for management of stress, identification and intervention of early signs of recurrence, and enhancing their social and occupational functioning.

2) Drug therapy

Treatment of acute manic episode :

Mood stabilizing drugs - Lithium carbonate, valproic acid, carbamazepine, and oxcarbazepine are highly effective in treatment of acute episode of mania and as prophylactics to prevent further episodes.

Lithium needs 6-8 days to reach its full efficacy. So antipsychotic drugs may be needed initially to take control of acute attack of behavioural changes.

Sedative benzodiazepine drugs also could be incorporated in treatment initially. Therapeutic range of lithium is narrow.

Various side effects are tremor, muscular weakness, rigidity, seizures, weight gain, polyuria, polydipsia, impaired cognition, renal impairment (interstitial fibrosis, tubular atrophy, and sometimes glomerular sclerosis), hypothyroidism. It has teratogenic effects on fetus, if administered in 1st trimester of pregnancy.

Blood level greater than 2.0 meq/L can cause lithium toxicity. So during treatment it is necessary to monitor blood lithium levels at regular intervals.

Treatment of choice for acute lithium toxicity is haemodialysis.

Antiepileptic drugs Sodium Valproate, Carbamazepine, Oxcarbazepine are used for patients who are refractory to lithium.

Side effects of valproate are less including nausea, anorexia, drowsiness and tremor. Loss of hair, curling of hair, and hyperammonaemia (causing encephalopathy) have been observed. It should be avoided in pregnancy (particularly in 1st trimester), because it has produced neural tube defects in the offspring.

Carbamazepine and oxcarbazepine have clinical efficacy in the treatment of acute mania. Serious side effects of these drugs are hepatic failure, exfoliative dermatitis, pancreatitis and agranulocytosis. Dose related side effects are drowsiness, vertigo, double vision, ataxia, vomiting, diarrhoea. Along with blood monitoring, educating patients about the early signs and symptoms of side effects is also essential.

Another anticonvulsant drug Lamotrigine is also used in bipolar mood disorder, particularly to check recurrent depressive episodes of bipolar disorder.

However, fatal skin allergic reaction is a serious side effect of this drug (occurrence is 0.8 in 1000 cases of users). Other side effects of this drug are, blurred vision, headache, drowsiness, constipation or diarrhoea, runny nose, stomach upset, weight loss, painful menstrual periods.

Antipsychotics (olanzapine, risperidone, quetiapine, haloperidol) are used to treat severe behavioural attacks. Though risk of tardive dyskinesia is significantly lower with atypical antipsychotics, increased risk of weight gain and other metabolic abnormalities is a concern for using these drugs for long term. Some patients however may require maintenance treatment with antipsychotic medication. Antipsychotic quetiapine particularly have been found to be effective in treating bipolar depression, reducing the rate of a switch to mania or hypomania.

Treatment of acute depressive episode :

To combat depression in bipolar disorder is a challenging task, as antidepressants increase the risk for precipitation of manic episode and accelerate the cycling. SSRIs (fluoxetine) are first to be considered. In patients resistant to SSRIs, other antidepressants (mirtazapine, venlafaxine, bupropion) or anti psychotics (quetiapine, olanzapine) should be considered.

Antidepressants are tapered off following remission of depressive symptoms after 8 wks of maintenance treatment.

Prophylactic treatment with mood stabilizers is to be continued if there is closely recurrent episodes of mania and depression.

(3) ECT

It is used in treatment of severe acute mania, major depressive episodes particularly with suicidal risk, and cases refractory to medication.

It can also be used in specific situations where pharmacological treatment may not be possible as in pregnancy or severe cardiac diseases.

Prognosis or Outcome

Bipolar disorder is a serious, chronic illness, and needs life long surveillance by a psychiatrist. Within the first two years of 1st episode, 40-50% of patients experience another episode. 50-60% of patients on lithium gain control of their symptoms.

There is high rate of alcohol and substance use associated with bipolar mood disorder.

Patients with bipolar disorder have increased rate of suicide by 15-20% compared to that of general population.

Recurrent Depressive Disorder

This is characterised by at least two depressive episodes, each episode lasting for minimum of 2 weeks, at the interval of at least 2 months.

The depressive episodes may be mild, moderate, or severe (with or without psychotic symptoms).

Persistent Mood Disorder

This is characterised by a period of at least 2 years of instability of mood involving several episodes of mild depression and/or mild elation with or without intervening period of normal mood.

None of the manifestations of depression or elation during such period should be severe or long lasting enough to meet the criteria for manic episode or, moderate and severe depressive episode. However, manic and major depressive disorder may have occurred before, or may develop later after such persistent mood disorder.

Persistent mild depression for more than 2 years is termed as **dysthymia.**

If mood instability cycles between mild depression and mild elation persistently, then it is called **cyclothymia.**

A significant number of dysthymic disorders progress to a major depressive episode. 20% or more develop double depression (major depressive episode superimposed on dysthimic disorder). Prognosis of this is grave with higher risk of recurrence and treatment resistance.

Treatment is psychotherapy, antidepressants and mood stabilizing drugs.

Other Mood Disorders

1) Other single mood disorders

Mixed Affective episode

This is characterised by either a mixture or rapid alteration (i.e. within a few hours) of hypomania, mania, and depressive symptoms, which are prominent most of the time during a period of at least two weeks.

There is no history of previous manic, depressive, or mixed episodes.

2) Other recurrent mood disorders

Recurrent brief depressive disorder

This disorder is characterised by either mild, moderate or severe depressive episodes which occur about once a month over the past one year.

Individual episodes last less than two weeks (typically two to three days).

And it is not solely related with the menstruation (that is in premenstrual depression) in case of females.

3) Other specified mood disorders

Seasonal Mood Disorder

This is characterised by depressive symptoms found during a particular season (usually in winter months) and absence of symptoms during other time. Specific features associated with this depression are lack of energy, decreased activity and atypical depressive symptoms including overeating, weight gain, hypersomnia and craving for carbohydrate foods. As many as 20% of patients may have a bipolar mood disorder. In this case, the patient experiences depression in some particular season (usually winter months), and hypomania or mania in some other season (usually summer months).

This disorder is believed to be related with the changes in the length of the day (i.e. hours of light) and its effects on hypothalamus with inappropriate melatonin secretion. Melatonin is produced in dim light and darkness by the pineal gland under the influence of suprachiasmatic nucleus of hypothalamus which receives light-dark sensation via retinohypothalamic nerve fibers from retina.

The treatment of this disorder is bright light therapy, using artificial bright light (white, full spectrum light at 2500-10000 lux intensity) with the patient sitting at a distance, commonly 30-60 cm. from the light box, eyes open but not staring at the light source for 30-60 minutes.

Other effective therapies are dawn simulation and negative air ionization.

Dawn simulation is a technique which creates timed lights in the bedroom mimicking sunrise 30 minutes to 2 hours before awakening. To many patients dawn simulation is a more convenient alternative, because the therapy is completed before awakening and it is, as studies show, equally effective as bright light therapy.

Negative air ionization, which involves releasing charged particles into the sleep environment, has also been found to be effective.

Masked depression

A state in which depressed mood is not particularly prominent, but somatic features of depressive disorder are present, e.g. sleep disturbance, diurnal mood variation, vague pains (headache, back pain, abdominal pain etc.), paresthesias.

Though this may occur at any age, it is more common after mid-life.

Pathological behaviour, masking depression may develop in the form of impulsive sexual behaviour, drug and alcohol abuse, or pathological (compulsive) gambling.

Treatment is antidepressants.

Atypical Depression

This disorder is applied to a variety of presentations with mild to moderate depression, but the symptoms do not present with classical or typical features of depression.

They usually occur in teens and are characterised by overeating, fatigue (leaden paralysis - i.e. heavy leaden feelings in arms or legs), hypersomnia, 'rejection sensitivity'.

The patient with atypical depression are more likely to suffer from anxiety disorders, phobic disorders, obsessive compulsive disorder, personality disorders (such as avoidant, borderline and histrionic personality disorders).

Medicinal trials show that older class of antidepressants mono amine oxidase inhibitors (MAOIs) are more effective at treating atypical depression. More modern antidepressants SSRIs and SNRIs are also quite effective in the treatment, but tricyclic antidepressants typically are less effective.

The wakefulness-promoting agent Modafinil has also shown considerable effectiveness in the treatment of atypical depression.

Premenstrual Tension

This disorder, also known as premenstrual syndrome, occurs in the premenstrual phase of the menstrual cycle. Most women experience premenstrual symptoms 7-10 days before the onset of bleeding. Features are non-specific somatic and psychological symptoms including depression, irritability, malaise, headache, gastrointestinal upsets such as colonic spasms and constipation, frequency of micturition, breast engorgement, fullness of abdomen, and edema of the face and feet. In some cases there is demonstrable water retention, and weight gain of 1 to 1.5 kg. or even up to 5 kg. can be measured with accompanying edema of the legs.

Aetiology of this syndrome is obscure. Cyclical hormonal change with excessive estrogen production, genetic vulnerability, imbalanced neurohormonal system, poor diet, underlying depression all may be causative factors.

Treatment is healthy diet, diuretics (spironolactone) for the fluid retention, hormonal treatment with oral contraceptive pill and treatment of underlying depression.

Postpartum Depression

Postpartum Blues or 'Baby Blues' occurs after delivery of baby, usually by the third post-partum day and is characterised by mild depression.

This usually resolves within two weeks and no treatment is necessary.

Postpartum depression is a more severe form which occurs with increased incidence following subsequent child birth. This disorder is associated with severe depression with no mother care about the baby and also with thoughts of hurting the baby.

The disorder may last for several months or even a year.

Treatment is antidepressants and psychotherapy.

Postpartum psychosis develops in 0.1 - 0.2% cases of postpartum depression. Rate is higher in women with bipolar mood disorder or a previous history of postpartum psychosis. Symptoms are those of postpartum depression associated with psychotic symptoms and mood instability. Psychotic symptoms can take the form of schizophrenia like illness (thought disorders, hallucinations, delusions, and/or disorganised speech or behaviour).

Treatment includes antidepressants, mood stabilizers, antipsychotics and ECT (highly effective).

Prognostic indicators in Mood Disorders

Good prognostic indicators are :
1. Acute or abrupt onset.
2. Typical features of the illness.
3. Severe depressive illnesses.

4. Previous record of good occupational and social adjustment.

5. Previous stable personality.

6. Absence of associated other physical disease.

7. Good response to the treatment.

Poor prognostic indicators are :

1. Chronic or recurrent onset.

2. Social and occupational maladjustment.

3. Unstable personality.

4. Presence of other physical disease.

5. Gross hypochondriacal ideas and mood-incongruent delusions.

6. Double depression.

7. Poor response to the treatment.

CHAPTER IV

OBSESSIVE COMPULSIVE DISORDERS

An obsession is an unwanted thought or impulse which enters the mind of a person repeatedly despite his or her conscious resistance.

And a compulsion is the act which is taken by the person to prevent or neutralise the distress, arising out of obsession.

It affects 4-5% of population. Though the percentage could be higher as a majority of patients do not admit or show willingness to reveal the facts of having their obsessive habits, and do not seek for help. It is commoner in higher social class and high intelligence groups.

It could be : -

1) predominantly obsessive
2) predominantly compulsive
3) mixed - where obsessive and compulsive components are both present.

In this disorder the subject's insight is usually present.

The subject can recognise the idea as his own idea, but alien to his personality (ego-alien). And failure to resist it causes marked distress in the subject's mind (ego-dystonic).

It is different from delusion, because in delusion the subject firmly believes that the idea his own and does not try to resist it.

But sometimes the subjects may possess over-valued ideas, that is the subjects are uncertain about their beliefs regarding their obsessions or compulsions. In these cases, it becomes difficult to differentiate the disorder from delusion or psychotic disorder.

This disorder may cause serious restrictions in life style. It affects the subject's interpersonal and social relationships. The subject may avoid close relationship with others.

In severe disease, the subject may be completely housebound.

Depression and anxiety are usually found to be associated with obsessive compulsive disorders. There is increased evidence of alcohol and substance use among the sufferers of this disorder.

There may be delayed onset of sleep and reduction of total sleep time due to excessive compulsive behaviour. Impaired sleep continuity, increased awakenings during sleep, are constant findings. However, in OCD, despite some initial confusing findings, there has not been recorded any specific alteration in the sleep structure.

After long-term habituation the person's resistance to obsessive thoughts or compulsive acts may diminish.

For that, the patient of OCD without significant anxiety or distress, signifies as a poor indicator in prognosis.

As I have told already (read Ch. 4, Part II), in these cases, nearly complete adaptation occurs. More the time, and more continuous, will the person live with the object or situation of his obsession, the more incomplete adaptation will proceed to complete adaptation, and more he will be subjugated to the object or situation. In imaginary cases, and less frequently occurring cases, the symptoms of obsession, that is fear, anxiety, distress, remain strong. Again, too much infrequently or rarely occurring cases, or where one episode is not too much severe to scar the person's mind for a prolonged time, the obsessive symptoms may gradually disappear due to expressing out of the emotional memories, either consciously or subconsciously, producing in neutral memories with faded out attached emotional memories.

In case of more complete adaptation, the subject's insight is also gradually diminished.

Diagnosis

To diagnose OCD, either obsessions or compulsions, or both should be present on most of days for a period of at least 2 weeks.

Following types of OCDs are commonly seen.

1) Intrusive Thoughts

Here obsessional thoughts come into the subject's mind, that does not follow any compulsive act.

Obsessional thoughts may be some ideas, words, images, past events, and aggressive or sexual thoughts. Superstitions with excessive attention to something that is considered lucky or unlucky with respect to some aspects of the person's life, or any religious or moral issue, may also be encountered in the subject's obsessive thoughts. These thoughts come into the subject's mind repeatedly despite the subject's strong resistance or efforts of avoidance to it.

Rumination - Rumination is a situation where the subject continuously ponders over some person, object, thought, or doubts. It causes obsessive slowness in daily activities.

Obsessive thoughts create great distress upon the subject's mind.

2) Washing and Cleansing

This is the most common obsessive compulsive form.

The subject fears of contamination with germs, dirt etc. and washes his hands, body, personal possessions, bed sheet, clothes repetitively. In severe form of this disorder, the subject starts to clean repetitively room, bathroom, even door knobs or wherever he or she feels there is a chance of contamination that can affect them.

Excessive hand washings make their skin raw and chapped and vulnerable to secondary dermatitis.

3) Checking

The subject has checking habits on many things like whether the doors are locked when leaving, or whether the electric switches are off, or whether the gas and water taps are turned off, and many such others.

4) Arithmomania

This is an obsessive desire of counting. The subject repetitively counts his money, or other articles; counts the stairs while ascending or descending, counts the steps while walking etc.

5) Rituals

In these cases, the subject possesses various obsessive ideas which follow compulsive performance of various rituals. The person attaches good luck or bad luck with different particular activities or situations, and counteracts those by undertaking different rituals.

For example, stopping of walking for a while when a black cat crosses the road , a silent prayer or repeating a phrase in some specific situations, or closing the door three times before leaving, and numerous such things.

The subject may also be obsessive of doing something in a specific way. Like, dress should be worn in a particular fashion, hair should be parted in a distinct pattern, food should be eaten in a precise manner, things should be arranged in a particular order and so others.

This causes marked slowness of regular and daily activities.

6) Hoarding

The subjects fear that things may be required in future, or something bad will happen if they throw anything away. So, they compulsively hoard many things that they do not need, or are of no use.

7) Onomatomania

This is an obsession to utter repetitively a particular word.

Various compulsive habits, such as nail biting, hair pulling, skin pricking, excessive masturbation have been found to be associated with different obsessive compulsive disorders.

Yale–Brown Obsessive Compulsive Scale (scored by clinician rated questionnaire; but self-report version is also available) can be used for psychometric measurement of obsessive compulsive disorder.

Onset

Usually 2nd decade of life. 65% of cases manifest before age 25. Boys are more commonly affected than girls and men have slightly earlier age of onset than women. This disorder can also develop in childhood.

Causes

¤ Underlying conditioning of fear - incomplete to near complete adaptation - as has been discussed in Ch. VII. In case of complete adaptation, the subject would not experience the symptoms of mental distress in obsession.

¤ There is evidence of positive family history. 3-7% of first degree relatives of the patients with OCD are affected. Twin concordance studies have consistently found higher concordance rates of this disorder among monozygotic twins compared to dizygotic twins.

In family of OCD patients, an increased incidence of both OCD and Tourette's syndrome have been reported.

Tourette's disorder is a type of tic disorder which first appear in childhood or adolescence and is characterised by 1) motor tics - repetition of specific motor movements, e.g. grimacing, eye-blinking etc.; and 2)vocal tics - repetition of specific vocalization, e.g. throat clearing, coughing, sniffing etc. In later stage of this disorder, some characteristic symptoms may develop, like coprolalia (use of obscene words) and mental coprolalia (thinking of obscene words). Obsessions and compulsions are often found to occur in this disorder, but they are usually last to appear. However premediating urges and pattern of tic behaviours, closely resembles that of obsessions and compulsions.

¤ Different neurohumoral systems have been reported to be involved in different studies. Abnormality in 5-HT or serotonergic system, dopamine system, glutamet system, noradrenergic system, all have been implicated to be involved in different researches. But no clear conclusion regarding involvement of any particular system has been drawn so far.

¤ Neuroimaging studies have pointed to the involvement of some specific brain areas. These are orbitofrontal cortex, caudate nucleus, dorsolateral prefrontal cortex, and thalamus. Functional neuroimaging studies with PET (Positron emission tomography) have found increased functional activities (blood flow and metabolism) in the regions of frontal lobe, basal ganglia specially caudate lobes and cingulum, in the brain of the patients with OCD. Recent MRI study also reported abnormalities in frontal lobe region of the brain.

¤ Autoimmunity disorder following Group A beta haemolytic streptococcal infection has been found to be connected with childhood-onset obsessive compulsive disorder (PANDAS). But inflammation of specific brain areas, such as basal ganglia, causing disruption of cortico-striatal-thalamic axis functioning has been supposed to be the factor for causation of the disease in these cases.

¤ Obsession and depression co-exist frequently. On mental status examination, 50% of all patients of OCD have shown to have symptoms of depressive disorders.

Treatment

(1) Psychotherapy

Individual psychotherapy and family therapy are both advocated to support other modalities of therapy.

(2) Behaviour Therapy

Aim of behaviour therapy is deconditioning of underlying fear. Desensitization, flooding, aversion therapy have all been used with variable success.

Cognitive behaviour therapy has been proved to be most effective. Here the subjects are helped to modify or change their pattern of thinking and reactions to situations.

To prevent compulsive acts, the subjects are exposed to situations, and subsequently prevented from taking compulsive acts. Their anxiety and tension gradually wear off, and they get assurance to modify their behaviour.

(3) Drug Therapy

Antidepressants - Tricyclic drug Clomipramine and Selective Serotonin Reuptake Inhibitors (Sertraline, Fluoxetine, Fluvoxamine, Paroxetine) have efficacy in treating OCD. Clomipramine has specific anti-obsessional action. Drugs should be continued for at least 3 months. But longer therapy may be needed. Relapse of the disorder after discontinuation of the drug is very common. Other drugs which have been found to be effective in OCD, are venlafaxine(selective serotonin norepinephrine reuptake inhibitor), buspirone (serotonin receptor agonist, dopamine receptor agonist/antagonist), riluzole (antiglutaminergic).

Dopamine receptor inhibitors (DRIs), dextroamphetamine, or dopamine receptor agonist pramipexole can be tried in the severe cases of OCD where anxiety component is less featuring.

Antipsychotics - Antipsychotic drugs, added to SSRIs, have shown effectiveness in some resistant cases. Risperidone, Quetiapine, Haloperidol, and Pimozide are usually used.

Anxiolytic - sedative anxiolytic drugs benzodiazepines are to be used on short term basis if there is marked anxiety.

However, a combination of therapies, drug and behaviour therapy, is more useful than individual one.

(4) Electroconvulsive Therapy (ECT)

ECT has been found to be effective in severe cases (specially with suicidal risk), and cases refractory to medicine.

(5) Deep Brain Stimulation (DBS)

It is a neurosurgical procedure (which is also known as cerebral pace-maker), where electrodes are implanted using MRI guided techniques in specific areas of the brain through small holes on top of the skull, both on left and right sides. Electrodes are connected through extension wires to battery-powered pulse generators implanted under skin in sub-clavicular regions on both sides.

Through programmable (can be calibrated by outside remote control) pulse generator, controlled electrical impulses are sent to the specific areas of brain to control and modulate the activity of those regions.

Stimulation setting is done by the neurologist and adjusted in future depending upon the patient's condition.

It may be used in refractory cases of obsessive compulsive disorder.

Complications of DBS include infection, bleeding at implant site, and development of seizures.

Other indications of DBS are parkinson's disease, chronic neurological pain, major depression, and Tourette's disorder.

(6) Psychosurgery

Rarely used to treat extremely refractory cases.

Stereotactic limbic leucotomy or cingulotomy is the choice. Subcaudate tractotomy or capsulotomy has also been performed for this purpose.

Prognosis or outcome

Long term prognosis is variable. Some patients show chronic unremitting course. But the majority of patients show episodic course with intermediate periods of incomplete remission.

Factors indicating poor prognosis are :
- lack of resistance to compulsion
- absence of distress or anxiety
- childhood onset
- co-morbid depression
- associated personality disorder.

Good prognostic indicators are :

◻ presence of clear precipitating factor

◻ episodic symptoms

◻ stable personality

◻ good social and occupational adjustment.

The content of obsession does not seem to have any relation with prognosis of the disease

CHAPTER V

DISSOCIATIVE AND CONVERSION DISORDERS

Conversion Disorders

'Hysteria' this term is no longer in use, currently it is known as 'Conversion disorder'. In ICD-10, it has been included in 'Dissociative (Conversion) disorders', which include both conversion and dissociative disorders. Though the term 'Conversion' was used differently in past in different disease scenarios, it was specifically introduced for this disorder by Sigmund Freud. But the concepts of conversion disorder came from Paul Briquet, Jean Martin Charcot and Pierre Janet. According to Charcot, 'hysteria' is a hereditary neurodegenerative disorder and usually associated with a traumatic situation that the patient is going through for that time. Janet elaborated this disorder as being related to underlying unconscious stressful conflicts creating a dissociated state of the conscious mind. Freud explained it as to be the physical expression of the intrapsychic traumatic imprint which possibly results from repressed feelings, mostly sexual in nature, entrenched in distant childhood. However, now it has been concluded, that 'hysteria' is more psychological in nature related with stressful situations in life, rather than a disorder having a neurological background.

In this disorder the patient develops some signs and symptoms of illness (physical or mental or both) to escape from some difficult underlying stress factor, or stress situation, for some imagined or real gain, though the patient is not fully aware of the motive. And the motive should not be for some intended purpose, such as money, legal issue, or any social advantage.

Development of hysterical symptoms enables the patient to be detached from the original state of the mind. This is known as primary gain.

And the symptoms usually confer some advantages on the patient, e.g. reduced workload; reduced responsibility; gathering support, attention and favoring change in attitude and behaviour of other persons. It is called secondary gain. However, by ICD-10 secondary gain is not essential for the diagnosis of the disease.

Though all the manifestations of symptoms involve functions under the control of volition, the patient does not produce them intentionally. This results from severe stress which the patients are unable to cope with on their own.

Conversion disorder constitutes 5-15% of all psychiatric outpatient diagnosis. But the prevalence of conversion disorder vary from community to community. Prevalence rate ranges from 11 to 300 per 100000 population. This is more common in women than men. The ratio may be as high as 10 : 1. Most cases begin before the age of 35 years, with average age of onset of 10-25 years. Statistics indicate that conversion disorder is more common among rural people, persons with low educational level and low socio-economic background, and persons with low intelligence quotient.

Common conversion symptoms are :

1) Mutism
Inability or refusal to speak.

2) Paralysis of the limbs
It may be monoplegia, paraplegia, or quadriplegia, classically depends on the patient's previous knowledge on the neurological diseases. On neurological examination, muscle reflexes are seen normal. EMG (Electromyography) study is also found normal.

3) Abnormal movements
Variety of movements may occur in conversion disorder.

Tremor; jerky, dramatic, exaggerated movements of any part of the body or limbs; or violent, forceful movements of the limbs.

Movements may disappear when unobserved.

4) Abnormal gait (astasia-abasia)

Staggering, irregular gait with jerky body movements, and thrashing and waving of arm movements.

5) Laughing and crying.

6) Continuous sighing and difficulty in breathing.

7) Globus hystericus

Feeling of a foreign body to have lodged in the throat.

8) Blindness or contracted visual field (tunnel vision), and deafness.

9) Loss of sensation or anaesthesia

The most common sensory loss is anaesthesia of skin, particularly glove and stocking anaesthesia. The patient presents with loss of sensations in wrists and ankles. The distribution of sensory loss is not concomitant with the sensory loss caused by the affection of any sensory nerve.

10) Partial loss of consciousness.

11) Dissociative convulsions (Hysterical fits).

Hysterical fits or pseudoseizures should be distinguished from true seizures or epileptic fits on the points that −

¤ Hysterical fits never occur when the patient is alone or in sleep, and usually occur in safe places.

¤ Tongue bite is usually present in case of epileptic fits, but in hysterical fits, it is absent.

¤ On opening the eyes, the avoidance gaze is seen in hysterical fits, whereas in case of epileptic seizures a staring, fixed gaze is observed.

Arctic Hysteria (Piblokto or Pibloktoq)

This is a culture bound hysterical reaction seen in Inuit societies, living within the arctic circle.

The affected person is often a woman. The subject tears off her clothes; shouts, curses, breaks items, runs out and throws herself on ice in extreme cold condition.

The episode usually lasts 1-2 hours followed by amnesia for the events.

It has been found that this disorder did not begin until the native people met the outsiders from Europe and America.

So, the reason may be that out-weighing stress resulting from the pressure of cultural mixing affected the susceptible people.

Causes of conversion disorders

Once it was thought that genetical factors are mainly responsible for this disease. But now it has been clear that severe environmental stress situations and adjustment problems play the key role for the precipitation of this disease. But hereditary predisposition cannot be altogether ruled out. There are some reports of increased frequency of conversion disorder among first degree relative of the patients with this disorder. Increased risk of this disorder among monozygotic twins compared to dizygotic twins has also been reported.

It has also a part of conditioning process through secondary reinforcement. Because the first time, the symptoms are learned by the patient from the surrounding environment, e.g. seeing an epileptic patient or an unconscious patient.

A poorly educated family background with faulty emotional training in the upbringing of the child play a role. Childhood trauma, emotional or sexual abuse also count for later development of conversion disorder.

Some studies have found that associated other physical illness has been discovered later with the patients primarily diagnosed as 'hysteria'.

'Hysteria' is often found to be associated with histrionic personality (5-21% of cases). This personality is characterised by exaggerating, attention-seeking behaviour with shallow emotional responses which often outbursts in a dramatic, histrionic nature. Other personality disorders which have been related with conversion disorder, are dependent, antisocial and borderline personality disorders. However, conversion disorder can also occur without any premorbid personality disorder.

Biological factors have also been implicated in the disease. Several studies have reported hypermetabolism of dominant hemisphere compared to non-dominant hemisphere, producing hemispheric communicative impairment, which is responsible for the causation of the disease.

La Belle Indifference : La belle indifference is a person's indifference and casual attitude to serious symptoms. The patient seems to be unconcerned to what appears to be major impairment or disability for him or her. This may occur in patients suffering from other severe medical disorders also, but it is frequently seen to be associated with conversion disorders. Although some patients with conversion disorder describe their symptoms with exaggeration and elaboration.

Dissociative disorders

These are the disorders where fragmentation or separation of the integrity of conscious mind occurs. These are characterised by disruption in identity, memory, or perception, which are often precipitated by a psychological trauma or stressful situation. This is an unconscious defense mechanism where a particular group of person's mental functions is isolated and separated from the rest of the person's mental activities. Usually the onset is sudden and recovery is abrupt, but the disturbance may be gradual and the course may take up a recurrent chronic form.

The following types of dissociative disorders are seen.

(a) Dissociative Amnesia

The person is unable to recall important memories suddenly, but he is aware of this loss.

It occurs equally in men and women, most commonly begins in late adolescent or young adulthood.

The memory loss is patchy and inconsistent. This can not be on account of everyday forgetfulness. And this disturbance should not be attributable to any neurological disease (e.g. head injury, partial complex seizures), physiological effects of a substance (alcohol or other drugs of abuse, or a medication), or any other medical condition. A characteristic feature of this amnesia is loss of memories of personal events, such as details of weddings, birthdays, graduations, pregnancies, birth of children, and so on. The patient may be unable to recall significant personal events during a certain period of time (circumscribed amnesia, which is most common) or some selected events (selective amnesia). Continuous or generalised amnesia occurs very rarely.

Types of Dissociative Amnesias –

i) Circumscribed Amnesia : Inability to recall events during a particular or circumscribed period of time.

ii) Selective Amnesia : Inability to recall some selected but not all events, during a circumscribed period of time.

iii) Generalized Amnesia : Failure to recall a person's entire life.

iv) Continuous Amnesia : Inability to recall the successive events as they are happening continuously after a certain point of time, which is often preceded by a psychological trauma or stressful event.

v) Systematized Amnesia : Inability to recall a certain association of memory, like all memories related to a particular person, or a particular organization, or some particular family.

Recovery from amnesia is usually abrupt. Some patients may develop chronic form of the disease, which seriously disable their social functioning.

(b) Dissociative Fugue

Here the subject wanders away far from his home or usual surroundings, being forgotten of the past identity, and takes up a new identity. Though the subject forgets his normal past identity, he can perform all the mental higher functions, like booking tickets, paying bills etc.

The etiology is supposed to be traumatic intrapsychic conflicts or emotional stress, which, dominating a desire to escape, leads to an altered state of consciousness. The emotional stress usually comes from the subject's surroundings, which the subject was struggling with, like overwhelming fear, guilt, shame, incestuous urges, relationship problems, which are in conflict with the subject's conscious ego ideals.

Dissociative Fugue may last from some hours to months. Return to the past is sudden, and usually the subject remains amnestic about the dissociative period. Some patients experience perplexity, confusion, derealization and depersonalization symptoms in addition to amnesia. The patient may suffer from one episode of fugue, or some patients exhibit multiple fugues.

(c) Multiple Personality Disorder or Dissociative Identity Disorder

The subject lives with two or more personalities, but can experience only one at a time, being completely unaware of the existence of the others.

The person alters personality through an amnestic barrier, and the onset and termination of a personality is sudden.

Each personality has its own individuality with own pattern of thinking, believing, and relating internal self to environment or outside world. And with every personality, the subject maintains all the higher mental functions taking full control of them.

With respect to amnesia, the patients of dissociative personality disorder exhibit a complex form of amnesia which includes fluctuations in skills, habits, and knowledge.

Various factors have been linked with dissociative personality disorder. Childhood trauma, violent family subculture, physical or sexual abuse, traumatic life incidents in adulthood like rape, torture, harm, injury, loss, recurrent severe stressful conditions, all may be responsible for this disorder. Genetical contribution has also been assessed, but there is no significant data to support in favour of it.

(d) Trance and Possession Disorder

Trance : Trance is a temporary alteration of the state of consciousness with loss of usual sense of identity. But in trance loss of sense of identity is not replaced by an alternative sense of identity.

Possession disorder : This is a single or episodic alterations of the state of consciousness where the loss of usual identity is replaced by an alternate one. The subject feels to be taken over by another identity, such as a deity, a spirit, or another person. In trance and possession disorder, there is partial or full amnesia of the event.

(e) Dissociative Stupor

Dissociative stupor is characterised by marked reduction of voluntary muscular movements and speech, with diminished reaction to external stimuli, which manifest in a subject with preservation of conscious awareness, but with awareness somewhat detached from the external world. The onset is usually sudden, and it is related to a psychological trauma or stressful event.

(f) Depersonalization and Derealization Disorder

Depersonalization is characterised by recurrent and persistent feeling of detachment from one's self, so that the feeling of one's own reality is changed or lost temporarily. The person feels he is another one, not his true self.

Derealization is change in one's perception about the external world. That is the outside world seems to the subject different than what people normally feel. It may seem to the subject colorless, joyless, lifeless, distorted, uninteresting, or like a stage where everyone is acting.

In both the cases, the subject's insight is present. That means the subject can realize the change within him.

(g) Other Non-specific Dissociative Disorder

Brain Washing

This has been specifically applied to in the setting of political, cultural, or religious reforms. This is performed under the coercive forces by those in power. The minds are subjected to subjugation by induction of fear by various means, such as isolation, control over activities, exemplary punishments, etc. Subjugation on other emotional scales also occurs through isolation and deprivation of pleasurable activities. And in the stress of this severely subjugated state, there occurs metamorphosis or major changes in beliefs, behaviours and personality, producing a dissociative pseudoidentity altered from true identity, which is made to comply with serving for the demands of the authority. But besides this authoritative power, brainwashing can also be performed by tricky persons by various means. As explained in chapter VII, part I, seduction is also a process of brainwashing, where the seduced persons are made obliged to fulfill the desire of the seducers. But in case of seduction, the seducer must have some other emotion satisfying quality. Often children or adolescents with tender mind are overpowered by the manipulators by various ways and are subjugated to serve for them.

Diagnosis

Absence of underlying physical illnesses must be confirmed. Neurological disorders e.g., dementia and other degenerative disorders, brain tumors, basal ganglia diseases must be ruled out. But the diagnosis should not be made on negative grounds.

Proper history taking with specific attention to evidence of recent traumatic or stressful life events should be accomplished. And physical examinations should be carried out on positive grounds to reach the diagnosis.

Treatment

The hysterical symptoms should be ignored as far as possible, because giving attention to it would make the patient more habituated to it.

But if there is any improvement that should be encouraged.

An acute attack of conversion disorder may be reverted by giving painful stimuli e.g., pressing over supra-orbital ridges, or on the sternum; or by closing the nose and mouth.

Anxiolytic drugs may help. If there is presence of co-morbid depression or other associated psychiatric disorders, that should be treated.

Individual psychotherapy, family therapy, supportive psychotherapy, cognitive behaviour therapy all may be helpful.

In case of dissociative disorders, the symptoms usually resolve spontaneously when the patient is removed from the traumatic or stressful circumstances, but some patients may develop chronic form. No known drug treatment exists for the treatment of dissociative disorders. Treatment should be done for associated depression which is often present. Severe subjugation responds to dopamine receptor agonist (pramipexole, dextroamphetamine), or dopamine reuptake inhibitors. But these drugs have the risk of abuse potentials. ECT (Electroconvulsive therapy) may be considered in those cases where the patients have refractory depression or suicide ideation.

Insight oriented psychotherapy, Cognitive therapy, hypnotherapy, family therapy, group psychotherapy are varyingly responsive to recover memory, identity, and in reducing recurrence in this type of disorders.

Psychotherapy with Abreaction

Abreaction means bringing the patient's repressed thoughts, emotions, ideas, to conscious awareness through verbalization specially in the presence of and by the guide of a therapist. It is applied for conversion disorders and for recovering memories.

This process may be done by
1. Hypnosis
2. Free Association
3. Intravenous barbiturate (amobarbital), or diazepam.

In conversion disorder, once the patients come to their conscious awareness, they have to face their conflicts in reality. It may be difficult for them, but proper psychotherapy to educate them about solving the problems and coping with the situations, would eventually lead them to attain complete cure. If repressed emotions are released they get relieved from them.

This could also be helpful in some cases of dissociative amnesias, to recover the patient's forgotten memories, when the patients are refractory to other interventions.

Prognosis

In case of acute conversion disorder with clear precipitating factors and previous history of good social and occupational adjustment, the prognosis is good. Prognosis is poor in long lasting, recurring, well established cases and in patients associated with other comorbid organic or non-organic mental disorders. Besides depression, other comorbid disorders which have been found to be associated with conversion disorder, are substance abuse disorder, post traumatic stress disorder and different personality disorders.

CHAPTER VI

PERSONALITY DISORDER

Personality is an ingrained manner of a person's thought, behaviour, and reaction to the outside world, that relates the person's thinking about his or her own image and that of the surrounding world.

And personality traits are the different prominent features of a person's personality.

Both personality and personality traits are normal and unique to a person's individuality.

We call it personality disorder only when these traits become maladaptive to the society and become harmful to the person himself as well as the society he lives in.

Classically, personality disorder is ego-syntonic. That means, though in some cases, this disorder may cause some degree of distress to the person, but in most of the cases, the disorder does not make the subject suffer from any significant psychological stress or discomfort, and the person with personality disorder usually does not seek for psychological and professional help, if there is no other associated psychological illness.

This is in sharp contrast with the neurotic type of disorders, like obsessive compulsive disorders, where the disorder is ego-dystonic; that means the subject suffers from marked distress for his or her behaviour and tries consciously to resist it. And in severe case, the subject may seek for professional or other help.

For that reason, the diagnosis of a personality disorder is made separately from diagnosis of other psychiatric illnesses.

So, the personality disorder can be defined as an individual's characteristic and enduring ways of thought, behaviour, and inner experience, that markedly deviate from the expected and accepted cultural range or norm and is manifested in more than one of the followings,

(1) Inappropriate cognition (ways of perceiving and interpreting things, people and events around and forming images about one's self and surrounding others);

(2) Inappropriate affect (range and intensity of emotional responses);

(3) Inappropriate control over impulses;

(4) Inappropriate attitude (manner of handling others and interpersonal relationships).

Causes of Personality disorders

Aetiological factors of personality disorders are not well established. Being a member of deprived family, deprived of parental love, being subjected to childhood physical and emotional trauma and abuses, result in development of an individual's maladaptive personality traits.

Lower social class, poor parenting, misguided reinforcement of abnormal behaviour by family and surrounding others, are important factors.

And finally, genetical factors also play their roles in the background.

Prevalence of personality disorder in general population is 5-15%.

Usually personality disorders are not diagnosed until the child reaches his adolescence or >18 years of age.

Classification

Personality disorders are divided into three clusters.

Cluster A : Odd and Eccentric
Cluster B : Dramatic and Emotional
Cluster C : Fearful and Anxious

Cluster A : Odd and Eccentric

This may be of following sub-types.

(1) Paranoid Personality

The key features of this type of personality are :-

The subjects are suspicious, jealous; suspicious about fidelity of spouse or sexual partner; bear grudges; attributes responsibilities of something gone wrong to others; are hypersensitive and argumentative; have exaggerated sense of self-importance; have tendency to distort experience by misconstruing the neutral or friendly actions of others as hostile or contemptuous.

(2) Schizoid Personality

In this type, the subjects are emotionally cold, isolated, and indifferent; have little interest in sex; lack confidence; and are indifferent to praise or criticism.

They are insensitive to social norm, humour, and introspection.

(3) Schizotypal Personality

Here, the persons are eccentric and superstitious having magical thinking and unusual beliefs (not delusions); have inappropriate and constricted affect; poor in rapport formation with others and have tendency to withdraw socially; possesses vague circumstantial, tangential thinking.

This personality disorder is more closely related to schizophrenia than schizoid type.

Cluster B : Dramatic and Emotional

(1) Antisocial Personality

This personality is also known as psychopathic personality.

The subjects are violent and aggressive; use other people to achieve their own purposes; engage in exploitative and manipulative behaviour with no sense of remorse; callously disregard the rights or safety of other people; have low frustration tolerance and aggressive threshold; prone to blame others; do not take lessons from unpleasant experiences.

(2) Borderline (Impulsive) Personality

This type of characters shows marked variations of mood. They have impulsive behaviour (e.g. reckless driving, spending, binge eating or sex); lack control of anger; have identity confusion and unstable interpersonal relationships; suffer from chronic anhedonia and feelings of emptiness; afeared of abandonment; prone to self harm in the form of self-mutilation and suicidal gestures.

(3) Histrionic Personality

The subjects belonging to this type are dramatic, self-centric and attention seeking; have emotional shallowness and short-lived enthusiasm; get easily influenced by others. They are overtly concerned with physical beauties and attractiveness; behave sexually in a provocative manner but lack mature sexuality; continuously seek excitement and activities in which the subjects are the center of attention; use other people for their needs and seek instant satisfaction and approval.

This personality is more common in females.

This personality has some relationship to develop hysterical conversion symptoms (9-21% of cases of conversion disorders.

(4) Narcissistic Personality

The persons of this variant possess inflated self-image and self-importance. They are preoccupied with fantasies of unlimited success; self-centered and prone to demean others; have underlying sense of inferiority and are sensitive to criticism; need constant admiration and easily get depressed or raged by minor events.

Cluster C : Fearful and Anxious

(1) Avoidant (anxious) Personality

In this type, the subjects are anxious about social contacts. They have inferiority complex regarding their look, appeal, and competence; and are unwilling to grow relationship with people except some particular ones being liked. They are sensitive to criticism; avoidant of social or occupational activities that involve significant interpersonal contacts for the fear of criticism, disapproval and rejection; and are restrictive in life style for those reasons.

(2) Dependent Personality

In this case, the persons are indecisive and have difficulty in coping with their problems; engages others to make important life decisions; need persistent support from other people in everyday activities; tend to comply with the wishes of authority figures; are afraid of being left alone and taking care of themselves; and feel uncomfortable and helpless when they are alone.

(3) Obsessive (Anankastic) Personality

Here, the subjects are meticulous, perfectionistic, and pedantic; they are rigid and stubborn; preoccupied with rules, order, and schedules; have excessive doubt and caution about everything; unreasonably insistent that other should follow their way of doing things and reluctant to allow others to do things.

Diagnosis

According to ICD-10, the diagnosis of a personality disorder should be made on the following basis.

(1) An individual's characteristic and enduring pattern of inner experience and behaviour must deviate markedly, as a whole, from the cultural norm in more than one of the following areas :
    (a) Cognition.
    (b) Affectivity.
    (c) Control over impulses and need of gratification.
    (d) Relating to others and manner of handling interpersonal situations.

(2) The deviation should be stable and of long duration, having its onset in late childhood or adolescence.
(3) The deviation should not be manifestation of other adult mental disorders.

(4) Organic brain disease, injury, or dysfunction must be excluded as possible cause of the deviation.

Treatment of Personality Disorders

By their nature personality disorders cannot be radically cured, but individuals can be helped to make necessary changes to their behaviour, so that their behaviour become less distressful to themselves as well as to the surrounding others.

Following therapies are used for the personality disorders.

(1) Individual psychotherapy.
(2) Group psychotherapy.
(3) Therapeutic community : A group based residential therapy.
(4) Cognitive analytic therapy : It has both cognitive and analytic approaches. It helps the patients to learn procedural events that developed the target problem. It also assesses reciprocal roles that is the pattern of relationships that the subject learned through earlier life. It has been proved to be effective in borderline personality disorder and other mental disorders like anorexia nervosa.
(5) Cognitive behavioural therapy : It aims at solving target-oriented problems by modifying or restructuring thinking and behavioural pattern.
(6) Dialectical behavioural therapy : It is a type of cognitive behaviour therapy, used in borderline personality disorder to reduce self-harm and suicidal gestures.
(7) Drug therapy : Drugs used in personality disorders are –

a) low dose antipsychotic drugs to control impulsivity and brief psychotic episode in borderline and schizotypal personality disorders.

b) antidepressant drugs to check co-morbid depression with personality disorders.

c) lithium and carbamazepine may be used for episodic behavioral changes in Cluster B personality disorders.

Prognosis and Outcome

Prognosis varies according to the types of the personality disorders. Following prognosis have been recorded in different types of personality disorders.

◻ Paranoid and Schizoid personality disorders worsen with age.

◻ Schizotypal PD has variable prognosis. It may improve on treatment. But a significant number of patients develop schizophrenia.

◻ Antisocial and borderline PD may improve with age. But there are opinions that antisocial personalities with maturation just change the nature of their behaviour from overtness to covertness, but underlying traits and inclinations remain unchanged.

◻ Dependent PD - though the traits of the personality cannot be changed, but the treatment of the dependent PD helps the person to deal with the situations and learn in more productive ways.

◻ Anxious and Anankastic PD may develop into social phobia and obsessive compulsive disorder respectively.

Habit and Impulse Disorders

These are a group of heterogeneous disorders, where the subject is unable to resist impulsive behaviour that is harmful to themselves and also to the other people.

Here the subject feels release of tension by taking the action and may feel guilt after completing the act.

Following types are seen.

Kleptomania

Kleptomania is an irresistible impulse to steal things without any apparent motive or gain. The person may be affordable and may not need the object, but the action of stealing gives him pleasure.

The act is not done in retaliation, or for any revenge, or on a result of anger. The person may feel guilt and anxiety after the act. Most patients with kleptomania steal from retail stores, but they can steal from family members in their own household also.

Pyromania

Pyromania is an impulse to set fire to things repetitively, without any motive.

The person feels an intense urge to set fire to objects and get relieved in tension by the act. Pyromania is significantly associated with substance abuse disorders, specially alcoholism. Fire setters also likely to be mildly mentally retarded and tend to have an antisocial trait.

Pathological Gambling

This is characterised by an irresistible urge or impulse to gambling.

The person takes the action repetitively and though the outcome is not profitable, the person cannot resist it.

It negatively affects family and work relationships.

Trichotillomania

This is an impulse of pulling out hairs, and the person suffers from noticeable hair loss. An estimated 35 to 40 percent of the patients chew or swallow their hairs which they pull out, posing a dangerous hazard of developing bezoars - accumulating hairballs in the alimentary tract.

Patients usually deny the behaviour and try to conceal their resultant alopecia.

Intermittent Explosive Disorder (IED)

This is characterised by episodes in which the person loses control of himself and attacks another without any adequate cause or show explosive behaviours (like breaking or throwing chairs) without any reason or for trivial cause.

Internet Addiction

The subject spends most of their waking time, sitting before computer surfing web. They feel an irresistible, constant and repetitive urge to go on web and get released of their tension after that act.

The person may be attracted to different contents of internet material, such as interactive gaming, social sites, shopping sites, sex sites and many others.

It adversely affects family and social relationships and 40% of internet addicts get less than four hours sleep per night

Treatment of Impulsive disorders

(1) Behaviour therapy

i) Aversion therapy : A noxious stimuli is presented immediately after a specific behavioral response to reduce the occurrence of the behaviour and to ultimately extinguish it. The unwanted behaviour is paired with a negative stimulus to be conditioned. The noxious stimuli used are nausea stimulating drugs, electric shock, physical pain, and many others. The unwanted behaviour may disappear after a series of such sequences.

ii) Cognitive behaviour therapy : To change thinking and behavioural pattern.

(2) Individual psychotherapy.
(3) Family therapy in some cases.
(4) Treatment of associated psychiatric disorder, if it is there.
(5) Drug therapy :

SSRIs, carbamazepine, and low-dose antipsychotics may be helpful in some cases.

Munchausen's Syndrome (Factitious Disorder)

This disorder is named after Baron Von Munchausen, a German nobleman, who was legendary for his inventing lies.

In this disorder, the patient seeks medical attention presenting some dramatic symptoms of medical emergency, such as acute chest pain or intra-abdominal distress.

The patient is addicted to be under medical supervision and hospital admission. He fabricates some convincing history to persuade the doctor and lead him to conduct detailed investigations and exploratory surgery. The patient usually possesses a superficial medical knowledge about the diseases and sometimes may distort any investigation report to support his lies.

When suspicion arises, the person angrily discharges himself and present himself in similar manner to other doctors or in other hospital.

Their abdomen may show multiple scars of previous surgeries (grid-iron abdomen).

This disorder is different from malingering, because in malingering the person has a clear motive - that is the person pretends to be sick or injured in order to avoid doing work, or for other purposes. But in this disorder, there is no back-up motive for the subject's addiction.

There is no specific treatment for these patients. Any associated psychiatric disorder (depression, anxiety, mood disorder) should be treated.

CHAPTER VII

ANXIETY AND STRESS RELATED DISORDERS AND OTHER NEUROTIC DISORDERS

Anxiety is a very common feeling among all of us. We all felt anxiety in various situations in our lives. It is an universal experience.

However, in some situations, it takes some form that may significantly impact on a person's normal regular activities. In this condition care and treatment from the professionals become necessary for the person.

Anxiety disorder may be of two types. Some patients feel anxiety for a significant period of time, which impairs their social and occupational works. And ultimately treatment becomes necessary for them. It is called trait anxiety.

Another type is, in certain situation the person feels acute precipitation of anxiety. It is called state anxiety.

1. Generalized Anxiety Disorder

This disorder is diagnosed when feelings of apprehension, worry and tension is present for at least a period of six month.

This is the commonest psychiatric disorder in general population.

One year prevalence of generalised anxiety disorder is 3-8%. Disorder mostly begins in adolescence and early adulthood. They occur slightly more often in women than in men.

Anxiety disorder may occur along with other mental or physical illnesses. It is necessary to treat these other problems, while treating the anxiety disorder.

Signs and Symptoms of anxiety are :

A. Psychological
  ¤ Feeling of apprehension
  ¤ Restlessness and inability to relax
  ¤ Feeling of choking
  ¤ Irritability
  ¤ Feeling dizzy, unsteady, or light-headed
  ¤ Distractibility and lack of concentration
  ¤ Exaggerated startle response.
  ¤ Derealization (feeling of reality of the external world being temporarily lost), and depersonalization (feeling of detachment from self).
  ¤ Fear of loosing control and passing out.
  ¤ Fear of impending disaster.

B. Physical
  ¤ Increased heart rate
  ¤ Sweating
  ¤ Trembling and shaking
  ¤ Chest pain or discomfort
  ¤ Hot flushes or cold chills
  ¤ Dry mouth
  ¤ Sensation of lump in throat and difficulty in swallowing
  ¤ Muscle tension and pain
  ¤ Numbness and tingling sensations
  ¤ Nausea or abdominal discomfort
  ¤ Frequency of micturition
  ¤ Insomnia.

Secondary depression may be associated with the disorder.

Causes

The aetiology of anxiety disorder is not well established. Several theories are there and the research is underway to find the actual cause of the anxiety disorder.

Anxiety is the expression of the emotion 'fear' associated with a hyper-wakeful state. The opposite end of emotion 'fear' is 'confidence'. 'Anxiety' results when the object or cause of the fear is unknown, but the situation is unavoidable or unescapable. 'Stress' occurs when the object or cause of the fear is known, and also the situation is unavoidable or unescapable. Both are associated with concomitant hyperwakeful state, but this state is more pronounced in anxiety and less in stress.

It is also a protective mechanism of vigilance and alertness, preparing oneself for future possible danger.

Hereditary factors are strongly evidenced to be implicated in anxiety disorder. Almost half of the patients suffering from panic disorder have at least one affected relative. In case of other anxiety disorders, data shows higher frequency of disorder among first degree relatives of the affected patients.

But improper family background, faulty upbringing and emotional training, poor learning in the skills of situational management, unstable and uncertain family or social surroundings, hostility and adversity of the environment, cultivate trends in a person with high emotionality to suffer from anxiety and stress related disorders.

People with high emotionality are more prone to anxiety disorder. Higher activity of amygdala and limbic system in response to external stimuli in people suffering from anxiety has been found in different studies.

Biological factors responsible for anxiety disorder :

(a) Autonomic Nervous System

Anxiety is a hyper-autonomic state. In anxiety sympathetic autonomic nervous system is over-activated, as a result of which symptoms manifested in the patient are - increased heart rate (tachycardia), increased sweating, dilatation of pupil etc. Patients suffering from anxiety disorder, specifically panic disorder, show increased sympathetic tone, and respond exaggeratedly to normally moderate stimuli.

(b) Neurotransmitters

On the basis of animal studies and respond to drug treatment, it has been ensured three major neurotransmitters are associated with anxiety disorders -

Norepinephrine (or Noradrenaline), Serotonin and gamma aminobutyric acid (GABA). Sympathetic arousal is mediated through increased noradrenergic function. It has been postulated that the patients suffering from anxiety disorder have poorly regulated noradrenergic system. In patients with panic disorder beta adrenergic receptor agonists e.g. isoproterenol and alpha2 adrenergic receptor antagonist e.g. yohimbine can provoke severe panic attacks.

The involvement of serotonin in anxiety disorder has been conferred from the effectiveness of buspirone, a serotonin 5HT-IA receptor agonist, in the treatment of anxiety disorder, and serotonergic antidepressant clomipramine in the treatment of obsessive compulsive disorder. Many reports also indicate that serotonergic hallucinogens and stimulants - for example, lysergic acid diethylamide (LSD) and 3,4-methylenedioxymethamphetamine (MDMA) - are associated with development of acute and chronic anxiety disorders in the users of these drugs.

It has been inferred that GABA has a role in the causation of anxiety disorder because of the fact that benzodiazepines, which enhance the activity of GABA at the GABA type A receptor, are indisputably effective in several anxiety disorders. But this connection has not been proved directly.

(c) Hormones

In stress situation, cortisol synthesis and release is increased. Besides many metabolic functions, cortisol contributes to increased arousal and vigilance. Alterations in hypothalamic-pituitary-adrenal (HPA) axis function with resulted increase in cortisol has been demonstrated in post traumatic stress disorder. Hypothalamic secretion of corticotropin-releasing hormone (CRH) is also increased during stress, resulting in activation of HPA axis and increased release of cortisol.

Treatment

(1) Psychotherapy.
(2) Relaxation techniques
     ¤ Jacobson's progressive relaxation techniques
     ¤ Yoga
     ¤ Meditation.

(3) Behaviour therapy

Cognitive behaviour therapy has a good efficacy in the treatment of anxiety disorders.

Here the subject is helped to change his thinking pattern, behaviour and reactions to anxiety provocating factors, supervised by a group of trained therapists.

The subject is encouraged to face the situations which he usually avoided, and is helped to be adjusted to those situations.

Treatment takes 3-4 months with 1-2 hours session in several days in a week.

Therapy may be conducted individually or with a group of patients suffering from the similar disorder. Group therapy is specially helpful in the case of social phobia.

(4) Drug therapy

Selective serotonin reuptake inhibitors (SSRIs) - Citalopram, Escitalopram, Fluoxetine, Paroxetine, Sertraline - are the first line of medications.

SSRIs have side effects of headache, nausea, insomnia, and low sexual drive. But the symptoms improve with the course, except sexual dysfunctions.

Selective serotonin-norepinephrine reuptake inhibitors (SNRIs) - Venlafaxine and Duloxetine can also be considered as first-line pharmacological option for treating GAD.

Pregabaline, an original antiepileptic drug, is effective in treatment of anxiety disorder. It has less effect on sexual dysfunction than SSRIs.

Mono amine oxidase inhibitors (Phenelzine and Tranylcypromine) are effective in anxiety. But their drug-food, and drug-drug interactions and other side effects including insomnia, orthostatic hypotension, anorgasmia, weight gain have restricted their use. They are specifically helpful in treating panic disorders.

Benzodiazepines (alprazolam, clonazepam, oxazepam) can be used on short-term basis, because patients develop psychological dependency on these drugs. Their sedative effects also impair generalised alertness, cognitive and psychomotor functions. The patient should be careful to drive and do other risky machinery jobs while under these drugs.

Buspirone, a 5-HT 1A receptor partial agonist, is less sedative anxiolytic drug and after long-term use, it has been found to have no dependency effect on the part of the patient. But it takes 2-3 weeks initially to work. It is not effective in children.

Beta-blocker (propanolol) are mainly useful for the control of somatic symptoms like, tachycardia, palpitations, etc. The care must be taken in the patients with asthma, bradycardia, or heart block, when treating with beta-blockers.

Prognosis and Outcome

Prognosis of anxiety disorders are variable. Good prognostic indicators are recent onset, short duration, stable personality, and good work record.

Poor indicators are childhood onset, history of neurotic diseases in family, unstable personality, and poor performance record.

2. Panic Disorder

This is characterised by recurrent attacks of severe intense anxiety which are sudden and unpredictable. Panic attacks are not associated with exposure to dangerous life threatening situations.

It affects 1-2% of general populations. Women are more (2-3 times) vulnerable. Age of onset has a bimodal distribution with highest peak incidence at 15-24 yrs. and second peak at 45-54 yrs.

Attack lasts for 10-20 minutes and then gradually wanes off. There may or may not be underlying generalized anxiety disorder.

Condition that can mimic panic disorder, include hyperthyroidism, hypoparathyroidism, pheochromocytoma, mitral valve prolapse, hypoglycemia, Cushing's syndrome, carcinoid syndrome, myocardial infarction, chronic obstructive pulmonary disease (COPD), complex partial seizure, drug ingestion (amphetamine, cocaine, caffeine) and withdrawal (alcohol, barbiturates, opioids, sedative hypnotics, steroids).

To diagnose panic disorder, there should be at least 4 attacks within the period of 4 weeks, and should include at least 4 of the following symptoms, one of which must be from the first 4 symptoms (ICD-10).

1. Increased heart rate or palpitations
2. Sweating
3. Trembling or shaking
4. Dry mouth (not due to medication or dehydration)
5. Difficulty in breathing
6. Feeling of choking
7. Nausea or abdominal discomfort (e.g. churning in stomach)
8. Chest pain or discomfort
9. Dizziness or light-headedness
10. Derealization or depersonalization
11. Fear of loosing control or passing out
12. Hot flushes or cold chills
13. Numbness or tingling sensations
14. Fear of dying.

Causes

Genetic factors are involved. First degree relatives of the patients with panic disorder have 5-7 times greater chance of having panic disorder than general population.

Patients with panic disorder have a higher incidence of stressful life events. Childhood abuse, physical or sexual, is another important factor for the development of disorder. About 60% of women with panic disorder have a history of childhood sexual abuse.

Neurohumoral mechanisms which may be responsible for panic attacks are : 1) Increased serotoninergic activity. 2) Decreased inhibitory neurotransmitter GABA (gamma-amino butyric acid) level or reduced GABA receptor sensitivity. 3) Increased adrenergic activity.

All these, causing overactivity in limbic system particularly amygdala, produce 'fear effect' of panic disorder.

Panic episode can be precipitated in patients suffering from this disorder, by I.V infusion of sodium lactate, ingestion of caffeine, yohimbine, and inhalation of CO_2 in clinical settings.

Comorbidity

The patients suffering from panic disorder are commonly found to be having other associated psychiatric disorders. 91% of the patients have at least one other psychiatric disorder. Most common is depression. Concomitant depression is present in 50% of the patients with panic disorder. Other disorders that are common with panic disorder, are social phobia (15 - 30%), other specific phobia (2 - 10%), generalized anxiety disorder (15 - 30%), obsessive compulsive disorder (20 - 30%) and post traumatic stress disorder (2 - 10%).

Treatment

(1) Psychotherapy.
(2) Cognitive behaviour therapy.
(3) Relaxation techniques and breathing exercises.
(4) Drug therapy :

Antidepressants - Selective serotonin reuptake inhibitors (SSRIs) are the first line of treatment. Other antidepressants monoamine oxidase inhibitors (MAOIs), tricyclic antidepressants (TCAs), selective noradrenergic receptor inhibitors (SNRIs) are also effective.

Use of benzodiazepines is controversial as they develop dependence on long-term use. But they may be used on short-term basis to control the severity of acute symptoms.

For treatment of severe symptoms atypical antipsychotics (olanzapine, risperidone) may be used.

Treatment should be continued for 12-18 months. Then the dose of the drugs should be gradually tapered off over 2-4 months. If symptoms recur after discontinuation of drugs, treatment should be carried on for longer period.

Panic disorder if neglected or untreated, the patient gradually develops avoidant behaviour, which may culminate into social phobia or other types of phobia.

3. Acute Stress Reaction

Acute stress reaction occurs following exposure to an exaggerated mental or physical stressor (e.g. severe harm, loss, injury or any catastrophe). And it is manifested by a number of symptoms, from mild to moderate judging the nature of reaction.

If the stress factor is released then symptoms last for not more than 8 hours. But if the stress factor is not released, it gradually dissolves within 48 hours.

Mild form of the reaction is manifested by any symptom of generalized anxiety disorder. But moderate and severe reaction has associated symptoms of the followings.

(1) Withdrawal from expected social interactions.
(2) Narrowing of attention
(3) Apparent disorientation
(4) Anger or Verbal aggression
(5) Despair or hopelessness
(6) Inappropriate or purposeless over-activity
(7) Uncontrolled and extreme grief.

Treatment

Treatment is supportive psychotherapy to help the patient to overcome the stressful experience.
Benzodiazepines for tranquillizing effect.

4. Post Traumatic Stress Disorder

This disorder occurs when a catastrophic life-threatening event scars the patient's mind. Traumatic events include witnessing or being involved in a violent accident or crime, military combat in war, assault, physical or sexual abuse including rape and natural disaster e.g. earthquake, flood, tsunami.

Life time incidence of PTSD is estimated to be 9 - 15% and life time prevalence of PTSD is estimated at about 8% of general population. Women have a greater tendency to suffer from PTSD than men (5:2).

Although PTSD can appear at any age, young adults are more prone to suffer from this disorder as they are more exposed to precipitating events. Children can also develop this disorder.

Etiology

Risk factors for the development of PTSD include a past psychiatric history and personality characteristics of high neuroticism. Twin studies show a substantial genetic influence on all symptoms associated with PTSD, with less evidence for an environmental effect. Neurophysiological theory suggests that there is excessive release of noradrenaline from locus ceruleus in response to stress and increased noradrenergic activity in hippocampus and amygdala in patients with PTSD. Overactivity of hypothalamic-pituitary-adrenal (HPA) axis has also been implicated in the development of the disorder.

Symptoms

There are three sets of symptoms.

(A) Repeated recollection
The patient suffers from repeated recollection of the catastrophic event unwillingly. The patient cannot resist it.

(B) Avoidance
The patient reduces involvement with the external world. Activities are diminished, specially those which may evoke the memory of past experience. There is reduced emotional feelings or emotional numbness.

(C) Hyperarousal state
The patient is hyperalert or hypervigilant with exaggerated startle response.

The symptoms may appear after a latent period following the incident.

Diagnosis

According to ICD-10, essential criteria for diagnosis of PTSD is :

(A) Exposure to a stressful event or situation (either short or long duration) of exceptionally threatening or catastrophic in nature, which is likely to cause pervasive distress in almost any one.

(B) Persistent remembering or reliving the stressful event by intrusive flash backs, vivid memories, recurring dreams, or experiencing distress when exposed to circumstances resembling or associated with the stressor.

(C) Actual or preferred avoidance of circumstances resembling or associated with the stressor.

(D) Either (1) or (2)

(1) Inability to recall either partially or completely, some of the period of exposure to the stressful event.

(2) Persistent symptoms of increased psychological sensitivity and arousal exposure to the stressor shown by any two of the followings -

    (a) difficulty in falling or staying asleep.

    (b) irritability or outburst of anger

    (c) difficulty in concentrating

    (d) hypervigilance

    (e) exaggerated startle response.

Symptoms should occur within 6 months of the stressful event.

Treatment

(1) Drug therapy

SSRIs (sertraline, fluoxetine, paroxetine), and SNRIs (venlafaxine) are the first line of management. TCAs (imipramine and amitriptyline) are also effective but have less tolerance. MAOIs (phenelzine) are effective, but should not be considered as first line drugs because of their side effects and necessary dietary restriction.

Short term benzodiazepines (alprazolam, clonazepam) may be used for anxiety symptoms, hyperarousal state and sleep disturbance. However some authorities are against the use of it in PTSD.

Mood stabilizers (carbamazepine, valproate or lithium) have been used to check intrusive thoughts and impulsiveness.

If there is sleep disturbance with recurrent nightmares, Prazosin may help to reduce the symptoms. Tazodone, a sedative antidepressant, is frequently used to combat insomnia.

Psychotic symptoms, behavioural aggression may need the use of antipsychotics (olanzapine, risperidone).

(2) Exposure therapy and Supportive therapy with relaxation techniques

There are two psychotherapeutic approaches to treat the patients with PTSD.

(a) Exposure therapy : Exposure therapy consists of imaginal exposure - where the patient is asked to relive the traumatic event imaginally and abreact the emotions associated with it; and also in vivo exposure - where the patient confronts the site or situation of traumatic event which the patient avoided because it reminds him or her of the trauma (like going to the site of traumatic event, driving again after a road accident etc.). Exposure is repeated until the patient no longer reacts with high level of distress.

(b) Supportive psychotherapy with relaxation techniques : The patient is taught about the methods of stress management and relaxation techniques.

Exposure therapy is superior to supportive psychotherapy and relaxation techniques and results of exposure therapy last longer.

(3) Cognitive behavioral therapy

Cognitive behavioral therapy is effective in the treatment of PTSD. This include an element of psychoeducation about the common reactions to trauma which helps to normalize the patient. The therapist helps the patient to have cognitive approaches towards the reactions to the memories of trauma and give up behaviours that maintain the problem.

(4) EMDR (Eye movement desensitization and reprocessing)

EMDR therapy is based on the observation that inducing saccadic eye movements (oscillatory movements of the eye when a person follows an object) while a person thinking or imagining an anxiety provoking event he is suffering from, helps to reduce anxiety in him. Several studies have concluded that EMDR is as effective as cognitive behaviour therapy or drug treatment in the treatment of post traumatic stress disorder.

(5) Disaster management by providing early help is a preventive measure.

Outcome depends on severity of initial symptoms. One half of the patients recover completely within one year. Near about 30% of cases develop chronic psychological illness.

[Phobic disorders and dissociative-conversion disorders have been described in Ch.-VII, Part I and Ch.-V, Part II respectively.]

Other Neurotic Disorders

1. Somatoform Disorders

Somatoform disorders are that group of disorders where the patient presents with experiences of physical symptoms of illness, though the doctor is unable to find and detect any underlying medical disease.

Despite the assurance of doctor, the patient remains persistent in his or her request to do further investigations and check-up.

Delusional belief disorder can occur in schizophrenia and other psychotic disorders, but that should be differentiated from somatoform disorder by the delusional intensity and the presence of other psychotic features.

It is differentiated from factitious disorder and malingering by the features that, in factitious disorder the patient fabricates the symptoms, but in somatoform disorder the patients do not pretend, or invent the symptoms, actually they feel the experience of the symptoms. In case of malingering, besides fabrication of the symptoms, the patients also nurture a definite purpose to gain from their produced illness.

Somatoform disorders may be of different subtypes as followingly.

(a) Somatization Disorder

In somatization disorder there is a history of complaints of multiple physical symptoms for at least two years, that cannot be explained by any detectable physical disorder.

Physical symptoms may involve any system of the body - such as gastro-intestinal system, cardiovascular system, respiratory system, genitourinary system and dermatological system. The physical symptoms commonly encountered are :

Gastro-intestinal symptoms

- Abdominal pain
- Nausea
- Feeling of bloating of abdomen
- Complaints of vomiting, loose stool, bad taste in mouth.

Cardio-vascular symptoms

- Breathlessness
- Chest pain

Genito-urinary symptoms

- Dysuria (pain during urination) or frequency of micturition (repeated urination).
- Unpleasant sensations in or around genitals.
- Complaints of unusual or copious vaginal discharge.

Skin and Pain symptoms

- Complaints of blotchiness or discolouration of the skin.
- Complaints of numbness or tingling sensations.
- Pain in the limbs or joints.

Life time prevalence of this disorder varies from 0.2 to 2% in case of females, but in males the prevalence is less than 0.2%. The disorder is more common in patients with low education and of lower occupational groups.

Exact etiology of somatization disorder is not known. Probably multiple factors are involved in the disorder. This include genetic, environmental and some defects in neurophysiological functions.

Familial association has been well established in somatization disorder. It has been found that the frequency of disorder is 10-20% higher in the first degree relatives of female somatizers. Though in case of male somatizers this affinity has not been strongly reflected in studies, it may be because of the fact that somatization in men is probably heterogeneous in character. Familial association may be both due to genetical and environmental elements.

Neurophysiological basis of the disorder has been supported by the findings of abnormalities in information processing technique in few studies - such as low threshold for pain, disturbed capacity to filter out trivial afferent stimuli, and enhanced central nervous system response to sensory input.

Treatment :

Treatment of the somatization disorder is difficult, as there is no definite therapy and the patients invariably have a constant and high expectation for removal of their symptoms. They have a high tendency to change their doctor frequently.

Following therapies may be helpful.

¤ Psychotherapy : The patient with somatization disorder usually resist psychiatric treatment, but some may accept the treatment if it is held up in a medical setting. The treatment is aimed at to educate the patient to cope with stressful situation and with their symptoms, and to resolve their interpersonal problems if those are there.

¤ Relaxation techniques : Various relaxation techniques such as yoga, meditation may be helpful.

¤ Drug therapy : Antidepressants and anxiolytics for the treatment of undercurrent depression and anxiety.

(b) Hypochondriacal Disorder

In hypochondriacal disorder there is a persistent belief of having or developing serious disease by the patient for at least six months.

This belief may be of any deformity or disfigurement of the body (e.g. his or her nose is deformed, or limbs are thinner than normal). In this case it is called body dysmorphic disorder.

The fear is often the result of the patient's exaggerated misinterpretation of trivial bodily signs and symptoms. The patients with hypochondriasis are profoundly preoccupied with their bodies and health condition, always scrutinizing their body functioning, body appearance and checking health considerations.

The patients refuse to accept doctor's assurance that there is nothing wrong with either their bodies or general physical conditions.

The prevalence of hypochondriasis is general medical clinic is reported to be 4-8%. Although the onset of symptoms can appear at any age, the disorder most commonly occurs in the persons between 20 to 30 years of age.

The etiology of hypochondriasis has been variably assumed. It may be a variant of anxiety and obsessive compulsive disorder, where the person is anxious and obsessive on excessive self-concern. Or the patient may pursue a 'sick role' for receiving attention and achieving secondary gain from the 'sick role'. The sick role enables the person to escape from obligations, duties and unsolvable situations.

Treatment :

¤ Psychotherapy : Like somatization disorder hypochondriasis is also most difficult to treat. Insight-oriented psychotherapy, cognitive behavioral therapy and hypnosis may be helpful.

¤ Treatment of underlying anxiety or depression.

(c) Somatoform Autonomic Dysfunction

In this disorder the patient attributes symptoms of autonomic hyperactivity to a physical illness.

The symptoms are, for example, palpitations, sweating, dry mouth, flushing, hyperventilation, hiccough, abdominal discomfort or bloating etc.

The patients are preoccupied with the thoughts that these trivial and insignificant symptoms are due to serious physical illness and adhere to their beliefs despite the repeated assurance from the quarter of the doctor.

The most common presentations are :

i) Hyperventilation syndrome

It is a syndrome of accelerated breathing, particularly when under stress or emotional pressure leading to hypocapnoea (decreased CO_2 in blood) and respiratory alkalosis. Hypocapnoea results in decreased cerebral circulation and decreased availability of O_2 of oxyhemoglobin in regions of low PCO_2 in brain, producing symptoms of dizziness, fatigue, confusion. Respiratory alkalosis results in hypocalcaemia producing symptoms of muscle twitching, paraesthesia, carpopedal spasm, and hypokalaemia producing symptoms of generalised weakness. Increased sympathetic arousal produces symptoms of anxiety, palpitations, sweating and chest pain.

Treatment :

¤ The attack can be aborted by having the patient breath from a paper bag and hold their breath as long as possible, which raises plasma PCO_2 and reverses physiological processes alleviating symptoms. But before that any pathological disease must be excluded.

¤ Relaxation technique and breathing exercises are helpful.

¤ Treatment of associated anxiety and depression.

¤ Supportive psychotherapy.

ii) Irritable bowel syndrome

It is very common. The patient complains of abdominal discomfort or pain, feeling of fullness, diarrhoea or constipation, or sensations of incomplete evacuation of stool.

There are no indicative findings in laboratory investigations. Studies and reports suggest physiological responsiveness of the gastro-intestinal system to associated anxiety and stress as an attributing factor for this disorder. Motility activity of intestinal muscles is reduced in small intestine and increased in large intestine during stress condition.

High gas producing foods and foods containing FODMAP (FODMAP are fermentable oligo-, di and mono saccharides and polyol, those are poorly absorbed and readily fermented, producing gas) can be responsible for unfavourable gastrointestinal symptoms.

Treatment :

¤ Dietary modification

Avoidance of high gas producing foods (e.g. cabbage, cauliflower).

Avoidance of food containing high FODMAP (high FODMAP containing foods include rye, barley, onion, garlic, asparagus, beetroot, some pulses, apples, apricots etc.

Dietary modification should be individualised on patient's personal experience of what food is causing symptoms, and on consultation with physician and nutritionist.

¤ Avoidance of smoking, caffeine, and caffeinated beverages.

¤ Drug therapy

For constipation : Bulk purgatives like Isobgula husk (Psyllium), Methyl cellulose. If uncontrolled Lactulose.

For diarrhoea : Bulk purgatives, Loperamide.

For abdominal cramps : Antispasmodics - Dicyclomine, Hyoscyamine, Mebeverine.

Alosteron can reduce symptoms in non-constipated IBS female patients, but its efficacy in males is not clear.

¤ Antianxiety and antidepressive treatment.

¤ Supportive psychotherapy.

iii) Premenstrual syndrome

This syndrome arises one or two weeks before menstruation and disappears during or after menstruation. Between the post menstruation and next ovulation the subject remains normal.

The syndrome is characterised by irritability, restlessness, headache, insomnia, breast tenderness, weight gain due to fluid retention, abdominal discomfort, mood swing, anxiety, depression, crying spells etc.

Causes are multifactorial. Cyclical hormonal change, genetic vulnerability, imbalanced neurohormonal system, poor diet, underlying depression all may be cultivative factors.

Treatment :

◻ Healthy diet.

◻ Exercises.

◻ Avoidance of caffeine and alcohol.

◻ Treatment of underlying depression and anxiety.

◻ Diuretics (Spironolactone) for the fluid retention.

◻ Hormonal treatment with oral contraceptive pill may be efficacious.

◻ In some cases supportive psychotherapy.

iv) Persistent somatoform pain disorder

The patient complaints of persistent pain from any part of the body for at least six months. There are a heterogeneous group of pain symptoms that patients may present; i.e., headache, musculoskeletal pain, joint pain, low back pain, abdominal and pelvic pain and other kinds of pain.

This pain cannot be attributed to any physical disorder by the doctor after all clinical check-up and sufficient investigations.

This is a common entity encountered in medical practice. Prevalence of this disorder is exactly not known, but on the basis of recent works 6 months and life time prevalence of this disorder has been roughly estimated to be 5% and 12% respectively. There is no age specific predilection for occurrence of this disorder. It can begin at any age and frequently found to be associated with anxiety and depressive disorders. Chronic pain is seemingly associated with depressive disorders whereas recent or short duration pain appears to be associated with anxiety disorders. There are also cases where the patients try to seek attention and achieve secondary gain from the sick role. Neurophysiological theory implicates serotonin and endorphins in this disorder. Serotonin has a inhibitory effect on pain perception and it is probably the neurotransmitter of the descending inhibitory pathways. Endorphins act for modulation of pain in central nervous system. Deficiency or chemical abnormalities of them subjects the patients to suffer from pain.

Treatment :

¤ Drug therapy : Analgesic medicine can be used but many patients develop dependence and abuse of them. Sedatives and anxiolytics should be avoided because of misuse and dependency risks. Tricyclic antidepressants (TCAs) and selective serotonin reuptake inhibitors (SSRIs) are most effective in the management. The mechanisms of action of antidepressants to reduce pain may be either due to their antidepressant action or direct pain inhibitory action (e.g., action of serotonin on pain inhibitory pathways).

¤ Psychotherapy : Individual psychotherapy, family therapy, group therapy along with other modalities of treatment are beneficial.

2. Neurasthenia

Neurasthenia is persistent feeling of tiredness and exhaustion after minor mental or physical effort.

For example, subject feels tired performing normal every day work that does not require too much either mental or physical effort. The subject takes longer than usual time to recover after work by rest, relaxation, entertainment etc.

There may be associated muscle aches and pain, tension headache, irritability, dizziness, and sleep disturbances.

No organic basis for this disorder has been found. Muscle testing usually reveals 'give-way weakness', characteristic of non-organic disorders.

Other medical and mental diseases must be excluded as to be the underlying cause of fatigue before diagnosis of neurasthenia.

Treatment is supportive. No effective medical treatment is known.

3. Depersonalization and Derealization Disorder

Depersonalization is characterised by recurrent and persistent feeling of detachment from one's self, so that the feeling of one's own reality is changed or lost temporarily. The person feels he is not himself, an another person.

Derealization is change in one's perception about the external world. That is the outside world seems to the subject different than what people normally feel. It may seem to the subject colorless, joyless, lifeless, distorted, uninteresting, or like a stage where everyone is acting.

In both the cases, the subject's insight is present. That means the subject can realize the change within him.

Severe psychological stress is the causative factor. Usual onset is 15 to 30 years of age. The disorder occurs suddenly and episodically. Termination of episode is also abrupt.

Depersonalization and derealization may also occur in a variety of psychological and medical disorders including schizophrenia, mood disorders, anxiety disorders, neurological disorders (cerebral tumor, complex partial seizure, migraine), alcohol and drug abuse, hyperventilation, hypoglycemia, grief etc.
Before diagnosis of the disorder as a pure entity, these other causes should be excluded first.

Treatment

This is poorly responsive to treatment. Followings may be tried.
¤ Treatment of underlying depression and anxiety. Drugs used are SSRIs (citalopram, escitalopram, fluoxetine) and benzodiazepines (clonazepam); clomipramine (if obsessional symptoms are marked); naltrexone.
¤ Supportive psychotherapy.

The course of the disorder is variable and depends on recurrence of stressful situations.

Grief

Grief is a natural response to all who have suffered separation. Grief occurs after the loss of a loved one, e.g. a close relative or a friend, specially a person who was occupying a significant position in his or her emotional life. Grief may also occur after the loss of a pet animal, a material thing which may be valuable or was attached with some emotional events in bereft person's life, and even after loss of status or reputation.

Normal Grief Reaction

Normal grief reaction is a natural phenomenon and is self-limiting. It constitutes both physical and psychological manifestations which may occur immediately after bereavement or be delayed. In some persons, symptoms may be exaggerated and in some persons, symptoms may be apparently absent.

Usual common features of grief reaction following bereavement are :

(1) State of Shock

Immediately following the loss, there is a state of bewilderment, with failure to realise the loss at full extent. This can last for a few hours to as long as two weeks and during this state, the individual may experience no distress, or there may be a sense of numbness or irritability to appreciate any emotional reactions.

(2) Full Grief Reaction

Full grief reaction occurs after realisation of the total extent of the loss. This includes a variety of physical symptoms and behavioural changes and continues to persist for two to six weeks, even up to six months. Feeling of grief may return on the anniversary of the loved one's death or other special days.

The physical symptoms which occur in grief reaction are feeling of tightness in throat, feeling of choking, repeated sighing and crying, breathlessness, empty feeling in abdomen, poor appetite and poor concentration.

Behavioural changes include restlessness, aimless movement, withdrawal from social contacts, disruption of normal routine work, and carrying out activities to keep the memories of the deceased alive.

(3) Preoccupation with Memories or Image of the Deceased Person

This is a characteristic feature of the grief reaction, which occurs during the early months of the grief reaction. Thoughts and image of the deceased person tends to dominate the mind of the bereft person. There is also a tendency to idealise the deceased person. The mourner often misinterprets others voices and faces as being that of the lost person and feels a sense of presence of the deceased in the surroundings.

(4) Depression

Depression with or without crying spells, loss of interest in work and activities, apathy, insomnia, anorexia, fatigue, weight loss, self-neglect, self-reproach and guilt feelings, panic attacks and suicidal ideas are frequent features of grief reaction.

These may be aggravated by reminding of the lost person.

There may also occur irritability, resentment and hostile feelings to others.

(5) Identification

Sometimes, the person, in a state of grief, takes on the personality of the deceased person - his qualities, mannerisms and characteristics. And he identifies himself with the deceased person.

Elisabeth Kübler-Ross in her book 'On Death and Dying' (1969) described five distinct stages of how people react in grief. These are : 1. Denial, 2. Anger, 3. Bargaining, 4. Depression, and 5. Acceptance.

Morbid or Pathological Grief

When there is exaggeration of one or more symptoms of normal grief, or further prolongation of the duration of normal grief for at least one month beyond six months after bereavement and without spontaneous recovery, the condition is called morbid or pathological grief.

Complicated Grief

In this case, grief is complicated by different neurotic or psychotic disorders, and mood or sleep disturbances, in addition to normal grief reactions. These may be hallucinations, delusions, anxiety, severe depression, suicidal thoughts or behaviour, significant sleep disturbances, and others.

Treatment

(1) Normal grief reaction does not need any specific treatment, either medical or psychiatric. Sometimes mild sedatives or anxiolytics may be needed on short term basis.

(2) For morbid and complicated grief, treatment may be required, either medication or psychotherapy, according to the presentation of symptoms. Morbid and complicated grief sometimes may result in severe depression, alcohol or drug abuse, if left untreated.

(3) Mental assistance to the bereft person should be concentrated on

¤ helping the person to adapt with the changed situation after loss. But it is not advisable to suppress emotional feelings of the grieved person; rather emotional catharsis should be encouraged.

¤ making the person understand that there are other members in his or her companions, and there are other parts and activities of life.

¤ encouraging the person to engage in new goal-oriented activities.

¤ bringing together similarly grieved persons for sharing experiences.

CHAPTER VIII

EATING DISORDERS

Anorexia Nervosa

This disorder typically appears in prepubertal adolescence, and girls are predominantly affected.

Average age of onset is 17 years, and prevalence is 1-2% in girls aged 12-18 yrs. 5-10% cases occur in males. Occasionally the disorder may develop in older women.

It is more common in white women with middle class background and in subjects who are aesthetic and perfectionistic.

There are a variety of socio-psychological factors that play in the background of the disorder.

Prevailing social norm of maintaining slim figure works as a supportive psychological factor on the minds of many of the subjects. In some cases, girls are anxious to play the woman's role and sexual maturation, and wish to remain in their prepubertal state. Disturbances in interpersonal relationships within the family, overweighing parental influences also contribute to the psychological factors for the disorder. The girls who were initially little fatter and were teased for their fatness, may take an extreme course.

Prevalence of the disease is also higher in certain professions, like dancing, modelling, stage performing, athletes (runners and gymnasts).

Studies have shown association of hereditary factors with this disorder. Chances of developing anorexia nervosa have been reported to be 30-50% higher in monozygotic twins compared to general population.

Essential diagnostic criteria of AN are :

(1) Weight loss at least 25% of the original body weight, or weight below 25% of the normal body weight for that age and height.

(2) Distortion of one's own image. That means the subject thinks she is fatter than she actually is.

(3) Avoidance of high calorie food, despite normal appetite. Anorexia is a misnomer for this reason.

(4) Menstrual cycle abnormalities (Primary or secondary amenorrhoea).

(5) Absence of any organic disease or mental illness, that may account for the weight loss.

Other associated features are, the subjects are often found to possess peculiar habits with handling foods, such as cutting food in very small bits, nibbling the food, hiding food in their pockets or all over the house, collecting recipes and cooking for others, and habits with involving themselves in vigorous exercises.

They may use purgatives or induce vomiting secretly after meals.

Though absence of mental illness is one of the criteria for the diagnosis of anorexia nervosa, depression is found to be associated with a large number of subjects.

Frequent mood change and obsessive compulsive traits are other co-morbid factors.

Extreme emaciation occurs in severe cases, when the subjects are untreated.

Death may occur from cardiac arrhythmias due to hypokalemia (low level of potassium in blood), which develop as a result of induced vomiting.

Clinical Signs and Symptoms :

Skin of the subjects are dry, yellowish, and scaly. Fine lanugo hairs develop over the body of them.

Body fat is undetectable, Body mass index [BMI = weight(kg)/ height(m)2] is reduced. Density of bone mass is reduced.

There may be bradycardia, hypotension, hypothermia, peripheral cyanosis.

Renal calculi may be formed.

Cardiac arrhythmias develop as a result of hypokalemia.

In rare cases, mitral valve prolapse may occur as a result of valve-ventricular volume mismatch, which is brought about by starvation induced reduced left ventricular volume.

Peripheral neuropathy may occur as neurological manifestation.

Other physical signs are atrophy of breasts, swelling of the parotid and submandibular glands, and swollen tender abdomen (due to intestinal dilatation resulting from reduced motility and constipation).

Laboratory Investigations

The blood picture of the patients shows anaemia, leucopenia (with bone marrow hypocellularity), hypoalbuminemia, increased blood urea nitrogen, low levels of IgG, IgM, and other complement factors.

Hyponatraemia, from excessive water intake or syndrome of inappropriate antidiuretic hormone [SIADH], affects 40% of cases. Hypokalaemic/hypochloraemic metabolic alkalosis occurs from vomiting, and metabolic acidosis occurs from laxative abuse. Hypocalcaemia, hypophosphataemia, hypomagnesaemia may also occur.

Hypoglycaemia may result from prolonged starvation and low glycogen stores.

Thyroid hormones T3 and T4 are low, rT3 is increased due to euthyroid sick syndrome (an adaptive mechanism).

Blood cholesterol level may be elevated.

Serum amylase may be elevated in absence of pancreatitis.

Basal levels of lutenizing hormone (LH) and follicle stimulating hormone (FSH) are low when there is severe weight loss, and response of LH secretion to lutenizing hormone releasing hormone (LHRH) is impaired.

Other endocrine abnormalities are hypercortisolaemia, increased growth hormone level, and decreased estrogens and progestogens levels.

Before diagnosis of anorexia nervosa other physical and mental illnesses must be excluded, such as, hypothyroidism, diabetes mellitus, disseminated tuberculosis, major depression, schizophrenia etc.

Severity of The Disorder

Body mass index (BMI) is used as an indicator to determine the severity of the disease.

Mild AN : BMI > 17
Moderate AN : BMI 16 - 16.99
Severe AN : BMI 15 - 15.99
Extreme AN : BMI < 15

Management

Patients with anorexia nervosa are very secretive and deny they have any symptom. Invariably they resist treatment and in all most all cases relatives and intimate acquaintances confirm a patient's history. The patient must have a thorough general physical and neurological examination and necessary laboratory investigations should be done. Once the diagnosis is confirmed the first objective of the treatment is restoration of body weight. Hospital admission is necessary for moderate to severe cases; and patients with impaired renal functions, hypokalemia, cardiac abnormalities.

The patient should be supervised under specific nursing care, preferably one nurse taking care of the patient.

Rapid re-feeding should be checked due to cardiac decompensation, when the heart muscles cannot withstand the stress of increased metabolic demand. Controlled diet is given to achieve a weight gain of approximately 1 kg per week. Multivitamins and adequate intake of vitamin D (400 IU/day) and calcium (1500 mg/day) should be provided with the meal. Patient should be encouraged during meal and supervised for one hour after meal to ensure vomiting does not occur.

Once the weight loss is recovered, menstruation returns, other signs gradually disappear. Amenorrhoea may persist for some time in few cases.

Concurrent psychotherapy is essential, but individual psychotherapy is often unfruitful. Family counselling and behaviour therapy, like positive reinforcement therapy, cognitive behavioural therapy may help.

Drug therapy :

Drugs used in anorexia nervosa are :

(1) Antidepressants

Selective serotonin reuptake inhibitors (SSRIs) – Fluoxetine, Citalopram, Escitalopram.

Tricyclic antidepressants (TCAs) – Amytriptyline, Imipramine, Clomipramine. Use of TCAs are restricted because of potential risk of developing cardiac arrhythmias in a low weight, depressed patient.

(2) Antihistaminics

Cyproheptadine. Cyproheptadine is useful in increasing appetite, weight gain, and decreasing depressive symptoms.

(3) Antipsychotics

Olanzapine, Pimozide. Chlorpromazine has been used previously for weight gain. Some preliminary studies indicated that use of atypical antipsychotics (olanzapine) may assist in the treatment by increasing rate of weight gain and decreasing the obsessive thinking. But large trials are necessary.

Prognosis and Outcome

Despite extensive attention, long-term prognosis of anorexia nervosa is poor. 20% of patients make a full recovery, 20% remain chronically ill, and 60% have recurrent episodes of anorexia.

Death occurs in 5-10% of all cases. The cause of death is either complications arising from the disorder (which is primarily cardiac arrhythmias due to hypokalemia), or suicide.

Poor prognostic factors are onset of the disorder later than age 20, longer duration of illness, extreme weight loss, and significant co-morbid depression.

Bulimia Nervosa

It is almost exclusively confined to women, and the age of onset is a little older than that of anorexia nervosa.

Prevalence has been estimated at 1-3% of women in their early twenties.

Bulimia nervosa is characterised by episodic ingestion of large amount of food (binge eating). The number of episodes vary but there should be at least two episodes per week over a period of three months for the diagnosis.

During the episode, the subject takes large amount of food compared to normal intake of food by the people, within a discrete period of time (average 1 to 2 hrs., but may last for 8 hrs.).

After the episode the subject becomes apprehensive about gaining weight and suffers from subsequent depression.

To counteract this effect, the subject takes the help of induced vomiting, laxative abuse, periods of starvation, and use of appetite suppressive drugs.

The secrecy about the eating and counteracting is characteristic of this disorder.

There is a persistent preoccupation with eating, and an irresistible craving for food. Distortion of self-body image occurs as in anorexia nervosa. However, weight loss is less prominent than anorexia nervosa and amenorrhoea may not be present.

On examination, erosion of teeth enamels are seen due to induced vomiting.

Esophageal erosions, gastric or duodenal ulcers, cardiac arrythmias are other findings related to vomiting and purgative abuse. Other features of anorexia nervosa may also be seen but in less severe form.

Lab investigation reveals hypokalemia and metabolic alkalosis due to vomiting, and metabolic acidosis due to purgative abuse.

Electrolyte and fluid disturbances can be sufficiently severe to cause cardiac arrythmias and renal damage.

Treatment

The patients are treated on outpatient basis. Hospitalization is rarely needed in cases of severe complications or in patients associated with other psychiatric disorders. Treatment modalities used are :

(1) Psychotherapy

Individual and family therapy. Group therapy is also helpful.
(2) Behaviour Therapy
    Cognitive behaviour therapy.
(3) Drug therapy
    Fluoxetine (20-60 mg/day) is particularly useful as it decreases appetite and also treats co-morbid depression. Long-term treatment (>1 yr.) is necessary.

Prognosis is generally good, unless there is significant severe personality disorder.

Psychogenic Vomiting

Psychogenic vomiting is defined as vomiting without any organic pathology or medical reason, and which results from psychological mechanism.

Anxiety, depression and conversion disorder have mostly been found to be associated with the psychogenic vomiting.

Symptoms include absence of nausea, occurrence of vomiting usually after meal, and limited control over emesis.

Despite repeated vomiting weight loss is insignificant. Stressful life events induce acute exacerbations of vomiting.

The course of the disorder is usually chronic with frequent remissions and relapses.

Treatment

(1) Identification of psychological stressor.
(2) Educating the patient to cope with the stressful situation.
(3) Psychotherapy. Individual and family counselling.
(4) Anxiolytic and antiemetic drugs have a secondary place in management.

CHAPTER IX

SEXUAL DISORDERS

Sexual disorders can be classified into four groups.

(A) Gender Identity Disorders
(B) Psychological and Behavioural Disorders associated with Sexual Development and Orientation
(C) Disorders of Sexual Preference
(D) Sexual Dysfunctional Disorders.

A. Gender Identity Disorders

In this disorder the subject is confused with the identification of his own gender and wishes to achieve sexual features of the opposite sex.

These are of following subtypes :
1) Transsexualism
2) Dual role transvestism
3) Gender identity disorder of childhood.

Transsexualism

Transsexualism is a phenomenon when a person identifies him with a physical sex that is different to his own biological sex.

As a result of this, a consistent desire in the person's mind is formed to get rid of his primary anatomical sexual structures and secondary sexual features and to adopt the sexual features of opposite sex.

That means a person, born male wants to be a female and a female wants to be a male.

According to ICD-10, there are three diagnostic criteria for transsexualism.

(1) The desire to live and be accepted as a member of the opposite sex, usually accompanied by the wish to make his or her body as congruent as possible with the preferred sex through surgery and hormone treatment.

(2) The transsexual identity has been present persistently for at least two years.

(3) The disorder is not a symptom of another mental disorder or a chromosomal abnormality.

Transsexualism could be primary or secondary.

Primary Transsexualism

Primary transsexualism occurs in early childhood and has stable course over time.

Primary transsexuals are more consistent in their desire from the very beginning of their life, and are not variable. Their distress is more prominent and they are more insistent on their desire of changing their sexual structures and features according to the opposite sex.

Genetical factors play more significant role in case of primary transsexualism than environmental factors.

Secondary Transsexualism

The onset of secondary transsexualism is later in life compared to primary transsexualism. This is less severe form and the desire of the patient is less consistent (that is heterogeneous in desire).

Majority of these patients are male.

Environmental factors play more role in the psyche of the patients, than genetical factors.

Is transsexualism a mental disorder ?

There are a lot of recent controversies regarding this issue. Certain country like France has excluded transsexualism from the list of their mental diseases.

It depends on two factors, one environmental and another genetical.

Many environmental factors (that are heredity independent) are responsible for secondary transsexualism in all social order. Children and younger adults are more commonly vulnerable to the stress of this environmental factors which may trigger their overt expression to secondary transsexualism.

Bondage and Sado-Masochistic (BDSM) relationships are mainly responsible for this.

This relationship could be formed even in the same sex between teacher and student, employer and employee, dominant elderly and younger member in family, or in any other situation where one play a dominant role over the psyche of the other. There is established a strong sense of attachment or bondage from this relationship. And in this relationship recessive or dominated partner may grow the desire of being opposite sex to its dominant partner.

Follow-up studies have shown many children initially presented with indicators of gender identity disorder, but later in life their desires have gone. This is predominantly environmental, and cure may be ensued following correction of his environmental situation and proper therapy (psychotherapy, or behaviour therapy including aversion therapy).

But in case of Primary transsexualism, the cause lies in the genetical lineage. Genetical change through hormonal disturbance may promote to exhibition of transsexuality or homosexuality to a degree. But absolute primary transsexualism depends on the permanent change in the structure in brain. That is change in the brain's controlling area that determines sexual desire and activities (sexual act is a more psychic procedure).

Gender identity opposite to anatomical original sex structure results in from this change in brain structure. That means man and woman psyche are reversed opposite to body's structural composition.

Usually female sexuality is both common to male and female, which is determined by genes in X chromosome. Male sexuality is imposed which is determined by genes in Y chromosome.

These genes in Y chromosome not only determine the structural sexual features in a person, but also responsible for male psyche through specific structural changes in some centers of brain.

We know SRY gene in Y chromosome is responsible for the male's primary sexual structure formation, that is the development of testes, which in turn through differential hormonal action produces secondary sexual characters.

But male psyche is not controlled by SRY gene. In XX male syndrome, SRY gene is positive and X-Y interchange during meiosis appears to be the common cause of the disorder. But this interchange may or may not be associated with transfer of male psyche gene. Detailed psychological studies have not been done in XX male syndrome.

Male to Female (MTF) primary transsexuality can be occurred by dysfunction of male psyche gene in Y chromosome either by deletion, translocation, or mutation. Genes responsible for male psyche may be single or multiple in close proximity.

But female to male (FTM) primary transsexuality requires genetic recombination. Prevalence of MTF is higher than the FTM, also supports the fact.

Usually crossing over or recombination between X and Y chromosome is restricted to the pseudoautosomal regions, the regions which function for pairing of X and Y chromosomes and segregating them properly during the meiosis.

Pathogenic translocation between X and Y chromosome occurs in case of XX male syndrome, or XX true hermaphrodite, where sufficient genetic material from Y chromosome through translocation induces the development of testicular tissue. As these people are infertile recombinant chromosomes are never passed further.

But besides translocation or crossing over, gene conversion has also been evidenced between male specific region of the Y chromosome and X chromosome [Ref 72].

More research is needed with the sex chromosomes of transsexual persons. And that could explain the underlying cause of many gender identity disorders.

Most studies show overall psychological functioning and quality of life is better in the subjects of primary transsexualism who were treated, compared to those untreated. On the other hand various mental health problems, depression, anxiety, alcohol and drug abuse are common in the subjects untreated.

All these support the fact that defect lies in the mismatch of psyche and physique, but not in the psychological aberration. So the primary transsexualism may not be regarded as mental illness, and may be considered as quite natural taking his or her genetical make-up.

Sexual Reassignment Surgery (SRS) and Hormone therapy should be considered for them who want those to relieve them from their distress.

Treatment for Transsexualism

The treatment may be either Reconciliation with the Anatomical Sex or Gender Assignment Therapy.

(1) Reconciliation with the Anatomical Sex

This method is effective in secondary transsexualism. This could be done by

a) Individual psychological counselling or family counselling
b) Behaviour therapy (aversion therapy)
c) Management of stress, depression or other factors, if they are underlying.

(2) Gender Reassignment Therapy

This is indicated in the case of primary transsexualism. This comprises Hormonal Therapy and Sex Reassignment Surgery (SRS).

a) Hormonal Therapy

This is aimed at modifying their secondary sexual characteristics.

Detailed discussion with the patient covering the risk and benefits of hormonal therapy should be done before the start of the therapy.

Regular check-up for side effects and monitoring is necessary.

i) Female-to-Male hormonal therapy

It is provided to promote male characteristics, such as male muscularity, male voice, male arrangement of body hairs, and breast atrophy. The treatment also stops monthly menstruation.

Long-acting testosterone ester injection (e.g. testosterone enanthate or cypionate), testosterone gel or patches, or subcutaneoustestosterone implants are used.

ii) Male-to-Female hormonal therapy

It is provided to inhibit male characteristics and promote feminine characteristics, such as breast formation, reduction in body hair growth, thinning of the skin, and reduced muscle development.

Estrogens (e.g. estradiol valerate, estradiol cypionate, estradiol enanthate) and anti-androgen (e.g. finasteride or cyproterone acetate) are used.

b) Sex Reassignment Surgery (SRS)

SRS is an almost irreversible surgery. So before surgery

i) diagnosis of stable, long-standing primary transsexualism should be made.

ii) Proper psychological assessment to rule out any other mental abnormalities should be done.

iii) The subject may go through trial adaptation role through living as a member of the desired gender community for a period before surgery to assess his or her ability for future adjustment.

Sex Reassignment Surgery may be done in single or multiple stages. Standards of Care by WPATH (World Professional Association for Transgender Health) recommends one year hormonal therapy prior surgery.

Surgery includes :

a) For Male to Female

Penectomy, Orchidectomy, Labiaplasty, Tracheal Shave, Breast augmentation surgery, Laser hair removal.

b) For Female to Male

Hysterectomy with Oophorectomy, Metoidioplasty or Phalloplasty, Testicle implants, Mastectomy (breast removal surgery).

Hormone replacement therapy should be continued after surgery.

Dual role Transvestism

According to ICD-10 it has three criteria.

1. The individual wears clothes of the opposite sex in order to experience temporary membership in the opposite sex.
2. There is no sexual motivation for the cross-dressing.
3. The individual has no desire for a permanent change to the opposite sex.

Inter-sexuality

Intersexuality is not a primary mental disorder. There is gross anatomical and physiological alternations in the body, particularly with respect to sexual features either primary or secondary.

This include :

(1) Disorders of Chromosomal Sex

Klinefelter Syndrome :
(47 XXY or mosaic between 46XY/47XXY)
Features are : normal male, testes are small hyalinized, gynaecomastia (enlargement of breasts), infertility.

Turner Syndrome or Gonadal Dysgenesis :
(45X or mosaic of 46XX/45X or defect in X chromosome)
Features are : immature female, short stature, bilateral streak gonads, multiple congenital anomalies, primary amenorrhea.

True Hermaphroditism :
(46XX/46XY)

Features are : both an ovary and a testis or a gonad with histologic features of both (ovotestis) is present.

(2) Disorders of Hormonal Imbalance

Female pseudohermaphroditism :

Most common cause is congenital adrenal hyperplasia. Signs are : hypertrophy of clitoris, signs of virilization (coarsening of voice, frontal balding etc.).

Female internal structures and ovaries remain unaltered.

Male pseudohermaphroditism :

It may be due to abnormalities in androgen synthesis or abnormalities in androgen action (receptor disorders). Signs are : variable development of wolffian duct (from which develop male sex organs; epididymis, vas deferens, seminal vesicle, and ejaculatory duct).

(B) Psychological and behavioural disorders associated with Sexual Development and Orientation

(1) Sexual Maturation disorder

The subject is uncertain about his or her gender identity or sexual orientation, whether it is heterosexual, homosexual, or bisexual. Most commonly this occurs in adolescents, which often cause anxiety or depression. Sometimes after a period of apparently stable sexual orientation, the subject feels his or her sexual orientation is changing.

(2) Ego-dystonic Sexual Orientation

Here the gender identity or sexual orientation is not in doubt. But the subject wishes it were different, because of associated psychological and behavioural disorders, and may seek treatment to change it.

Homosexuality

On human rights ground, ICD-10 has excluded this from their list of mental disorders, and replaced it with Ego-dystonic sexual orientation, only where the subject seeks treatment or expresses a desire to develop heterosexual orientation.

Homosexuality is sexual attraction or behaviour between persons of the same sex. Female homosexuals are also called lesbians and male homosexuals are called gay.

However, homosexual behaviour is not uniform in all cases. In Kinsey scale, Heterosexuality-Homosexuality orientation has been graded as follows.

Grade	Description
0	Exclusively heterosexual
1	Predominantly heterosexual, only incidentally homosexual.
2	Predominantly heterosexual, but more than incidentally homosexual
3	Equally heterosexual and homosexual
4	Predominantly homosexual, but more than incidentally heterosexual
5	Predominantly homosexual, only incidentally heterosexual
6	Exclusively homosexual
X	No socio-sexual contacts or reactions

Homosexuality has different aetiological factors.

(1) genetical factors
(2) conditioning factors
(3) constitutional predisposition
(4) psychodynamic mechanisms
(5) influence of physiological and hormonal factors.

When we regard personality, we should remember that our personality is not 'all or none' phenomenon. As said earlier, women psyche is common to both men and women. Male psyche is imposed upon it. And either different genes or different level of expression of genes are responsible for it. So individuals show the personality in variable degrees between two extremities, in spite of their definitive primary and secondary sexual characteristics.

So one may be masculine female and another may be feminine male.

Different social and conditioning processes, playing upon this genetical pedestal, develop homosexual orientation in a particular person.

Treatment should be given to them whoever feels significant distress for their homosexual orientation and search for medical help.

Treatment includes :

(1) Psychotherapy
(2) Behaviour therapy
a) Aversion therapy

Aversion therapy is done by electrical shock or any painful stimuli or a nausea inducing drug, when the patient is confronted with photograph of nude or near nude attractive person of same sex.

Now the role of aversion therapy is very differential. It could be effective in the cases, where homosexuality has been developed through a conditioning process.

But the therapy, itself, acts as a conditioning process, where reason of homosexuality lies deeper, that is constitutional.

So the goal of the treatment should be objective, and based upon proper analysis.

The subject may be helped to be relieved from his guilt feelings, and social tension, and let to be adjusted to his homosexual orientation; and be helped to cope with work and surroundings to lead a reasonably worthwhile productive life.

b) Systemic desensitization therapy

If there is phobia for heterosexual relationship.

3) Antidepressant or anxiolytic – if there is associated depression or anxiety.

4) Hormone therapy (occasional).

(3) Sexual Relationship Disorder

Here the gender identity or sexual preference disorder is responsible for difficulties in establishing stable sexual relationship.

(C) Disorders of Sexual Preference

This is also called Paraphilias or sexual perversions or deviations. It has following three diagnostic criteria.

1. The subject experiences recurrent sexual urges and fantasies involving unusual objects or activities.

2. The subject either acts on the urges or is markedly distressed by them.

3. The preference has been present for at least 6 months.

Types include :

Masochism

The term came from the Austrian novelist Leopold Von SacherMasoch. He, after being whipped by his wife, used to be stimulated for his literary work.

The opposite of this phenomenon is named as Sadism.

In masochism, sexual gratification is obtained by the suffering of pain. Masochists get pleasure from being beaten, abused, tortured, humiliated, degraded, or dominated by their opposite sexual partners, and they tend to place themselves repeatedly in self-defeating positions.

They may even willingly expose themselves to severe bodily injuries to their partners.

Usually Sadism and Masochism are rarely found in pure state. They are found as a combination, where one partner dominates the other one. From this combination a special relationship of 'bondage' is developed.

They are found in all age groups and in all social levels.

In ICD-10 they have been conjointly classified as sadomasochism.

Generally mild degree of sadomasochistic stimulation is common in otherwise normal sexual activities. But it should be labelled as a disorder if this behaviour is persistent and become the only mode of sexual stimulation.

Fetishism

Here sexual arousal occurs by an inanimate object possessed by his or her loved one.

It is commonly seen in men. The object may be bra, underpants, handkerchief, shocks, shoes, or any other.

The subject may be sexually gratified by mere possessing it or touching and smelling it. Or he may masturbate in that object.

Exhibitionism

In this case, sexual arousal occurs by exposing one's external genitalia in public to an unsuspecting person, usually of opposite sex.

It is almost exclusively found in men. Sexual gratification occurs by attracting women in this act.

Relief occurs through masturbation.

Voyeurism

Here sexual gratification occurs by watching someone of opposite sex getting undressed, naked, or engaged in sexual activity; by peering, peeping, without making the observed person aware of this act.

This is almost seen in men, and relief occurs through masturbation.

Frotteurism

In this case, sexual gratification is achieved by rubbing against or touching the parts of an unsuspecting and non-consenting person of opposite sex, usually in crowded place, buses etc.

Here the victim may not protest, because she cannot prove, and for social embarrassment.

Paedophilia

This disorder occurs in a person, 16 years or older, who feels recurrent and intense sexual urges or fantasies and involves in sexual activity with a prepubescent child (generally age 13 or younger).

This may be associated with sadomasochistic relationship.

Bestiality

Bestiality is sexual intercourse by a human being with a lower animal.

The common animals are usually pet dogs, or farm animals like calves, sheep etc.

Zoophilia is sexual attraction and behaviour with animals. It is common in females, with household dogs or cats. The animal manipulates the genitalia with its mouth and actual coitus is very rare.

Partialism

Partialism is sexual attraction to a specific part of the body rather than genitalia.

For example,

Nasophilia : Here the person feels obsessive sexual attraction towards nose or nostrils.

The subject may desire to be watching, to be in contact, or manipulate the specific part; or he may desire to penetrate through nostrils.

Other types of partialisms are :

Podophilia - sexual attraction to foot
Occulophilia - eye
Maschalagnia - armpit
Mazophilia - breast
Pygophilia - butt

Alvinophilia - belly/navel.

Other Paraphilias

Necrophilia (sexual activities with dead bodies), Urophilia (sexual arousal with urine), Coprophilia (sexual arousal with faeces), Stigmatophilia (sexual arousal with body piercing, and tattoos).

Treatment of Paraphilias

(1) Psychotherapy
(2) Behaviour therapy
   Cognitive behavioral therapy is most helpful.
(3) Drug therapy
   Anti-androgens (Cyproterone acetate) or progestogen (Medroxyprogesterone acetate) are effective to reduce sexual drive. SSRIs are being used increasingly due to their relative lack of side effects. Antipsychotics have been used to treat dangerous or severe aggression associated with paraphilias.

(D) Sexual Dysfunctional Disorders

These are classified as :

1. Lack or loss of sexual desire
2. Sexual aversion and lack of sexual enjoyment
3. Failure of genital response
4. Orgasmic dysfunction
5. Premature ejaculation and delayed ejaculation
6. Non orgasmic vaginismus
7. Non orgasmic dyspareunia
8. Excessive sexual drive.

1. Lack or loss of sexual desire

Causes of lack or loss of sexual desire may be fear of pregnancy (in case of female), past unhappy experience of sexual activity, chronic medical illness, stress, marital disharmony, and due to side effects of some drugs. Abstinence from sex for a prolonged period of time, sometimes causes suppression of sexual impulses.

This disorder is more common in females.

2. Sexual aversion or lack of sexual enjoyment

Negative feelings and aversive attitude towards sexual activity may be developed by childhood traumatic and abusive experience, or similar experience in the past.

3. Failure of genital response

Male erectile disorder (Impotence)

Impotence is inability to get and maintain penile erection sufficient to complete satisfactory sexual activity.

Impotence may be primary or secondary. A person with primary impotence has never had an sufficient erection for sexual intercourse.

Secondary impotence occurs when there is loss of erectile response after a period of normal function.

The risk of secondary impotence increases with age.

There are a lot of medical diseases that may cause impotence particularly diabetes. Chronic medical illness, alcohol and tobacco use, obesity, prostate surgery, different drugs may cause impotence.

Excluding the biological factors, the psychological factors may count for impotence in following cases.

◻ Lack of knowledge or guilt feelings regarding the sexual act.
◻ Fear of failure or performance anxiety.
◻ Interpersonal relationship problem between the sexual partners.
◻ Inferiority complex.

¤ Underlying stress, depression, anxiety.

¤ Certain environmental factors, like unfamiliar surroundings, lack of privacy.

¤ Fear of damaging sexual partner.

Female sexual arousal disorder (Frigidity)

In this disorder, women feel difficulty in sexual arousal or maintaining the sexual arousal until the completion of the sexual activity.

It may result in inadequate vaginal lubrication during sexual act.

Life stresses, aging, menopause, deterioration of general health, medications, and marital discord or relationship problems are mostly responsible for female sexual arousal disorder.

4. Male and Female orgasmic dysfunction

(Male anorgasmia and Female anorgasmia)

Anorgasmia is inability or difficulty to achieve an orgasm during the process of sexual intercourse, despite sufficient initial sexual excitement.

In case of male, it presents as retarded ejaculation.

To understand what is orgasm, we will have to know first normal human sexual response cycle.

Human Sexual Response Cycle

Normal human sexual response cycle has four phases.

(1) Excitement phase

(2) Plateau phase

(3) Orgasmic phase

(4) Resolution phase

Excitement phase

It is the first phase of the cycle. In this phase following events occur.

In male : penile erection due to vasocongestion; elevation of testes with scrotal sac.

In female : erection of nipples; erection of clitoris; lubrication of vagina.

In both : increased muscle tension; skin flush; increased heart rate and blood pressure; accelerated breathing.

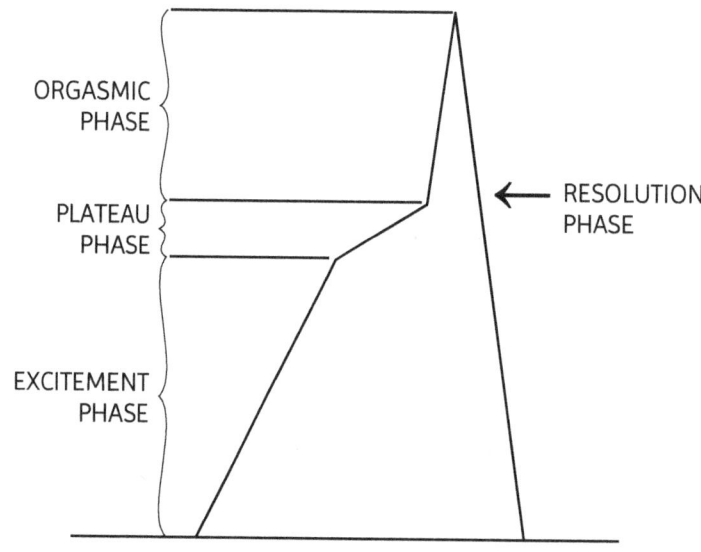

Fig. 39 : Human Sexual Response Cycle

Plateau phase

This is a very brief phase between excitement and orgasmic phase. In this phase following events occur.

In male : full engorgement of penis; elevation and enlargement of testes; appearance of few drops of transudate with spermatozoa on glans penis.

In female : retraction of clitoris under clitoral hood; engorgement of outer 1/3 of vagina with colour change; further increase in vaginal secretion.

Orgasmic phase

In this phase peak sexual excitement followed by release of sexual tension occurs. In this phase following events occur.

In male : contraction of prostrate, seminal vesicles, and vas deference so that semen and sperm can be discharged in the urethra; starting of ejaculation in spurts.

In female : contraction of urethra, cervix and lower 1/3rd of vagina.

In both : marked autonomic activity (heart rate, blood pressure reaches their peak); contraction of external and internal sphincters; quick rhythmic contractions of lower pelvic muscles; involuntary muscular spasms in other parts of the body; temporary brief clouding of consciousness.

Resolution phase

In this phase the body gradually returns to its original, unexcited state. Following events occur in this phase.

In both : sense of relaxation and general well being with enhanced intimacy and often feeling of fatigue; normalization of heart rate, blood pressure back to previous level; disappearance of sexual flush followed by perspiration; gradual diminution of vasocongestion in the sexual organs.

Refractory period for further orgasm in males vary from few minutes to many hours. But in case of females, there is actually no refractory period. Females are capable of reaching orgasm again from any point during resolution. Practically females have the potentiality to experience many orgasms during the whole intercourse process. But they may not always want it. Good understanding between the partners decreases the chance.

There are a number of medical diseases that may cause sexual dysfunction and anorgasmia both in male and female. Diabetes, peripheral vascular disease, multiple sclerosis, diseases of spinal cord, anterior temporal lobe lesion, are important.

Different drugs have their side effects of it too.

Psychological factors that has been stated under 'failure of genital response', may play their role here.

Recent study has also suggested genetical basis for female orgasmic dysfunctions.

5. Premature Ejaculation and Delayed Ejaculation

Premature Ejaculation : This is a disorder where ejaculation occurs either before the penetration or if penetration occurs before the partner can achieve orgasm.

It makes sex less enjoyable. In case of young inexperienced men, it may resolve in time. But in case of ongoing relationships, it greatly impacts in the relationship.

This disorder seldom has an organic cause. It is related with anxiety in sexual situation.

Delayed Ejaculation : In this disorder, the ejaculation is delayed or the male achieves ejaculation with great difficulty during coitus. A man with life long delayed ejaculation problem, can never ejaculate in time during partnered sexual activity. In acquired form of the disorder, it develops at a time after previously normal functioning.

There may be various causes of delayed ejaculation disorder. Spinal cord lesion and use of antidepressant drugs can cause ejaculation delayed. In other causes psychogenic factors dominates. Rigid, conservative family background may be responsible for life long delayed ejaculation problem, where the person perceives the sex as sinful. Use of excessive pornographic material may render a person suffer from delayed ejaculation when normal sexual activity takes place. In case of acquired disorder loss of attraction to the partner, demands for greater commitment by the partner, or unexpressed hostility towards the partner can play as psychogenic factors for delayed ejaculation.

6. Sexual disorders associated with pain

a) Non-orgasmic vaginismus

Vaginismus is due to spasm of the muscles surrounding the entrance of the vagina and adductor muscles of the thigh, which prevents full penetration.

It results from intense fear of penetration, even at the thought of intercourse, on the part of the woman. It is a conditioned response to previous imaginary or real frightening sexual experience.

b) Non-orgasmic dyspareunia

Dyspareunia means pain in the genital area during sexual intercourse on the part of either men or women.

Dyspareunia is more common in women. Causes are mostly organic ranging from infection, obstetrical trauma, scar, different local genital diseases including malignancy, endometriosis and adenomyosis.

When organic causes have been eliminated psychogenic possibility should be considered.

7. Excessive sexual drive

Sometimes there is exaggerated sexual desire in men and women. In case of men, it is known as satyriasis and in women, it is known as nymphomania.

Treatment

A. Treatment for hypoactive sexual disorder

a) Psychological Counselling : Either individual or couple counselling (couple counselling is better than individual counselling).

b) Behaviour therapy : Masters' and Johnson's dual sex therapy is most successful, where both of the couple are treated.

c) Mindfulness : Mindfulness is a technique where the patient is directed to focus on the present moment and nonjudgemental awareness of consciousness - that is accepting the present without judging or trying to change them. The patient is trained to focus on the moment and feel the awareness of sensations - visual, auditory, tactile, and olfactory, that he or she is experiencing at that moment. The aim is to make the patient concentrate on a focus, preventing distracting and judgmental thoughts. It has been helpful in treatment of sexual dysfunctions.

d) Treatment of underlying stress, anxiety, depression.

e) Treatment of underlying medical illness.

f) In a drug induced case, modification or change of the drugs, if possible.

g) Hormone therapy :

In case of female - Estrogen only or combined estrogen/progesterone for hysterectomised patients (undergone uterus removal surgery) and post menopausal women respectively.

Testosterone supplementation on short term basis for postmenopausal women. Systemic testosterone has various side effects. Transdermal testosterone patch has lesser side effects.

In case of male - Testosterone supplementation (if testosterone level is low).

h) Drug therapy :

Sildenafil (Viagra), Vardenafil, Tadalafil in case of men.

Recommended dose of Sildenafil 50-100 mg (for men >65 years 25 mg) one hour before intercourse.

Maximum dose frequency once a day.

These are contraindicated in patients of coronary heart disease and those taking nitrates. Caution is advised in presence of liver or kidney disease, peptic ulcer, bleeding disorders.

Flibanserin, a newer drug for premenopausal women, achieved approval by the US FDA in August 2015. Dose is 100 mg. once in a day at bedtime. It is serotonin 1A receptor agonist and serotonin 2A receptor antagonist. Women on flibanserin should be cautious about concomitant ingestion of alcohol. It has been reported to cause marked hypotension (low blood pressure) resulting in loss of consciousness after taking alcohol. Other side effects include mild to moderate nausea, dizziness, insomnia, drowsiness and dry mouth.

B. Treatment for male erectile dysfunction

a) Any organic cause, i.e. disease or surgery affecting blood supply of the penis should be excluded.

b) Psychotherapy for psychological factors (both of the couple counselling is better).

c) If it is due to side effects of medication which the patient is continuing, the dosage of the drug should be adjusted, or drug should be changed if alternative is available.

d) Drug therapy : Sildenafil (viagra), vardenafil; Papaverine or prostaglandin E1 injection into the penis prior to intercourse. Oral phentolamine and apomorphine are helpful as potency enhancers in minimal erectile dysfunction.

e) Vacuum constriction device (vacuum pump) to produce penile tumescence. Vacuum pump is a mechanical device that can be used by the patients suffering from vascular disease. The blood is drawn into the penis by the creation of vacuum and kept there by the use of a ring at the base of the penis. Semi-rigid or inflatable penile prostheses implantation are considered for those suffering from organic disease.

f) Bypass surgery of penile artery has been done in selected cases with some success where the cause of failure in penile erection is due to atherosclerosis or other blockage of artery.

g) Treatment should be done, if there is underlying stress, anxiety or depression.

C. Treatment for premature ejaculation and delayed ejaculation

For premature ejaculation Squeeze technique and Semans' technique are used.

Squeeze technique : Here the female partner helps her man to get an erection, and when the male partner feels the ejaculatory inevitability, he squeezes the penis on the coronal ridge, causing delayed ejaculation.

Semans' technique (stop-start technique) : The penis is stimulated to high arousal, but not to the ejaculation threshold. Then stimulation is stopped to subside the arousal. Repetition of the process is done 4-5 times until ejaculation is permitted.

Drug therapy :

Dapoxetin, a member of the SSRI drugs group, is used in premature ejaculation in men between 18-65 years of age. The dose is 30 to 60mg orally one to three hours before planned sexual activity only once a day.

For delayed ejaculation the male is advised to stimulate his penis extravaginally and then gradually enter into the vagina when the time of ejaculation is near. But medical cause and medication induced side effect should be ruled out first.

D. Treatment for vaginismus

a) Psychotherapy
b) Kegel's exercises to relax the pelvic floor muscles and muscles around vagina.
c) Vaginal vibrator under supervision.

E. Treatment for excessive sexual desire

a) Psychotherapy and behaviour therapy.
b) If it is secondary to mood disorder (e.g. mania), that should be treated.
c) Drug therapy : SSRIs; Anti-androgens (Cyproterone acetate) or progestogen (Medroxyprogesterone acetate).

CHAPTER X

PSYCHOLOGICAL THERAPIES

Psychotherapy is a mode of treatment where the therapist through communication between the patient and the therapist, tries to modify, remove, or retard patient's mental symptoms and disturbed pattern of behaviour and promotes positive personality, growth and development. In this type of treatment a deliberate professional relationship is fostered to be established between the patient and the therapist.

The way of communication in the treatment can be either verbal or non-verbal.

Psychotherapy is not new, and has been practiced in some form or other for thousands of years. Every culture has devised its individual ways of providing mental support, guidance and healing. Religious agencies, and spiritual advisors have also played a great role in it. But modern psychotherapy is based on more logistic, rational, and scientific approach and provided by the expert mental health care professionals in the related fields.

There are various forms of psychotherapies. These are :

(1) Supportive psychotherapy
(2) Group psychotherapy
(3) Hypnosis
(4) Psychoanalysis and psychoanalytic psychotherapy
(5) Family and marital therapy
(6) Behaviour therapy
(7) Cognitive Therapy or Cognitive Behaviour Therapy
(8) EMRD
(9) Biofeedback
(10) TRAM

Common ingredients of psychological treatment are :

Support factors	Learning factors	Action factors
Trust	Advice	Facing of fears and problems
Reassurance	Feedback	Mastery
Explanation	Insight	Working through
Acceptance	Rational exploration	Modeling
	Assimilation	Testing solutions
	Experiences	

Though there are various forms of psychotherapy, many therapies integrate more than one form of therapies.

Supportive Psychotherapy

Bloch (1979) describes supportive psychotherapy as a form of psychological treatment given to people with chronic and disabling psychiatric conditions for whom fundamental change is not a realistic goal. Gilbert and Ugelstad (1994) believe that the therapist's primary role in supportive psychotherapy is to support and strengthen the individual's potential for better and more mature ego functioning in both adaptational and developmental tasks. But the concept of supportive psychotherapy is still evolving.

In general agreement, supportive psychotherapy is any form of psychological treatment intended to relieve symptoms and help the patient to acquire a more sustained state of psychological well-being and psychological self-reliance, rather than attempt to change the subject's character structure.

Supportive psychotherapy is probably the most commonly used method to tackle with problems of emotional nature. The key factors in supportive psychotherapy are :

(1) Reassurance

(2) A thorough and detailed explanation to the patient of his illness focused on 'here and now'.

(3) Suggestion and guidance

(4) Direct advice

(5) Encouragement to achieve a more improved state of mind to carry on normal life and activities.

Here the clinician plays an important role. This is now recognised that mere interview can exercise a psychotherapeutic effect – that is the act of a doctor listening carefully to what the patient is saying and giving him a full account of his situation and problems, can result in significant improvement. Supportive psychotherapy includes guidance in various matters such as education, employment, financial crisis, health and social relationships, but it always let the subject to take the final decision.

In recent years, the value of ventilation of feelings based on old concept of catharsis, has been gaining more interest. The patients through expressing their emotions - fear, anger, sadness etc., can feel better and seek relief from their disturbed emotional state.

Group Psychotherapy

This therapy includes treatment of a number of persons, usually 6-10, experiencing and suffering from psychological problems of same nature. The persons are seated around a circle and after introduction, every one shares their experiences. Customarily the duration of group therapy is 1 - 1½ hours and held once or twice weekly. But group therapy is usually not advised for severely psychopathic personalities, persons in acute severe psychotic conditions, persons with low IQ or suffering from dementia.

The aim of group therapy is
(1) education and reorientation
(2) establishment of fellowship and spiritual strength
(3) guidance and practical advice
(4) socialization
(5) deeper analysis and understanding of the problems.

In group psychotherapy the therapist's task is :

(1) Establishing a therapy group :

To select the issue; to select the members of group; to prepare members for group therapy; deciding on time duration of each session and frequency of the sessions; to form appropriate goal.

(2) Constructing and maintaining a therapeutic environment :

To manage boundaries of the issue; allowing and cultivating free-floating discussions; using procedural aids as appropriate; locating and resolving common problems.

(3) Analysis and Interpretation :

To analyse transference issues and provide metaphorical constructions for defenses and resistances; to translate the language of unconscious (individual or group) behaviour to conscious behaviour. Here the therapist acts as both the therapist and a member of the group.

(4) Leadership activity :

To maintain therapeutic neutrality; to provide linking communications; to provide holding, containment and reflection; to clarify and confront with individuals; to attend omissions, avoidance and denial; to bring background events to foreground.

In group analytic psychotherapy developed by Foulks, all contribution come from the patients. Here the therapist retains a passive attitude equivalent to that of a psychoanalyst (described later).

Studies have shown that group therapy is more efficacious than individual therapy for higher intelligent individuals. But combination of group and individual psychotherapy is most effective for these patients.

Hypnosis

Hypnosis is a state of artificially induced increased suggestibility.

The term 'Hypnosis' was first used by James Braid in the 19th century. Later it was exclusively applied by Jean Martin Charcot (1825-1893) in France in the treatment of 'Hysteria'. Sigmund Freud and Josef Breuer was greatly influenced by his technique while working as students under him and thereafter started its practice in their treatment for mental patients also. But both Breuer and Freud noticed that during treatment, some female patients were falling in love with them. Both were alarmed by this but Freud soon realised that it was not for his personality, but the patient was taking him as a substitute for the person beloved to her. The love is being transferred to the physician and this process is known as 'transference'. Later Freud discontinued the practice of it and switched on to 'free association' where the patients were allowed to be relaxed on a couch and encouraged to tell everything that came into their minds.

The technique of 'hypnosis' aims at narrowing of the patient's concentration to the hypnotist. Though the condition may simulate sleep but physiologically it is different from sleep, for example, electroencephalographic recordings during hypnosed state are similar to those of the waking state. There are different levels of hypnosis, ranging from a light hypnotic state to deep trance. Not all the persons can be hypnotised and if hypnotized, cannot be to the same level. Though over 80% of general population can be hypnotised without difficulty, but only 10% reach deep hypnotic state.

Hypnotic Technique :

A variety of techniques are available for inducing 'hypnosis'. Following is an example of techniques used.

The subject is seated comfortably in a chair or lie down on a couch and encouraged to let his all muscles go loose and relaxed. Then the hypnotist asks the patient to pay attention to what he is saying. He then asks the patient to concentrate on his right and left hand consecutively and feel the sensations of touch coming from them. The patient is asked that as soon as he feels any movement in the thumb or fingers, to lift it up to indicate which one it is. Slight movements invariably occur and the subject lifts up the appropriate finger. This is then followed by suggestion that the hand and the arm are getting lighter and lighter and will rise upwards steadily to touch the forehead. As they rise, the patient gets sleepier. When the hand touches the forehead he goes into a deep sleep. The depth of hypnosis can then be further increased by asking the subject to count ten. By the time one has finished counting ten, he will be in a deep state of hypnosis.

Another technique is asking the subject to fix his vision on an object or a light source and giving suggestions that the eyelids are getting more and more tired and will close.

Following changes occur during hypnotic state :

(1) The person under hypnosis becomes highly suggestible to the commands of the hypnotist, without understanding their nature.

(2) Dissociation of a part of the body or emotions from the remainder may occur.

(3) There is a partial or complete amnesia (loss of memory) for the events happening during the hypnotic state.

(4) Post-hypnotic suggestion can be given to the subject just after the trance and it is followed by the subject.

The use of 'hypnosis' in the psychological treatment (hypnotherapy) has been applied in various disorders – Psychosomatic disorders, Conversion disorders (hysteria), dissociative disorders, eating disorders (anorexia nervosa and bulimia nervosa), habit disorders (smoking), pain management, anxiety disorders, sleep disorders, irritable bowel syndrome, post traumatic stress disorder, phobias. Besides medical uses, 'hypnosis' has also been used in education, sports, forensics, military services and for entertainment.

The objective of the hypnotherapy is :

(1) to resurface underlying conflicts and problems, and to facilitate recall of forgotten experiences which may be important.

(2) to abreact past experiences.

(3) to modify symptoms and mental attitudes to enable the patient to adopt a more healthy and socially acceptable norm of life.

Psychoanalysis and Psychoanalytical psychotherapy

Psychoanalysis was developed from the work of Sigmund Freud in the late 19th century. Later the method and ways of psychoanalytic interpretation has been worked through and modified by a number of workers like Curl Jung, Alfred Adler, Otto Rank, Harry Stack Sullivan, Melanie Klein and many others.

The principal aim of psychoanalysis is gradual removal of amnesias that was rooted in early childhood and the emotions attached with it being suppressed, on the assumption that when all the gaps in the memory have been filled up, the person will no longer need to be fixated at the past.

Freudian psychoanalysis typically needs 3-5 visits in a week and carried out over a period of 3-5 years.

During each session the patient is let lie on a couch relaxed and allowed to talk freely when the therapist remains out of his vision. Through this 'free association', the patient is encouraged to uncover his feelings, past experiences, problems and conflicts, and his wishes and impulses. Early therapy was based on the fact that suppression of motivation forces or innate drive such as sexual drive or libido which the subject is partially or completely unaware of, results in development of symptoms either physical or mental. Treatment is aimed at giving the patient an awareness or insight into these underlying conflicts and suppression which can be modified or resolved.

Interpretation is the pivotal factor in this therapy. But it is not any dogmatic theory by the therapist, rather it is used as a suggestion or tentative hypothesis, which the patient is allowed to consider either to agree or reject it. Another basis of this therapy is 'transference'. Through the established professional relationship the patients transfer their feelings and emotions - love, anger, fear, towards their therapist. In psychoanalytic therapy 'transference' is used as an important tool to understand an individual's feelings, difficulties and problems with relationships.

Analysis of dream is another important factor to consider in psychoanalytic treatment. Freud says, "interpretation of dreams is the royal road to the knowledge of the unconscious activities of the mind". According to him, dream represents the conflicts, fears, desires, unfulfilled wishes often related to repressed childhood memories or obsessions that had been undercovered in unconscious mind.

Defence mechanisms

Defense mechanisms are psychological strategies which are used to protect an individual from unbearable emotional distress. The defence mechanisms are evoked automatically without conscious control, but can be triggered by the psychological measures aimed at coping with stressful situation and adjusting with the reality. Even the normal individuals use defence mechanisms in some time or other. But the excessive use of any one or more defence mechanisms emphasizes the subject's suffering on a neurotic or psychotic state.

The defence mechanisms can be :

(1) Narcissistic or psychotic,

(2) Immature or neurotic and

(3) Mature.

Some of the commonly used defense mechanisms are --

Narcissistic or Psychotic :

These defence mechanisms are usually found as a part of a psychotic process, but they may also occur in children and in adult's fantasies. Like,

Regression - Reverting to the modes of psychological functioning which were characteristics of earlier stages of life.

Denial - Denying unpleasant or painful reality.

Projection - Internal anxiety or urges are attributed to an outside cause.

Immature or Neurotic :

These are commonly found in apparently normal and healthy individuals as well as neurotic disorders. Like,

Conversion - A repressed, forbidden feeling is expressed through some symbolic somatic disturbance as in conversion disorder (hysteria).

Displacement - Transference of an emotion from its original object or event onto a less threatening or more acceptable object or event.

Undoing - Unconsciously motivated acts to counteract unacceptable thoughts and impulses as in compulsive acts in obsessive compulsive disorders.

Mature :

These mechanisms are found in normal and healthy individuals throughout the life time. They are socially adaptive and useful in integration of personal needs and motives. Like,

Sublimation - Expression of socially unacceptable impulses or urges through socially acceptable behaviour pattern, such as forbidden sexual impulses into artistic paintings.

Anticipation - Thinking and planning for future to avoid difficult emotional state.

Altruism - Meeting one's own emotional needs by helping others.

Humor - Diffusing difficult emotional situation with seeing funny side of it.

Psychoanalytic psychotherapy :

Psychoanalytic psychotherapy is based on fundamental themes of psychoanalysis, but designed to expand its scope. The techniques vary widely from using explorative method (uncovering, interpretative, evocative) to adopting supportive method (suggestive, suppressive etc.). But all the treatment protocols maintain the common axis that it is insight-oriented psychotherapy.

Unlike psychoanalysis, here the patient and the therapist meet in face-to-face encounters. But 'free association' is encouraged. The therapy may take several months to several years, at times taking time as long as psychoanalysis.

Family and Marital Therapy

In family and marital therapy the focus of the treatment is laid not on the individual, but on the family as a unit or on the couple as a marital unit. Both family and marital therapy aims at some changes in relational functioning along with specific changes in individual functioning. The concept of a family with interpersonal relationships and role assignments among its members is not constant and varies in different cultures and societies. The therapy is targeted to fulfill individual goals as well as the goal of the family system.

The indications of family and marital therapy are wide, but whenever there is relational difficulties within the family or marital unit, the treatment should be sought for.

Many models of family therapy exist, such as McMaster model, Circumplex model, Bowen model, Darlington's model, General System model, Psychodynamically oriented model and others. None of them is superior to others, their use depends on clinician's choice and expertise in practice of the particular one.

The types of marital therapies include individual therapy, supportive marital therapy, conjoint therapy, combined therapy, group therapy and psychoanalytical therapy.

Sex therapy though different from marital therapy, should be considered conjointly in the treatment as in many cases sexual dysfunctions and disharmony in sexual relationship affect the marital relation also.

Behaviour Therapy

Behaviour therapy is a form of psychotherapy based on learning and aimed at changing maladaptive behaviour to an adaptive one.

A majority of behaviour therapy is based on operant conditioning model, that is a reward (positive reinforcement) or punishment (negative reinforcement) are linked with the behaviour for conditioning the behaviour in direction of achieving the desired adaptation.

Behaviour therapy is a short duration therapy and cost effective. Usual duration of therapy is 6-8 weeks.

Some important behaviour therapies are :

(A) Systematic Desensitization

It was introduced by Wolpe (1958), based on the principle of counterconditioning and most often used in the treatment of phobias. In this treatment the subject is gradually exposed to anxiety provoking object or situation and overcomes fear by learning through relaxation technique. A hierarchy of feared situations are set. For example, if the patient is suffering from acrophobia (the fear of height), the treatment starts from looking down from second floor to gradually looking down from the topmost floor of a skyscraper. The patient is taught relaxation techniques at exposure to feared object and when he is able to experience a anxiety-free state, next step in the hierarchy is climbed. The treatment is concluded when the patient faces the maximum level without anxiety.

A variety of relaxation methods have been developed since ancient times, like yoga, zenbuddhism, transcendental meditation, but Wolpe advocated progressive relaxation technique developed by Edmund Jacobson and it is mostly used in this therapy. The patients are trained to relax different groups of muscles in sequential order starting from feet to face.

Adjunctive use of drugs like anxiolytics or benzodiazepines has also been practiced to help relaxation, but the drugs should be used cautiously and only by the clinicians who are well experienced with the adverse effects of those. Drugs could also develop dependency on the drugs.

Along with phobia, this therapy has also been applied in the treatment of obsessive compulsive disorders and other anxiety related disorders.

(B) Flooding

This is also used in the treatment of phobias but here no hierarchy is maintained. The patient is directly exposed to the object of phobia and escape is made impossible. Through prolonged coexistence with the object of phobia along with the therapist's guidance and encouragement, the patient becomes gradually adapted to the situation and his anxiety slowly diminishes. Each session lasts for at least one hour. In a variant of this therapy, known as Imaginal flooding, the feared object is confronted only in imagination, not in real life. This treatment is however contraindicated where intense fear could be detrimental to the patient's health, like for the patients suffering from heart diseases.

(C) Aversion therapy

Aversion therapy is based on the principle of classical conditioning and involves pairing of an aversive stimulus with the unwanted behaviour. This aversive stimulus may be nausea stimulating drug (emetics), electrical shock and other stimulus inducing physical pain. For example, pairing a nausea stimulating drug with drinking of alcoholism in the treatment of alcoholism. This method is more powerful when the same physiological system is used. In this case both nausea and drinking involves gastro-intestinal system. One of the drawback of this method is classical conditioning tends to weaken over time in absence of repeated pairing. So the booster session is needed at time gaps to prevent the relapse.

Aversion therapy has been used in the treatment of alcohol and drug addiction, paraphilias, habit and impulse disorders like, pathological gambling, kleptomania etc.

Cognitive Therapy or Cognitive Behaviour Therapy (CBT)

Cognitive behaviour therapy is a type of therapy which is aimed at changing the pattern of thinking that is the underlying basis of the subject's mental distress and maladaptive behaviour.

Cognitive system (or information processing) intricately ties thoughts with other emotional and behavioural responses. According to Aaron T Beck, upon whose theory the cognitive therapy developed, the cognitive appraisal of internal or external stimuli influences these other systems also, making a cognitive triad of thoughts, emotions and behaviour. Cognitive therapy targets to correct the distortion of this triad to obtain a more adaptive and sustainable form.

Cognitive therapy is not the replacement of negative thoughts with the positive ones, rather it focuses on shifting the cognitive appraisal of stimuli from ones which are unhealthy and maladaptive to those which are evidence-based and adaptive.

Cognitive therapy rests on three main propositions :

(1) the access hypothesis - With appropriate training, motivation, and attention, the persons can identify the content and pattern of their thinking.

(2) The mediation hypothesis - The manner in which the persons think about, interpret and construe events influences their emotional and behavioural responses also.

(3) The change hypothesis - The persons can, on their own will, modify and change their thoughts and behavioural responses to adapt with the situations they face.

Cognitive behaviour therapy is time limited, structured and problem oriented.

Average length of cognitive behaviour therapy is between 12 to 24 weeks, with once-weekly meetings.

The cognitive therapist's approach includes four basic steps :
  (1) Eliciting automatic thoughts,
  (2) Testing automatic thoughts,
  (3) Identifying maladaptive underlying assumptions, and
  (4) Testing the validity of maladaptive assumptions.

The automatic thoughts are so called because they are habitual and reflexive that we make to ourselves not necessarily being fully conscious about it. Suppose someone did not say a 'Hello' when passed by and one thought he stopped liking him and felt a sinking sensation. In testing automatic thoughts, the therapist helps the patient to check the validity of the automatic thought. As the therapist and the patient continue to identify the automatic thoughts of the patient through collaborative empiricism (where the therapist and the patient act as coinvestigators), the pattern of the patient's thinking ultimately becomes apparent. And this pattern may represent the maladaptive assumptions that rule and guide the patient's life. For example, 'As he does not like me, my life is worthless.' In testing the validity of maladaptive assumptions, the therapist again urge the patient to check the validity of the assumption, like 'Why is he so important to you?'

The cognitive therapist's task is to help the patient to identify automatic thoughts which are responsible for his or her distress, challenge the validity of the automatic thoughts and maladaptive assumptions providing substitute alternative interpretations and correct the cognitive distortion which leads to the subject's distressful life. But the therapist should ask the patients to test their thinking through their own observations and experiments, rather than persuasions.

Homework assignments are an important component of cognitive behaviour therapy. It helps the patients to acquire mastery and skill from what they learned in weekly session by applying them in real world.

Another important work-up that helps the patients to evaluate the progress, is Daily records of thoughts (DRT). It consists of three columns representing – the situations encountered; emotions or symptoms experienced; and the resulting thoughts.

The final sessions of the treatment are concentrated on consolidation of skills which are learned, and prevention of relapse or recurrence.

Cognitive behavioral technique is similar in the process, designed to change the maladaptive behaviours to adaptive ones.

The cognitive therapy can be used alone or in conjunction with medications in the treatment of depression. Though the cognitive therapy was devised initially for the treatment of depression, but now it is applied to a number of other psychological disorders. It has been found to be effective in the treatment of anxiety disorders, personality disorders, substance use disorders, eating disorders, post traumatic stress disorder, obsessive compulsive disorders, schizophrenia and many others.

Interpersonal Psychotherapy

Interpersonal psychotherapy is a structured, time limited (12 - 20 sessions over a period of 4 to 5 months) psychotherapy based on resolving interpersonal problems and symptomatic recovery by improving the quality of the patient's current interpersonal relations and social functioning.

The concept of IPT dates back in the works of Harry Stack Sullivan (1953), according to whom psychotherapy includes study of a person along with the people surrounding him - society and individual as an unit - rather than focusing exclusively on a single individual mind.

IPT first appeared as the control treatment for studies investigating the efficacy of antidepressant medications (Klerman et al., 1984). Like many fortuitous findings in science, IPT was found to be of comparable efficacy to medication in these studies and was used initially like CBT, for the treatment of depression.

But later on, it was found to be effective in other medical disorders also, like bulimia nervosa and substance use disorders.

The curriculum of the therapy is divided into three phases :
(1) Initial phase (2) Middle phase and (3) Terminal phase.

The initial phase (sessions 1-5) :

Initial phase is devoted to the establishment of professional relationship between the patient and the therapist, identifying the problem areas of the patient along with the patient's interpersonal problem areas and setting the goal for the treatment.

There could be four areas from which the problems for the patient can emanate :

(1) grief reaction,
(2) interpersonal disputes,
(3) role transition, and
(4) interpersonal deficits.

Interpersonal disputes : This may be due to domestic violence, verbal abuse, betrayals, infidelity, impropriety, conflicting loyalties, unmet expectations at work or school.

Role transition : The person recognizes the need to cope with a normative role transition but finds difficulty to make necessary changes required to adopt the new role. Difficulty in coping with role transitions may occur in –

Situational role transition e.g., job loss, migration, promotion;

Relationship role transition e.g., marriage, divorce, loss of parents;

Illness related role transition e.g., diagnosis of chronic illness, adaptation to physical disabilities;

Post-event role transition e.g., post traumatic state, refugee status etc.

Interpersonal deficits : The person due to interpersonal deficit (or sensitivity) finds difficulties in formation and maintenance of relationships and often gets socially isolated and lonely.

Middle phase (sessions 6-15) :

The middle sessions of the treatment constitute the 'work' of the treatment. It is directed towards resolving the problem area or areas. Clarifying positive and negative feeling states, identifying past models for relationships, guiding and encouraging the patient in examining and choosing alternative course of action constitute the basic techniques for solving each problem area.

Terminal phase (sessions 16-20) :

Terminal phase of the treatment is focused on consolidating the gains made during the treatment and preparing the patient for future work on their own. IPT, contrary to traditional psychoanalytical method, does not hold the idea that end of the treatment concludes in severing the relationship between the therapist and the patient. It is often agreed that after the initial treatment is over as specified by the contract, the patient will continue to keep therapeutic contact as necessary, and have further visit via new negotiated contract. In the following contacts the therapist should review the progress and give necessary positive feedback as possible. For that, IPT is regarded as two-stage treatment, one is the initial intense stage, which is followed up by a maintenance stage providing guidance to prevent relapse or recurrence.

Along with cognitive behaviour therapy, IPT has found a definite place in modern psychotherapy and is used to treat a wide range of mental disorders as many of our psychological illnesses are based on problems arising from interpersonal relationships.

Eye movement desensitization and reprocessing therapy (EMDR)

EMDR is based on the idea that inducing saccadic eye movements (rapid oscillation of the eyes that occur when a person follows an object) while a person imagining or thinking about a past anxiety evoking event, results in a decrease of his anxiety and alleviates his disturbed mental state.

Eye movement desensitization and reprocessing therapy was developed by Francine Shapiro. In 1987 Shapiro made a chance observation that moving her eyes from side to side appeared to reduce the anxiety and disturbance of her mind that she was experiencing from a traumatic life event. After further research and randomised control studies with trauma victims, ultimately she developed this form of therapy for the patients suffering from post traumatic stress disorders.

EMDR is an eight-phased treatment. In the first three phases, history and treatment planning, preparation and assessment are accomplished. In the fourth phase desensitization of traumatic experience is done. Here the clinician induces saccadic eye movements while the person is imagining the traumatic event. For example, the clinician moves his fingers back and forth approximately 25 cm in front of the patient's eye asking the patient to follow the movements of the finger. After approximately 20 back and forth eye movements the clinician stops and asks the patient to go off the memory. Then the clinician asks the patient to provide feedback if there is any change in the traumatic image, body sensations, emotions or thoughts about the self. The process is repeated until the image of the traumatic event fades off. In the 5th phase a positive cognition is installed in the patient's mind - like 'I am now in control'. The goal of this stage is to make the patient accept the full truth of his or her positive self-statement. In the sixth stage (body scan), after the positive cognition has been installed, the clinician asks the patient to bring the original traumatic event to mind and check for any residual tension in his or her body. If so, these physical sensations are then targeted for reprocessing. In the following phases closure and reevaluation of therapy are conducted.

Shapiro first applied EMDR therapy for the patients suffering from post traumatic stress disorder. Later it had been applied for the therapy of phobia also. But there is controversy about the therapy as whether the eye movements are necessary for the treatment or not. And it has been postulated that EMDR works because it is an accelerated form of behaviour exposure and cognitive reprocessing. However after several meta-analystic studies, it has been concluded that EMDR is as effective as cognitive behaviour therapy or drug treatment in the treatment of post traumatic stress disorder.

Biofeedback

Biofeedback comes from the idea that autonomic nervous system can come under voluntary control through operant conditioning. As I have already said in my first chapter that the mind's conscious and subconscious faculties have also extensions in the involuntary mechanisms of the body, like 'fear' produces accelerated heart rate. So if a person is provided feedback of his involuntary actions of his body, he can change his emotional state to alter the involuntary actions which is being resulted from his emotional state. And through relaxation processes the subject can learn to control voluntarily the expression of the physical symptoms of his disturbing mental state. To think deeply it is a desensitization process for those inner disturbed feelings which the person was properly unaware of.

The feedback instruments used depends on the patient's specific problem. The most effective instruments that are used are –

(1) EEG (Electroencephalogram) : It records the electrical waves from the brain during sleep and awake state. There are different wave patterns (Fig. 16, Chapter 4, Part I) recorded in EEG in sleep, tensed and relaxed awake mental states. Variations of these waves are associated with different psychological and medical disorders.

(2) ECG (Electrocardiogram) : It records heart rate, rhythm, axis and the nature of cardiac complexes including the intervals between them. During stress, anxiety, panic state, asthma, chronic obstructive pulmonary disease (COPD) and different heart diseases all of them may vary.

(3) EMG (Electromyogram) : It measures the electrical potentials of muscle fibers.

(4) Galvanic Skin Response (GSR) gauge : It shows skin conductivity. Skin conductivity decreases during a relaxed state.

(5) Thermistor : It measures skin temperature. Skin temperature drops during tension because of peripheral vasoconstriction.

(6) Pneumograph : It estimates respiratory rate, and expansion and constriction of the chest during respiration. It is used to detect respiratory rate and altered breathing pattern which occur in anxiety, panic state, asthma and COPD.

Patients are attached to one of these instruments and provided feedback measurements of their physical condition through audible or visual signals, so that the patients can assess their responses and can gain control over them through relaxation processes.

Relaxation is characterised by (1) Immobility of the body. (2) Control over the focus of attention. (3) Low muscle tension. (4) Cultivation of a specific frame of mind.

Patients are reminded that relaxation involves no efforts, because making an effort would make them tense and that is not relaxation. In often more than 50 sessions, the patient works on different muscle groups till he experiences his whole body seems to be perfectly relaxed. Relaxation breathing exercises are helpful in panic disorder where the patient learns to control his breathing which is exacerbated during panic attacks.

Applied tension : Applied tension is a technique that is opposite to the relaxation process. Here the patient learn to contract a specific group of muscles for a period of time till he feels warmth develop in his face. The patient is then asked to release tension. The patient is provided feedback measurement of blood pressure as the blood pressure rises during contraction of muscles. Increased blood pressure informs the patient that appropriate muscle tension has been achieved. Applied tension has been used to counteract the fainting responses that occur in panic disorder and phobia.

Biofeedback, relaxation therapy and applied tension have been shown to be effective in a wide range of psychological disorders including different medical conditions such as phobias, anxiety and panic disorders, migraine, tension headaches, fecal and urinary incontinence, asthma, chronic obstructive pulmonary disease (COPD), cardiac arrhythmias, temporomandibular joint stiffness, idiopathic hypertension and orthostatic hypotension.

Therapeutic Reprocessing of Association of Memory (TRAM)

This is my own conceived idea and had not been practised widely. This therapy can be applied for phobia and also any other emotional disorders. The main concept of this therapy is our emotions are aroused by the sight or thought of an object, person or situation by a group of embedded memories associated with that object, person or situation. This embedded set of associated memories evokes stimulation at a particular point on an emotion scale away from the adaptive range when a person feels that particular emotion. It can evoke responses on more than one emotion scale, depending on the emotive memories included in that set of association. For example, one can feel 'fear' and 'disgust' after watching an object. Now if this stimulation occurs too much negativewards on any scale of emotion, we feel difficulties to cope with it. That is what occurs in phobia, but it may occur with any other emotion also besides 'fear'.

It can be successfully treated if we can deliberately change this association of memories. Attaching pleasurable memories with the object, person or situation to overweigh the unpleasurable memories.

It should be remembered that TRAM is not positive reinforcement, but it is reprocessing of association of memories, so that a particular set of memories can be altered where the memories of undesirable emotional experiences are overweighed by desirable and pleasurable emotional experiences.

Even in practical life anyone can try on this thing. For example, a certain person, owing to some awkward incident, made himself an object of laughter to my mind. Afterwards whenever I saw him, I could not check myself from laughing. It was embarrassing to both me and him, because he could feel it. To counter balance my reaction, I decided to sit down with him and talk on some serious subjects. I did it and it exposed his inner personality, knowledge, seriousness of mind. It altered my associated memories about him and I stopped laughing at the sight of him.

—————————O—————————

References

1. The ICD -10 Classification of Mental and Behavioural Disorders : Clinical descriptions and diagnostic guidelines. Geneva, World Health Organization, 1992.

2. DSM - 5 : Diagnostic and Statistical Manual of Mental Disorders, Fifth Edition, 2013. American Psychiatric Association.

3. Plato : Philebus.

4. Aristotle : De Anima, Book III, Ch. 3 & Ch. 9.

5. Philosophy of Mind - Ancient and Medieval. Science Encyclopedia, 2015.

6. 'Samkhya Hinduism'. EncyclopaediaBrittanica, 2015.

7. en.wikipedia.org/wiki/ancient_egyptian_concept_of_the_soul.html, 2015.

8. en.wikipedia.org/wiki/history_of_psychology.html, 2015.

9. 'Rene Descartes' by Richard A Watson. EncyclopaediaBrittannica, 2015.

10. Descartes and Pineal gland. Stanford Encyclopedia of Philosophy, Stanford University, 2015.

11. Morgan Clifford T, King Richard A & others : Introduction to Psychology. McGraw-Hill Education, 1986.

12. Keller Fred S, Schoenfeld William N : Principles of Psychology. Appleton-Century-Crofts, 1950.

13. Hebb Donald O : Textbook of Psychology. W. B. Saunders, Philadelphia, 1972.

14. Hunter Ian M L : Memory Facts and Fallacies. Pelican, 1962.

15. Ellis J R : Methods of learning and Techniques of teaching. Pitman, 1962.

16. Schacter Daniel L and others : Psychology. Worth Publishers, 2014.

17. Barrett Kim E and others : Ganong's Review of Medical Physiology. 24th Ed., McGraw-Hill Education, 2012.

18. Guyvon Arthur C, Hall John E : Textbook of Medical Physiology. 13th Ed., W. B. Saunders 2015.

19. Coren Stanley, Ward Lawrence M, Enns James T : Sensation and Perception. 6th Ed., Wiley, 2003.

20. Gleitman Henry, Gross James, Reisberg Daniel : Psychology. 8th Ed., W. W. Norton & Company, 2010.

21. Karama S and others : Positive association between cognitive ability and cortical thickness in a representative US sample of healthy 6 to 18 years-olds. Intelligence, 2009 March-April; 37(2) : 145 - 155.

22. Narr K L And others : Relationships between IQ and regional cortical gray matter thickness in healthy adults. Cerebral Cortex, 2007 Sep; 17(9) : 2163 - 2171.

23. Choi Y Y and others : Multiple cases of human intelligence revealed by cortical thickness and neural activation. Journal of Neuroscience, 2008 Oct, 28(41) : 10323 - 10329.

24. Adolphs R, Tranel D, Damasio H, Damasio AR : Fear and the human amygdala. Journal of Neuroscience, 1995; 15(9) : 5879 - 5891.

25. De Bellis MD and others : A pilot study of amygdala volumes in pediatric generalized anxiety disorder. Biological Psychiatry, 2000; 48(1) : 51 - 57.

26. Frodle T and others : Larger amygdala volumes in first depressive episode as compared to recurrent major depression and healthy control subjects. Biological Psychiatry, 2003; 53(4) : 338 - 344.

27. Tebartz van Elst L and others : Amygdala enlargement in dysthymia - a volumetric study of patients with temporal lobe epilepsy. Biological Psychiatry, 1999; 46(12) : 1614 - 1623.

28. Vyas A and others : Enhanced anxiety and hypertrophy in basolateral amygdala neurons following chronic stress in rats. Annals of the New York Academy of Sciences, 985 : 554 - 555.

29. Vyas A and others : Chronic stress induces contrasting patterns of dendritic remodeling in hippocampal and amygdaloid neurons. Journal of Neuroscience, 2002 Aug; 22(15) : 6810 - 6818.

30. Williams C L and others : Hypertrophy of basal forebrain neurons and enhanced visuospatial memory in perinatally choline-supplemented rats. Brain Research, 1998 Jun; 794(2) : 225 - 238.

31. www.stanfordbinet.net/stanfordbinettest.html

32. Kaufman Alan S : IQ Testing 101. Springer Publishing Company, 2009.

33. Strachey James (Editor and translator) : The Standard Edition of the Complete Psychological Works of Sigmund Freud. Vintage, 1999.

34. Longo Dan L, Kasper Dennis L and others : Harrison's Principles of Internal

Medicine. Vol 1 & 2, 18th Ed., McGraw Hill Medical, 2012.

35. Brain R Walker and others : Davidson's Principles and Practice of Medicine. 22nd Ed., Churchill Livingstone, 2014.

36. Sadock James B, Sadock Virginia A, Ruiz P : Kaplan &Sadock's Synopsis of Psychiatry, Behavioral Sciences/Clinical Psychiatry. 11th Ed., Wolters Kluwer, 2015.

37. Oswald Ian : Sleep. Penguin Books, 1966.

38. Turek F W, Zee PC (editors) : Regulation of Sleep and Circadian Rhythms. Marcel Dekker, 1999.

39. Darwin Charles : The Expression of the Emotions in Man and Animals. John Murray, 1872.

40. Shaw P, Greenstein D and others : Intellectual ability and cortical development in children and adolescents. Nature, 2006 Mar; 440(7084) : 676 - 679.

41. Schlaug G : The brain of musicians. A model for functional and structural adaptation. Ann N Y AcadSci, 2001 Jun; 930 : 281 - 299.

42. Schlaug G, Jancke L, Huang Y and others : Increased Corpus Callosum size in musicians. Neuropsychologia, 1995 Aug; 33(8) : 1047 - 1055.

43. Schlaug G, Jancke L, Huang Y, Steinman H : In vivo evidence of structural brain asymmetry in musicians. Science, 1995 Feb; 267(5198) : 699 - 701.

44. Gaser C and Schlaug G : Gray matter differences between musicians and nonmusicians. Ann N Y AcadSci, 2003 Nov; 999 : 514 - 517.

45. Bangert M and Schlaug G : Specialization of the specialized in features of external human brain morphology. European Journal of Neuroscience, 2006 Sep; 24(6) : 1832 - 1834.

46. Niraj Ahuja : A short text book of Psychiatry. 7th Ed., Jaypee Brothers Medical Publishers (P) Ltd., 2011.

47. Vyas J N and Ghimire Shree Ram (Editors) : Textbook of Postgraduate Psychiatry. Vol. 1 & 2, 3rd Ed., Jaypee Brothers Medical Publishers (P) Ltd., 2016.

48. SadockBenjamine J, Sadock Virginia A, Ruiz P : Kaplan &Sadock's Comprehensive Textbook of Psychiatry. Vol. 1 & 2, 9th Ed., Lippincott, Williams & Wilkins, 2009.

49. Gelder Michael G, Andreasen Nancy C and others (Editors) : New Oxford Textbook of Psychiatry. Vol. 1 & 2, 2nd Ed., Oxford University Press, 2012.

50. Rees W L Linford : A Short Textbook of Psychiatry. 3rd Ed., The English Language Book Society and Hodder & Stoughton, 1981.

51. David Semple and Roger Smyth : Oxford Handbook of Psychiatry. 3rd Ed., Oxford University Press, 2013.

52. Tripathi K D : Essentials of Medical Pharmacology. 7th Ed., Jaypee Brothers Medical Publishers (P) Ltd., 2013.

53. Mayer-Gross W, Slater E, Roth M : Clinical Psychology. 3rd Ed., Bailliere, Tindall &Cassell, 1969.   54. Hamilton Max : Fish's Schizophrenia. 3rd Ed., John Wright, 1984.

55. Torrey E Fuller : Surviving Schizophrenia. A manual for Families, Patients, and Providers. 5th Ed., Quill, 2006.

56. Picchioni Marco M and Murray Robin M : Schizophrenia. British Medical Journal, 2007 Jul; 335 (7610) : 91-95.

57. Velligan Dawn I, Alphs Larry D : Negative Symptoms in Schizophrenia : An Update on Identification and Treatment. Psychiatric Times, Nov 24, 2014.

58. Shenton M E, Whitford T J, Kubicki M : Structural neuroimaging in schizophrenia : from methods to insights to treatments. Dialogues in Clinical Neuroscience, 2010; 12 (3) : 317-332.

59. Erp T J M van, and others : Subcortical brain volume abnormalities in 2028 individuals with schizophrenia and 2540 healthy controls via the ENIGMA consortium. Molecular Psychiatry, 2016; 21 : 547-553.

60. Burton N : Living with Schizophrenia. Acheron Press, 2012.

61. Dauvermann Maria R and others : Computational neuropsychiatry - Schizophrenia as a cognitive brain network disorder. Front Psychiatry; 2014 Mar; 5 : 30.

62. Pelizza Lorenzo, and others : Anhedonia in schizophrenia and major depression : state or trait ?. Ann Gen Psychiatry, 2009; 8 : 22.

63. Bombin Igor, ArangoCelso and Buchanan Robert W : Significance and Meaning of Neurological Signs in Schizophrenia : Two decades later. Schizophrenia Bulletin, 2005 June.

64. Lam R W., Levitt A J, and others : The Can-SAD study : a randomized controlled trial of the effectiveness of light therapy and fluoxetine in patients with winter seasonal affective disorder. American Journal of Psychiatry, 2006 May; 163(5) : 805-812.

65. Avery D H, and others : Dawn simulation and bright light in the treatment of SAD : a controlled study. Biological Psychiatry, 2001 Aug; 50(3) : 205-216.

66. Terman M and Terman J S : Controlled trial of naturalistic dawn simulation and negative air ionization for seasonal affective disorder. American Journal of Psychiatry, 2006 Dec; 163(12) : 2126-2133.

67. Thase M E : Recognition and diagnosis of atypical depression. Journal of Clinical Psychiatry, 2007; 68(Supple8) : 11-16.

68. Moayyedi P, and others : The effect of fiber supplementation on irritable bowel syndrome : a systematic review and meta-analysis. American Journal of Gastroenterology, 2014 Sep; 109(9) : 1367-1377.

69. Levine Stephen B, and others : Handbook of Clinical Sexuality for Mental Health Professionals. 2nd Ed., Routledge, 2010.

70. Masters William H and Johnson Virginia E : Human Sexual Response. Ishi Press, 2010.

71. Howkins and Bourne : Shaw's Textbook of Gynaecology. 16th Ed., Elsevier Health, 2015.

72. Rosser Zoe H, and others : Gene conversion between the X chromosome and the male-specific region of the Y chromosome at a translocation hot spot. American Journal of Human Genetics, 2009 Jul; 85(1) : 130-134.

73. Hembree W C, and others : Endocrine treatment of transsexual persons : An Endocrine Society clinical practice guideline. Journal of Clinical Endocrinology & Metabolism, 2009 Sep; 94(9) : 3132-3154.

74. NappiRossella E, Martini Ellis, and others : Management of hypoactive sexual desire disorder in women : Current and emerging therapies. Int J Womens Health, 2010; 2 : 167-175.